BREAD MACHINE
COOKBOOK

Foolproof Guide with 1200 Days of Easy-to-Make Recipes to Help You Bake Fresh and Tasty Homemade Loaves with any Bread Maker

Kaylee Hooper

CONTENTS

INTRODUCTION

The bread machine is one of the most versatile kitchen appliances, which is easiest to use and lets you prepare a wide variety of delicious bread at home.

They are now created by a dozen different companies and come in dozens of versions, each with its own set of settings, functions and sizes. They're not only simple to use, but they also motivate you to create your baking cycles, resulting in bread with thin, crisp crusts that rival even some bakeries. Baking bread in a bread machine takes so little time that you can experience the luxury of fresh bread every day, as it should be.

However, it must be pointed out that not everything is so obvious. Every time we are faced with something new, failure is around the corner. In this book, you will find a lot of information to help you get great results from the first loaf of bread.

If you're using a bread machine for the first time, it's always good to start with the simple recipes, the one you will find in chapter 2 will be ideal. This is a straightforward and foolproof recipe tested on many types of bread machines and will also help you make the more sophisticated recipes in this book.

The bread machine has won over many people who were previously adept at baking by hand, as well as those who were not motivated to learn how to prepare bread using an earlier approach. They were introduced to the evocative aroma, taste, and texture of baked bread through the bread machine and are now hooked.

Additives, colorants, preservatives, and chemical fixatives are absent from homemade bread. The bread machine gives you complete control over what goes into your bread, and you can almost always count on it to be of high quality. A home bread machine is a bread machine that turns all of the ingredients into delicious bread. The beauty of an automatic bread maker is that it takes care of all of these tasks for you.

Loaves of bread are generally defined in baking by the type of flour used, whether they contain yeast or not, their shape, and any additional flavorings, all of which contribute to the bread's unique personality. The recipes in this book vary in these ways, with something for every type of baker— an astonishing diversity of loaves of bread ranging from easy and familiar to innovative and demanding. There is bread for health-conscious individuals, sweet-toothed individuals, and gluten-free individuals. Bread using familiar and unfamiliar ingredients, imaginative flatbreads, and even artisan bread employing classic techniques adapted for the bread machine is included.

I'll frequently ask you to add ingredients in the sequence advised by the maker of your bread machine. Every bread machine is different: some want you to add wet ingredients first, while others require you to begin with dry ingredients. Before you start, read the manual for your specific bread maker. The explanation of the recipes will be significantly simplified. However, thanks to the teachings of this book, you won't have any problems making them.

Many factors, such as the type of flour used (protein content), the type of yeast used, the temperature of the ingredients, and your measuring tools, will affect the completed loaf. Occasionally, your bread will be so exquisite that you will want to photograph it. A cooler kitchen temperature prevents a good rise when you make the same recipe.

Don't give up! Even the most inconspicuous loaf of bread may be delectable.

Chapter 1
THE BREAD
MACHINE

A bread machine is a kitchen tool that is used to make bread. The gadget comprises a bread pan or tin with built-in paddles that sit in the middle of a small multi-purpose oven. Matsushita Electric, now Panasonic, initially introduced the one-stop equipment for baking bread in Japan in 1986. Throughout the 1990s, the machine's popularity grew, and it found its way into American kitchens. Bread baking, which had previously been difficult and time-consuming, had become as simple as putting a few ingredients into a machine and pressing a button. After the yeast, flour, and wet ingredients are placed into the machine's bucket, a tiny blade mixes and kneads the dough. The temperature automatically adjusts to rise, prove, and bake the dough. The bread machine was supposed to be the next toaster, with 1 million units sold by the end of 1992.

Several families claimed possession of the device in 1996. Ten years later, the number of families claiming to own a bread machine has increased dramatically. The machine's utility has been expanded into manufacturing dough for pizza, dinner rolls, and baked goods.

Consumers who use the machine regularly have discovered that it can make practically any dough recipe. That can subsequently be cooked in a conventional oven. A slew of bread machine recipe books has been created, each with its own set of instructions.

Today's bread machine has become a household staple, allowing time-pressed cooks to provide their families a prepared supper that includes freshly baked bread.

The bread machine is essentially a small electric oven that houses a large bread pan. The tin itself is unique because it includes a bottom axle connected to an electric motor beneath it. The bottom of the tin has a little metal paddle attached to the axle. Kneading the dough is done with the paddle.

1.1 Pros of Bread Machine

1. Convenience

Preparing bread is a time-consuming operation. Making fresh bread on the weekend may be fun, but during the week, when you return from work and still need to take care of the house, the likelihood that you will have a sudden burst of energy to create fresh bread is slim. A bread machine is an excellent choice if you want fresh bread every day.

Most bread machines feature a timer that you can set to the middle of the night and wake up to ready fresh bread with a single button push. The range of these clocks is around 12 hours. That is, you can do all of the prep work 12 hours before your bread is due to be baked.

Some machines also feature automatic nut and fruit dispensers (as well as any other tastes you'd like to add to your bread). Choose a machine with this option if you want bread with nuts and dried fruits, for example, as these additional components are mechanically introduced into your dough at the proper time.

2. Kneading is not required.

Kneading the dough is possibly the most physically demanding aspect of bread baking. Many people lack the patience or ability to knead the dough for a variety of reasons, such as health problems, aging, fatigue, or any other reason you can think of. It automatically kneads the bread. So, even if you wish to handle everything else by hand, the kneading can indeed be left to the bread machine's expert hands.

3. Healthy

Making bread at home is far healthier than buying it from a shop or even specific bakeries, since most bread is created with some degree of baking improvements, as everyone who makes bread at home knows. You can choose healthier components for your bread, whether it's organic flour, whole wheat, gluten-free flour, or whatever your dietary restrictions or tastes are.

4. Economical

Making your own bread can save you money over time when you take into account the cost of supplies, time and effort, and other crucial aspects, even if you only use a small amount of bread each week and still create one loaf. Bread machines (the good ones, not the cheap ones) will endure a long time.

5. No Experience Required

If you've never done anything like this before and don't have the time to learn, this is the way to go. However, you still require freshly cooked bread. The bread machine will swiftly turn you into a baker. You may save money, time and be in charge of your diet (you know what you're putting into your body) while enjoying fresh bread.

6. Clean Process

The bread machine dramatically simplifies the process. It's simple: put the ingredients in the bread maker, press a button, and adjust the timer. The kitchen remains spotless, and all that remains is to wait for the bread to bake.

This issue becomes quite important if you make bread daily, especially given the hectic schedules that most of us maintain and are all too familiar with.

1.2 Cons of Bread Machine

1. No Crispy Crust

You don't receive the crispy, crunchy crust. These devices do not use steam and instead bake in a pan. If you wanted a thicker crust, you could use the bread machine for the mixing, first rise, and punch phases, then take it out for the shaping and final rise and bake it in your oven. In that sense, a bread machine can help you out a little.

2. Common Problems

On paper, bread machines appear to be straightforward to use, but they can pose difficulties for bakers and create a lot of aggravation.

Bread does not rise totally or partially; the bread turns out dense and hefty, the inside of the bread is sticky, the top of the bread isn't browned. These are some of the most common problems beginners experience while making their first loaves of bread. Later we will look specifically at each one and how to solve them.

3. Sourdough in Bread Machine is difficult.

Using sourdough bread in a bread machine is not impossible. Keep in mind that your bread machine is unlikely to have a preset program for sourdough bread.

Sourdough bread has a different rise and proofing

time (usually much longer than bread made with commercial yeast), which is why bread machines don't work well with these recipes. Bread machines have manual modes to alter the times manually to avoid this problem. However, it will take some time and trial and error on your part to find out how to produce sourdough bread in a bread machine.

4. Only one loaf of bread per day

One loaf of bread per day may not be enough if you have a large household. You can bake numerous loaves at once in a standard oven, but it will take a long time and effort to make the bread.

5. Fixed kneading paddles

Most bread machines feature fixed kneading paddles that stay in the center of the dough while baking, resulting in a hole in the center of the loaf. However, there are a few new bread machines with collapsible paddles on the market.

1.3 Cycles and Setting of Bread Machine

When you start the bread machine, it goes through several stages. Cycles are the various processes that your bread machine goes through. These bread machine cycles are, for the most part, the same across the board.

Kneading

The kneading cycle is the first and, by far, the most crucial stage in preparing yeast bread. The kneading cycle incorporates all ingredients and is likely your bread machine's noisiest cycle. This cycle can take anywhere between 15 and 45 minutes. The time will vary depending on your bread machine and the type of bread you're baking. There are usually kneading paddles at the bottom of your baking pan that thoroughly mix everything.

Rest Cycle

Before continuing to knead, the dough can rest throughout the rest cycle. In the world of baking, this process is called autolyzing the dough. In other words, it enables all of the moisture in the air to be absorbed by the gluten and starch in the dough. This cycle may last only a few seconds or up to 35 minutes.

Rise Cycle

The fluffy, airy texture of bread is a result of this. It involves allowing the yeasts to ferment and gently boosting the temperature of the dough. Depending on your bread machine, this cycle will last between 40 and 50 minutes. Sometimes, especially if you're baking French bread, it could take a while.

Punch Cycle

Once the dough has finished rising, the Punch Cycle starts. The punching cycle got its name because during this cycle, your bread maker starts creating dough repeatedly. The difference is because at this stage, the tiny gas bubbles produced by yeast fermentation during the rise cycle are released much more gently. Punch, often referred to as the form cycle, is a brief but crucial cycle that takes only a few seconds to complete.

Baking cycle

When your breadmaker begins making your bread, that is. This cycle can take anywhere from 30 minutes to over 90 minutes, depending on your bread maker and the type of bread you're baking.

Setting

Different bread makers will employ a combination of various settings. Some bread will need more than 1 rising cycle to rise correctly. Some do, while others do not.

Now, allow me to explain the various cycles and settings available on the most common bread machine.

The Basic Bread

It is the most common setting on the bread machine, and it allows you to make standard bread. This process takes three to four hours, depending on the size of the loaf and the type of bread. This setting can also be used when making bread with whole wheat flour.

The Sweet Bread

As the name implies, this cycle is for bread with a more significant sugar or fat content than ordinary bread. When using components like cheese and eggs, the setting is also used. Because the components may cause the crust to burn or deepen in color, this function permits the bread to bake at a lower temperature than other functions. The approximate baking time is around 3 hours.

The Whole Wheat Bread

Whole wheat bread requires more time to knead and churn than conventional loaves. As a result, this cycle is ideal for bread that requires this type of flour. This feature helps the bread rise to the proper height while preventing it from getting overly dense.

The French Bread

Most Mediterranean bread, such as those from Italy and France, is far better when this function is used instead of the basic cycle. Many French-style loaves contain no or only a little amount of sugar.

Those loaves of bread require a longer rising time as well as a lower and longer temperature. It can produce the textures and crusts we've come to like. The approximate baking time is around 4 hours

The Dough

This setting is ideal for generating pizza dough and dinner roll dough. The machine will mix and knead your ingredients, allowing you to extract the dough, top with your choice toppings or fillings, and bake them in your regular oven. It eliminates the need to knead the dough manually and reduces the cleanup required, which is a great win for everyone.

Bake in a hurry

It is for bread bakers who utilize quick-rise yeast in their recipes.

Compared to the basic bread cycle, the quick cycle can save you anything from 30 minutes to two hours. It's worth noting that the quick bake cycle varies with each machine.

Quick Cycle/Cake

This cycle is great for yeast-free recipes, such as cakes. Unlike the other cycles, the bread machine does not knead the ingredients together. It merely combines the ingredients and bakes them. This cycle and baking time may differ from machine to machine.

Delayed Cycle or Time-Bake

Some bread machines have a unique setting for this. It allows you to put the ingredients in the bread maker and then configure it to bake conveniently.

To avoid difficulties with foodborne pathogens, bread that contains milk or eggs should only be delayed for one to two hours.

The functionality of the crust

When using a bread machine, the crust capability allows the user to choose their preferred crust. There are three crust settings: soft, medium, and dark. When it comes to white bread variations, a soft crust is always a winner. The medium and dark crusts will appeal to you if you desire a crispier crust. It's possible that adding sugars, nuts, or grains to your bread will cause it to brown faster. As a result, a light crust setting is suggested.

1.4 Common bread-making issues

Do you wish to learn how to make outstanding bread? Then it would be beneficial if you learned as much as you could about some of the challenges you might face while using the bread machine. Written down tricks will help you avoid typical bread machine baking errors, resulting in more delicious outcomes.

1. Small loaf

Reasons could be:

» There isn't enough sugar.
» There wasn't enough yeast, or the yeast was

old or kept incorrectly.

» The ingredients were placed in the pan with the timer set such that the salt or water came into contact with the yeast for an extended period.
» Short, heavier loaves are common when utilizing whole grain flours or all-purpose flour instead of bread flour.
» The pan was too big for the size of the recipe. Insufficient dough to fill the pan.

2. Bread does not increase in size

Reasons could be:

» The yeast used was either old or inadequately stored, or it had been forgotten or measured incorrectly.
» Other essential elements were overlooked or miscalculated.
» The ingredients were placed in the pan wrongly, and a timer was used.
» The yeast was killed because the water temperature was too high.
» The yeast was killed because there was too much salt in the recipe.
» The yeast was killed because there was too much sugar in the recipe.

3. Mushroom Shaped Top

Reasons could be:

» It usually means that the proportions of the ingredients were off. If you use too much yeast, sugar, flour, liquid, or a combination of these ingredients, the dough may rise above the pan's capacity.
» For the amount of dough, the bread pan was too little.
» There were much too many sweet substances

employed.

» There was no salt in bread or too much salt utilized.

4. The Top of Bread Sunk

Reasons could be:

» The proportions of the ingredients were off.
» You forgot the salt.
» The bread pan was insufficiently large.
» The dough perhaps reached the top of the machine, obstructing the baking and chilling process.
» During the baking cycle, you perhaps opened the bread machine.
» Warm weather, excessive humidity, and hot liquids accelerate yeast action, causing the dough to rise too quickly and the bread to collapse before or shortly after baking. Baking at the coolest part of the day and using cool or cold liquids can assist in avoiding this.
» There's a lot of liquid in the dough. When the baking began, it was too mushy to hold its shape.

5. Gummy Areas in Bread

Reasons could be:

» There are too many moist or rich components in this recipe, such as applesauce, eggs, oil, and so on.
» There is much too much sugar in the recipe.
» The room where the bread machine was kept was too chilly, which influenced the baking temperature and resulted in the loaf not being fully cooked.
» Your machine's thermostat is broken in rare circumstances, and the loaf does not bake correctly. It is most likely to be the case if it

occurs often.

6. Bread with Coarse Texture

Reasons could be:

» There is much too much water.
» Yeast activity was enhanced by hot, humid conditions, overheated substances, or both. Or too much yeast has been added.
» The salt was left out.
» Before adding the fruit and vegetables to the bread dough, drain them well and pat them dry.

7. Bread becomes heavy

Reasons could be:

» There isn't enough water.
» There isn't enough sweetness.
» There isn't enough yeast.
» There is much too much flour in the recipe.
» Check to see whether you did put salt in bread or not.
» You used an overabundance of whole-grain flour and entire grains. Alternatively, half of the bread flour you may use instead.
» There were too many dried fruits or other additional substances.

Other things to look into:

Check to see whether your yeast is still active. If you don't keep the yeast in the freezer, pay attention to the expiry date, or keep your yeast in the freezer (which is the best location to keep it). It may be kept fresh for a long time after it has passed its expiry date by freezing yeast. Please remove it from its container and put it in a tightly closed moisture-proof container to freeze. You do not need to thaw the yeast before using it; you can use it straight from the freezer.

Whether you're not sure if your yeast is good, combine 1 teaspoon yeast with 1/2 cup warm water plus 1 teaspoon white sugar in a glass basin. Allow 15 minutes for the mixture to settle. If the yeast is healthy, it will bubble and foam. It's dead if it doesn't replace your yeast.

Thaw them before using them if you keep flour, sugar, or other ingredients in the refrigerator or freezer. You can either let it reach room temperature completely or reheat it up in the microwave for 15 to 20 seconds. But you don't want it to become too hot.

Make sure you don't use more than 1/4 cup of sweetener in your recipe. If you use more than this, the yeast will suffer. Sugar, honey, and other sweeteners are all unhealthy for yeast. If you want to use more than 1/4 cup, use a yeast called "Brown Yeast," which is developed for doughs with a lot of sugar and acid. The yeast used may be ordered through the King Arthur Baker's Catalog.

Chapter 2

THE BEGINNERS
BIBLE

2.1 The Absolute Beginner's Loaf

Whether you have a new bread machine, a used one, or one given to you by a friend, you must test it and ensure it functions properly. Although it is a solid start, it isn't enough to plug it in.

You're the First Loaf Made from Scratch

This recipe has been tested with different types of bread machines and never had it fail; you can also use it to make whole wheat bread.

White Bread (1-1/2 Pound Loaf) in a Bread Machine

» 1 1/8 cup water
» 1 1/2 teaspoon of butter
» 3 cups flour for bread
» 2 teaspoons of sugar
» 1 teaspoon salt
» 1 1/2 teaspoons milk (dry)
» 2 1/2 tablespoons active dry yeast (instant)

Place all ingredients in the sequence specified in your machine's user handbook. You can start the basic or white bread cycle by hitting the start button.

Open the cover after 3 minutes of mixing and scrape along the sides of the pan with a spatula, avoiding the paddle. Any flour gathered on the edges should be pushed into the center. During kneading, scrape the edges, corners, and under the dough once or twice more

Checking the Consistency of the Dough

Open the lid after the machine has worked for about 10 minutes and check the consistency of the dough. The dough should be forming a nice spherical ball at this point. The dough should be somewhat tacky to the touch when you touch it with your finger, but no dough should remain on your finger when you draw it away. The consistency of the dough is crucial, and all bread machine doughs should look and feel like this, with a few exceptions.

If your dough becomes too dry, add 1 tablespoon of water until it reaches the desired consistency (leaving the machine to knead for a minute or so between additions). Or if the dough is too moist, add 1 tbsp. Flour until it reaches the desired consistency (allowing the machine to knead for a minute or so between additions). These changes aren't uncommon, and they don't necessarily indicate a problem with the recipe. What happens is that the moisture content of the flour varies depending on the weather. You'll need to check the dough consistency every time you create this or any other recipe unless you're using the timer, in which case you'll need to use a recipe you've used before and found to work well for you.

Note: The recipe is probably inaccurate if you need to add more than 3 tablespoons of water or flour to make the dough appropriately. Make a note of how much more water or flour you need to add, and include that amount the next time you make the recipe. If the amount is less than 3 tbsp, don›t do it.

When the Loaf is Fully Cooked

When the machine makes a beep sound, it indicates that the bread is done, open the top and let it rest for 10 minutes. Then take the bread pan out of the machine and gently remove the bread from the pan (invert and shake until it slides out). Cool for a minimum of 20 minutes before slicing it on a cooling rack.

Final Thoughts

You've just cooked your first loaf of bread, which is a huge accomplishment. You now know how to run your machine and make the dough look and feel right. You're all set to go on to the next recipe. If your loaf does not turn out as you had hoped, see if you can figure out what happened in the Common Bread-Making Issue chapter.

2.2 Seven steps to convert your favorite recipes

A bread machine is a gadget with a strong following among those who value the machine's ability to produce loaf after loaf with little more effort than pressing a button.

With so many different brands, quality levels, and sizes of bread machines on the market, not to mention the vast array of yeast bread recipes, it's hard to provide a one-size-fits-all solution for baking classic handcrafted recipes in a machine. It will help if you first learn some fundamental rules before experimenting with your favorite dishes.

Understand that baked in a bread machine, your favorite yeast bread recipes will be drier and less tender than the original. The price you pay for the ease of machine baking is a tiny reduction in the quality of the finished loaf. However, if you regularly eat your bread toasted or grilled, you won't notice the difference.

So, how do you choose which of your favorite dishes to make first? If you follow these guidelines, you'll soon be able to tell whether a recipe can be easily converted to a bread machine and when it's preferable to continue creating the recipe by hand.

1. **Find out how much bread your machine can make.**

You do not want to open your bread machine to find half-baked dough leaking out of the bucket into the machine's bottom because you used too much flour in the recipe. How do you tell if the flour in your proposed recipe is the correct amount?

While you can quickly know that your machine supports loaves of bread that weigh 1 pound, 1 1/2 pound, or 2 pounds, what you really want to know is its flour capacity.

Examine the recipe booklet that came with your machine to determine how much flour it can hold. For example, suppose you'll notice that the manufacturer's recipes always call for flour between 3 and 4 cups. In that case, this will be your machine's capacity. The following are the flour capacity for the most common bread machine sizes:

» 2 to 2 3/4 cups flour for a 1-pound machine
» 3 to 4 cups flour for a 1 1/2-pound machine
» 4 to 5 1/2 cups flour for a 2-pound machine

2. **Choose recipes that correspond to the flour capacity of your bread maker**

Many standard single-loaf recipes call for 3 to 4 cups of flour; they are ideal for your 1 1/2-pound machine (or for your 2-pound machine set to 1 1/2-pound).

If a recipe calls for less flour than your machine can handle, try baking it nonetheless; you'll probably end up with a loaf that's a little shorter than usual. If the recipe is greater, figure out how much flour you'll need to reduce to fit your machine's capacity, and stick to that quantity; lower the rest of the components by the same proportion.

3. Keep an eye on the add-ins.

Do you have a homemade recipe that calls for both rolled oats and nuts? Dry components such as nuts, fruit, flaked or chopped whole grains, and seeds will reduce the adequate capacity of your machine.

A recipe requiring 3 3/4 cups flour, 1 cup rolled oats, and 1/2 cup chopped walnuts would most likely exceed the capacity of your 1 1/2-pound machine; try a different recipe instead.

4. Instant yeast vs. active dry yeast vs. quick yeast

A package of active dry yeast is used in many recipes, whereas "quick" yeast is used in others. We're big fans of instant yeast in all kinds of bread baking, including machine baking. Instant yeast is robust and powerful; it's far less expensive than the supermarket's small sachets of active dried yeast, and it's virtually certainly fresher.

What's the best way to figure out how much instant yeast to use? It's a straightforward change:

2 1/4 teaspoons quick yeast can also be used in place of a packet of active dry or rapid yeast.

If you don't have any instant yeast on hand?

After that, you'll need to use active dry. Don't use active dry yeast in your machine's fast cycle because it may take longer to function.

Also, there's no need to "proof" active dry yeast before using it; its formulation has altered in recent years, and it's no longer required to dissolve it in warm water before using it.

Finally, if your bread machine loafs are consistently rising and then collapsing, reduce the yeast by one-third (for example, if you used 2 1/4 teaspoons yeast, reduce to 1 1/2 teaspoons). Your machine's rising cycles may be too heated or too long, causing the bread to rise too much before baking.

5. How do I choose a cycle?

Your machine offers a variety of settings, ranging from basic to wheat to manual. Which one do you think you should pick?

Begin with a medium crust and the basic cycle. It's a versatile cycle that can be used in various bread recipes, including whole-grain bread. Try the quick cycle if you're in a rush (but only if you're using rapid or instant yeast; it won't work with active dry yeast).

Isn't it possible to use the wheat cycle for whole-grain bread? Try it; I've found that the basic cycle bakes my 100 percent whole-wheat bread just as well as the wheat cycle, so I just use the basic cycle.

6. In the order listed, combine the ingredients.

The order for adding ingredients to the bowl will be specified in your machine's instruction handbook; follow those instructions, disregarding any mixing instructions provided by your recipe. If you don't have that information in your booklet, start with the liquids, then the flour, and finally the other dry ingredients.

Some ancient recipes will instruct you to "scald" the milk before using it; do not follow this instruction. Back in the day, bakers routinely scalded milk to destroy bacteria; nowadays, pasteurization takes care of that. Bring your milk to room temperature or slightly reheat it to remove the chill from the refrigerator.

7. For obstinate recipes, there's a simple remedy.

If you're disappointed with the way your favorite bread machine recipe turned out, there's an easy cure. Create the dough using the machine dough (manual) cycle, then remove it once it's fully risen. Continue with the recipe until it says to "deflate the dough," then shape and bake the bread in your standard oven.

The dough cycle on your machine provides a hands-free, convenient way to get any yeast dough prepared for shaping and baking: no hand-kneading ultra-sticky dough, no standing over a stand mixer or finding a warm location for the dough to rise. While you should check on the dough as it kneads and rises from time to time and adjust it by adding the liquid or flour if it appears too dry or sticky, you can set it and forget it.

2.3 How to store your bread

Just after the baking (and eating), the bread must be stored to keep it as fresh as long as possible. Below are the most commonly used preservation methods:

1. Put your bread in the freezer

Freezing bread is the greatest technique to keep it in its original state: crusty crust and soft interior. Freezing the bread delays the staling process significantly, and warming it in an oven or toaster re-gelatinizes the starches, making the bread springy and chewy once more. Place your bread in a sealed zip bag and freeze it, pressing out as much air as possible. Take it out, and then reheat it in the oven when you're ready to eat it. A great thing to do is divide the bread into slices before freezing it. This way, you won't have to thaw the whole bread. Bread can be stored fresh in the freezer for up to three months.

2. Wrap the bread in plastic

For people who easily eat through a loaf of bread, wrapping it in plastic is the simplest way to ensure a fresh loaf. It is a reliable short-term storage solution because the bread will not be sitting on the counter for an extended amount of time. Bread can be stored in reusable plastic or a glass-sealed container to keep it fresher for longer. Keep the bread on the counter in an airtight container if you want to eat it within three or four days.

3. Store in paper

You should eat a fresh loaf of bread within two to three days of buying it. It is best to keep food in a paper bag on the counter if you plan to consume it right immediately. Bread spoils significantly more quickly when it is stored in plastic, despite the fact that it could seem like a smart idea. You can use the bread heels to cover the cut side of the loaf if you want to keep them. By keeping the cut side of your bread as little exposed as possible, you can maintain its freshness.

4. Breadbox to Store Your Bread

A perfect breadbox will create a climate that strikes a balance between air movement and humidity, which you want for a soft interior (which you need to maintain a crusty crust). A larger box is preferable since it allows for better air circulation. The more bread you put in, the higher the moisture level in the bread box will be, so don't overfill it. Also, don't store the bread in the bread box in a paper bag—this can trap moisture and ruin the crust.

5. Purchase reusable bread bags

If you're looking for a more flexible or sustainable way to store your bread, consider using a reusable bread bag. These days, there are a lot more options available, and many of them freeze well. These bags can serve as an effective replacement for paper bags, which frequently tear and seem to allow crumbs to fall onto the counter. Reusable bags perform similarly to paper bags but don't produce waste because they are made of permeable textiles. They're a terrific investment for a bread (and environment) enthusiast of any level, with prices ranging from $7 to $20.

2.4 Five special tips for beginners

Although bread machines are supposed to be infallible, they aren't. Bread machines appeal to me because of their ease and simplicity.

Despite the convenience and all due respect to the inventors and engineers who create bread-making machines, some considerations and consequences should be avoided when misusing them.

1. The location

The location of your bread machine in the kitchen has a significant impact on the outcome of the baking process. High-humidity or low-humidity can affect how yeast rises as well as proofing times before baking. The temperature in the kitchen has an impact on the baking qualities of the bread. The surface of the bread can crack and crevice if the kitchen is too hot. The yeast will not rise if the kitchen is too cool, and bread proofing will take longer.

2. Make sure the dough is well combined

Some bread machines do not have view windows in the lid, whereas others do. In the first case, it's tough to see if the dough is processing properly. Even bread machines with windows may not provide a clear view of the finished product. Don't worry; lifting the top to see what's going on is perfectly fine.

It's crucial to determine whether yeast is active and living, and the best method to do so is to examine it closely. It's also crucial to double-check that the mixing and kneading stages have been completed completely. Take a look for yourself and check to see if the dough is too wet or too dry.

3. Shape the dough

The bread dough typically gets misshapen and

off-balance as it expands due to yeast expansion. After the final rise, reshaping the bread loaf to a symmetric and appealing appearance aids the bread machine's performance. You can execute this step using a bread machine, and the result would be much more appealing and evenly baked, with no pockets of gooey, undercooked dough.

4. Overcome the want to remove the loaf too soon after it is done

Unfortunately, many bakers remove the bread before it has cooled down in their eagerness to taste and admire it. Allow the bread to cool completely inside the machine.

If you don't, condensation will build up beneath the loaf, causing the crust to turn mushy. Removing the bred too soon will wrinkle on the surface, making the loaf look like dinosaur scales.

5. Remove the mixing paddles

While it may not be a significant deal to some bakers, the bread machine's mixing paddles will leave a small hole in the loaf if they aren't removed after mixing.
The hole can alter the loaf's appearance and provide an unwelcome moisture escape inside the loaf. It is good to remove them because no one likes a stale loaf of freshly baked bread.

So, once the dough is combined, just before it rises, take it out, give it a nice shape if necessary, remove the mixing paddles/paddles, and re-insert the dough, and it's ready to

go. Another trick is to place the small silicon matt under the dough at the bottom.

1. COUNTRY WHITE BREAD

READY IN ABOUT: 2 HOURS
YIELDS: 2 LB LOAF

INGREDIENTS

- 1 1/2 cups lukewarm Water
- 1 teaspoon salt
- 1/4 teaspoon Baking Soda
- 2 1/2 cups All-Purpose Flour   *1 tbsp. wheat gluten*
- 1 cup Bread Flour
- 2 1/2 teaspoons Active Machine Bread Yeast
- 1 tablespoon + 1 teaspoon Olive Oil
- 1 1/2 teaspoons Sugar

INSTRUCTIONS

Collect the necessary components. In the sequence advised by your bread machine manufacturer, add all of the ingredients to your bread machine pan. Set the crust to Medium and the quick setting. Start by pressing the start button. When the bake cycle ends, bread is ready; take it out and turn the bread out onto a cooling rack once it's done. Cut into slices and eat.

2. MULTIGRAIN LOAF BREAD

READY IN ABOUT: 2 HOURS
YIELDS: 2 LB LOAF

INGREDIENTS

- 1 1/4 cups water
- 1 cup 7 grain or multigrain cereal
- 1 1/3 cups bread flour
- 2 tablespoons unsalted butter
- 3 tablespoons brown sugar
- 1 1/4 teaspoons salt
- 1 1/3 cups whole wheat flour
- 2 1/2 teaspoons bread machine yeast

INSTRUCTIONS

In the bread machine pan, combine the water, melted butter, bread flour, whole wheat flour, multigrain cereal, and brown sugar, salt, and bread machine yeast in the sequence suggested by the machine maker. Choose between the Whole Wheat and the Basic/White Cycles. Start the machine with the Medium or Light Crust Color option. Allow the machine to prepare the dough, knead the bread, rise, and bake the bread. Remove it from the bread machine and cool fully on a wire rack when the bread is done.

3. HOMEMADE EASY CHALLAH

READY IN ABOUT: 3 HOURS
YIELDS: 1 1/2 LB LOAF

INGREDIENTS

- 3/4 cup Milk
- 1 1/2 teaspoon salt
- 2 Eggs
- 1 1/2 teaspoon active dry yeast
- 3 tablespoon margarine
- 3 cup Bread Flour
- 1/4 cup white sugar

INSTRUCTIONS

Add all dry and wet ingredients to the bread machine pan in the manufacturer's recommended order. Select the parameters for Basic Bread and Light Crust. Start by pressing the Start button. When the bake cycle ends, the bread is ready; take it out and allow it to cool after baking.

4. CLASSICAL BREAD

READY IN ABOUT: 3 HOURS
YIELDS: 1 1/2 LB LOAF

INGREDIENTS

- » 1 cup warm water (110 degrees)
- » 2 tablespoon White Sugar
- » .25 oz. Active Bread Machine Yeast
- » 1/4 Cup Vegetable Oil
- » 3 Cup Bread Flour
- » 1 teaspoon salt

INSTRUCTIONS

Place water, sugar, and yeast in the bread machine's pan. Allow 10 minutes for the yeast to dissolve and foam. Toss the yeast with the oil, flour, and salt. Press Start after selecting the Basic or White Bread setting. When the bake cycle ends, the bread is done; set it aside to cool before serving.

5. BASIL OREGANO AND ROSEMARY BREAD

READY IN ABOUT: 3 HOURS
YIELDS: 1 1/2 LB LOAF

INGREDIENTS

- » 1 cup warm Water
- » 1 Egg (beaten)
- » 1 teaspoon salt
- » 2 tablespoon White Sugar
- » 2 tablespoon Extra-Virgin Olive Oil
- » 2 teaspoon Dried Rosemary Leaves (crushed)
- » 1 teaspoon Dried Oregano
- » 1 teaspoon Dried Basil
- » 3 cup + 2 tablespoons All-Purpose Flour
- » 2 teaspoon Bread Machine Yeast

INSTRUCTIONS

Place the warm water in the bread machine pan. Add the remaining ingredients to the manufacturer's recommended order. Press Start after setting the machine to bake a big loaf with the Light Crust. When the bake cycle ends, the bread is done. Let your bread cool down before serving.

6. HONEY SPELT BREAD

READY IN ABOUT: 2 HOURS
YIELDS: 1 1/2 LB LOAF

INGREDIENTS

- » 1 cup water
- » 1 and 1/2 teaspoon vegetable Oil
- » 1 and 1/2 teaspoon honey
- » 1 and 1/2 teaspoon salt
- » 1/2 teaspoon Lecithin
- » 3 Cup white spelt Flour
- » 3 tablespoon dry milk powder
- » 2 teaspoon active dry yeast

INSTRUCTIONS

Add all of the ingredients in the bread machine pan in the manufacturer's recommended order. Press Start after selecting the Normal or Basic cycle. When the bake cycle ends, take it out and set it aside to cool before serving.

7. PUMPERNICKEL

READY IN ABOUT: 4 HOURS
YIELDS: 1 1/2 LB LOAF

INGREDIENTS

- » 1 1/8 cup warm Water
- » 1 1/2 tablespoon Vegetable Oil
- » 1/3 Cup Molasses
- » 3 tablespoon Cocoa
- » 1 tablespoon Caraway Seed (optional)
- » 1 1/2 teaspoon salt
- » 1 1/2 Cup Bread Flour
- » 1 Cup Rye Flour
- » 1 cup Whole Wheat Flour
- » 2 1/2 teaspoon Bread Machine Yeast

INSTRUCTIONS

Add all of the ingredients in the bread machine pan in the sequence specified by the manufacturer. Select the Basic cycle and hit the Start button. When the bake cycle ends, the

bread is done; remove it from the machine and set it aside to cool before serving.

8. BACK TO SCHOOL BREAD

READY IN ABOUT: 3 HOURS
YIELDS: 1 LB LOAF

INGREDIENTS

- » 7/8 cup warm water
- » 2 tablespoon lard
- » 0.25 oz. Active Dry Yeast
- » 2 3/4 Cup Bread Flour
- » 1 teaspoon salt
- » 1 teaspoon Ground Cinnamon (optional)

INSTRUCTIONS

Place the warm water and grease in the bread machine pan. Sprinkle the yeast over the top. Combine the flour, salt, and cinnamon in a mixing bowl. Choose a cycle and press the Start button. When the bake cycle ends, bread is done. Take the bread from the oven and set it aside to cool before serving.

9. ARTISANAL BREAD

READY IN ABOUT: 3 HOURS
YIELDS: 1 1/2 LB LOAF

INGREDIENTS

- » 1 cup warm Water
- » 3 tablespoon White Sugar

- » 1 1/2 teaspoon salt
- » 3 tablespoon Vegetable Oil
- » 3 Cup Bread Flour
- » 2 1/4 teaspoon Active Dry Yeast

INSTRUCTIONS

Add all of the ingredients in the bread machine pan in the manufacturer's recommended order. Choose the White Bread option. When the bake cycle ends, the bread is done. Take the bread out of the bread machine with care. Before slicing the bread, let it cool on wire racks.

10. FLAVORSOME BREAD

READY IN ABOUT: 3 HOURS
YIELDS: 1 1/2 LB LOAF

INGREDIENTS

- » 1 cup warm water (110 degrees F)
- » 3 Cup Bread Flour
- » 1 tablespoon butter
- » 1 tablespoon Dry Milk Powder
- » 1 tablespoon White Sugar
- » 1 1/2 teaspoon salt
- » 1 1/2 tablespoon Dried Parsley
- » 2 teaspoon Garlic Powder
- » 2 teaspoon Active Dry Yeast

INSTRUCTIONS

Add all of the ingredients in the bread machine pan in the manufacturer's recommended order. Press Start after selecting the Basic Bread cycle. When the bake cycle ends, the bread is ready. Remove the bread from the machine and set it aside to cool before serving.

11. STEAKHOUSE WHEAT BREAD

READY IN ABOUT: 3 HOURS
YIELDS: 1 LB LOAF

INGREDIENTS

- » 3/4 cup warm Water
- » 1 tablespoon butter (melted)
- » 1/4 cup honey
- » 1/2 teaspoon salt
- » 1 teaspoon instant coffee granules
- » 1 tablespoon white sugar
- » 1 cup bread flour
- » 1 cup whole wheat flour
- » 1 1/4 teaspoon bread machine yeast
- » 1 tablespoon unsweetened cocoa powder

INSTRUCTIONS

Add all dry and wet ingredients to the bread machine pan in the manufacturer's recommended order. Press Start after selecting the Regular or Basic cycle with Light Crust. When the bake cycle ends, the bread is ready. Take the bread from the machine and set it aside to cool before serving.

12. OLIVE OIL WHITE BREAD

READY IN ABOUT: 2 HOURS
YIELDS: 1 1/2 LB LOAF

INGREDIENTS

- » 0.25 oz. Active Dry Yeast
- » 1 tablespoon Olive Oil
- » 1 Cup Skim milk (warm)
- » 2 tablespoon warm water (110 degrees F/45 degrees C)
- » 1/2 teaspoon salt
- » 2 cup All-Purpose Flour
- » 1 1/4 Cup Whole Wheat Flour

INSTRUCTIONS

Add all dry and wet ingredients to the bread machine pan in the manufacturer's recommended order. Press Start after selecting the lightest setting. When the bake cycle ends, the bread is done. Pull it from the bread machine and set it aside to cool before serving.

13. BUSH BREAD

READY IN ABOUT: 3 HOURS
YIELDS: 1 1/2 LB LOAF

INGREDIENTS

- » 1 cup warm water
- » 1/2 teaspoon ground thyme
- » 2 1/2 teaspoon Active Dry Yeast
- » 1/2 teaspoon Garlic Powder
- » 3 cup All-Purpose Flour
- » 1 1/2 teaspoon salt
- » 3 tablespoon olive oil
- » 2 teaspoon crushed dried rosemary
- » 3 tablespoon white sugar

INSTRUCTIONS

Pour the water into the pan of the bread machine and add the yeast and sugar. Wait for 10 minutes to activate the yeast. Add the olive oil, thyme, garlic powder, rosemary, and flour after the salt. Press Start after selecting the Light Crust setting on the machine. When the bake cycle ends, the bread is done. Take the bread from the oven and set it aside to cool before serving.

14. EVERYDAY WHITE BREAD

READY IN ABOUT: 3 HOURS
YIELDS: 1 LB LOAF

INGREDIENTS

- » 3/4 cup water
- » 1 tablespoon butter (melted)
- » 2 tablespoons Skim Milk powder
- » 1 tablespoon Sugar
- » 3/4 teaspoon Salt
- » 2 cups White Bread Flour
- » 3/4 teaspoon Bread Machine Yeast

INSTRUCTIONS

Put the ingredients in your bread maker according to the manufacturer's instructions. Press Start after programming the machine for Basic/White bread and selecting light or medium crust. When the bake cycle ends, the bread is ready. Remove the bucket from the machine after the loaf is done. Allow 5 minutes for the bread to cool. Remove the loaf from the bucket with a little shake and place it on a cooling rack.

15. CRACKED WHEAT BREAD

READY IN ABOUT: 3 HOURS
YIELDS: 1 1/2 LB LOAF

INGREDIENTS

» 1 1/4 cup + 1 tablespoon Water
» 2 tablespoons Vegetable Oil
» 3 cups Bread Flour
» 2 tablespoons sugar
» 3/4 cup Cracked Wheat
» 1 1/2 teaspoons Salt
» 2 1/4 teaspoons Active Dry Yeast

INSTRUCTIONS

Boil a pot of water. Pour water over cracked wheat in a small mixing basin and whisk. Reduce the temperature to 80 degrees Fahrenheit (27 degrees Celsius). Place the cracked wheat mixture in the pan, and then add the rest of the ingredients except the yeast. In the center of these dry ingredients (above mentioned), with a spoon, make a well and add the yeast. Press Start after selecting the Basic Bread cycle with a medium color crust. After 5 minutes of kneading, check for the dough consistency. It should be a soft, tacky ball of dough. If it's dry and stiff, add 12 tablespoons of water at a time until it's sticky. If the dough is excessively wet and sticky, add 1 tablespoon of flour to add it until it is no longer sticky. When the cycle is through, remove the bread and set it aside to cool before serving.

16. SOFT EGG BREAD

READY IN ABOUT: 2 HOURS
YIELDS: 1 LB LOAF

INGREDIENTS

» 1/2 cup plus 2 tablespoons milk
» 2 2/3 tablespoons (melted) butter
» 1 egg
» 1 teaspoon salt
» 2 2/3 tablespoons sugar
» 2 cups white bread flour
» 3/4 teaspoon bread machine yeast

INSTRUCTIONS

Put the ingredients in your bread maker according to the manufacturer's instructions. Press Start after programming the machine for Basic/White bread and selecting light or medium crust. When the bake cycle ends, bread is ready. Remove the bucket from the machine. Allow 5 minutes for the bread to cool. Remove the loaf from the bucket with a little shake and place it on a cooling rack.

17. CRUSTED FRENCH BREAD

READY IN ABOUT: 2 HOURS
YIELDS: 1 LB LOAF

INGREDIENTS

» 2/3 cup water
» 2 teaspoons olive oil
» 1 tablespoon sugar
» 2/3 teaspoon salt
» 2 cups white bread flour
» 1 teaspoon bread machine yeast

INSTRUCTIONS

Put the ingredients in your bread maker according to the manufacturer's instructions. Press Start after programming the machine for Basic or White bread and selecting light or medium crust. When the bake cycle ends, the bread is ready. Remove the bucket from the machine after the loaf is done. Allow 5 minutes for the bread to cool. Remove the loaf from the bucket with a little shake and place it on a cooling rack.

18. TRADITIONAL ITALIAN BREAD

READY IN ABOUT: 2 HOURS
YIELDS: 1 LB LOAF

INGREDIENTS

» 2/3 cup water (27°C to 32°C)
» 2 cups white bread flour
» 1 tablespoon olive oil
» 1 tablespoon sugar
» 3/4 teaspoon salt
» 1 teaspoon bread machine yeast

INSTRUCTIONS

Put the ingredients in your bread maker according to the manufacturer's instructions. Press Start after programming the machine for Basic/White bread and selecting light or medium crust. Lift the bucket from the machine after the loaf is done when the bake cycle ends. Allow 5 minutes for the bread to cool. Remove the loaf from the pan with a little shake and place it on a cooling rack.

19. POTATO BREAD

READY IN ABOUT: 2 1/2 HOURS
YIELDS: 1 1/2 LB LOAF

INGREDIENTS

» 3/4 cup water
» 1 egg
» 2/3 cup instant mashed potatoes
» 2 tablespoons butter, unsalted
» 2 tablespoons white sugar
» 1/4 cup dry milk powder
» 3 cups bread flour
» 1 1/2 teaspoons active dry yeast

INSTRUCTIONS

Add the ingredients to the bread machine. Select light to medium crust color and start the Basic bread cycle. When the bake cycle ends, the bread is ready. Before serving, remove the bread from the pan and cool on a wire rack.

20. RUSTIC BREAD

READY IN ABOUT: 2 HOURS
YIELDS: 1 1/2 LB LOAF

INGREDIENTS

» 2 tablespoons full rounded yeast
» 3 cups white bread flour
» 1 tablespoon salt
» 1 1/2 tablespoons sugar
» 1 cup water

For the Topping:
» Olive oil
» Poppy seeds

INSTRUCTIONS

Add the water first in the pan, then the dry ingredients except for the yeast. In the center of these ingredients, make a well with a spoon and add the yeast. Select the French cycle and the light crust color, then press the Start button. When the bake cycle ends, the bread is done; brush the top with olive oil and a little dusting of poppy seeds. Allow cooling slightly before serving warm with a drizzle of extra virgin olive oil for dipping.

21. BEER BREAD

READY IN ABOUT: 2 1/2 HOURS
YIELDS: 1 1/2 LB LOAF

INGREDIENTS

» 1 1/8 cups (9 ounces) beer
» 2 tablespoons olive oil
» 3 1/2 cups bread flour
» 1/4 cup sugar
» 3/4 teaspoon salt
» 2 1/4 teaspoons bread machine yeast

INSTRUCTIONS

Pour the beer into a bowl and set it aside to flatten for a few hours at room temperature. Place all of the ingredients in the pan in the sequence specified by the maker. Set the crust too dark and begin the Basic cycle by pressing the Start button. Take the bread out from the pan and place it on a rack when the baking cycle is finished. Before slicing, allow it cool to room temperature.

22. SIMPLE SANDWICH BREAD

READY IN ABOUT: 2 1/2 HOURS
YIELDS: 1 1/2 LB LOAF

INGREDIENTS

» 2 tablespoons active dry yeast
» 3 cups Light Flour Blend
» 1/4 cup granulated cane sugar
» 1 tablespoon baking powder
» 2 teaspoons xanthan gum
» 1 teaspoon kosher salt
» 1/8 teaspoon ascorbic acid (optional)

Wet ingredients
» 1 cup plus 2 tablespoons 1% milk
» 1/4 cup olive oil
» 2 teaspoons apple cider vinegar
» 3 large eggs

INSTRUCTIONS

Place the bread pan on the counter with the beater paddle inside. Add the water first in the pan, then the dry ingredients except for the yeast. In the center of these ingredients, make a well with a spoon and add the yeast. Insert the bread pan into the machine, center it, and lock it in place. Close the lid and choose from the following option: Cycle gluten-free with 1 12 pound/750 g Loaf size: pick Medium crust, and then hit Start. When the baking is finished, take the bread pan from the machine and place it on a wire cooling rack on its side. Allow for a few minutes in the pan before turning it upside down and sliding the loaf onto the wire rack. Allow the bread to cool before slicing it upside down.

23. TENDER BUTTERMILK BREAD

READY IN ABOUT: 2 1/2 HOURS
YIELDS: 1 1/2 LB LOAF

INSTRUCTIONS

» 2 tablespoons) active dry yeast
» 3 cups) Light Flour Blend
» 1/2 cup) buttermilk powder
» 3 tablespoons) granulated cane sugar
» 1 tablespoon baking powder
» 2 teaspoons xanthan gum
» 2 teaspoons kosher or fine salt
» 1/8 teaspoon ascorbic acid (optional)

Wet Ingredients
» 4 tablespoons unsalted butter
» 3 large eggs
» 1 cup plus 2 tablespoons water
» 1 teaspoon apple cider vinegar

INSTRUCTIONS

Place the bread pan on the counter with the beater paddle inside. Add the water first in the pan, then the dry ingredients except for the yeast. In the center of these ingredients, make a well with a spoon and add the yeast. Insert the bread pan into the machine, center it, and lock it in place. Close the lid and choose from the following option: Cycle gluten-free with 1 12 pound/750 g Loaf size: pick Medium crust, and then hit Start. When the baking is finished, take the bread pan from the machine and place it on a wire cooling rack on its side. Allow for a few minutes in the pan before turning it upside down and sliding the loaf onto the wire rack. Allow the bread to cool before slicing it upside down.

24. TRADITIONAL EGG BREAD

READY IN ABOUT: 2 1/2 HOURS
YIELDS: 1 1/2 LB LOAF

INGREDIENTS

» 2 tablespoons active dry yeast
» 2 1/4 cups Light Flour Blend
» 1 1/4 cups millet flour
» 1/4 cup milk powder
» 2 tablespoons granulated cane sugar
» 2 1/2 teaspoons baking powder
» 1 teaspoon xanthan gum
» 1/2 teaspoon salt
» 1/8 teaspoon ascorbic acid, optional

Wet Ingredients

» 1 tablespoon honey
» 3/4 cup water
» 3 large eggs
» 6 tablespoons salted butter
» 2 teaspoons apple cider vinegar

INSTRUCTIONS

Place the bread pan on the counter with the beater paddle inside. Add the water first in the pan, then the dry ingredients except for the yeast. In the center of these ingredients, make a well with a spoon and add the yeast. Insert the bread pan into the machine, center it, and lock it in place. Close the lid and choose from the following option: Cycle gluten-free with 1 12 pound/750 g Loaf size: pick Medium crust, and then hit Start. When the baking is finished, take the bread pan from the machine and place it on a wire cooling rack on its side. Allow for a few minutes in the pan before turning it upside down and sliding the loaf onto the wire rack. Allow the bread to cool before slicing it upside down.

25. MALT BREAD LOAF

READY IN ABOUT: 3 HOURS
YIELDS: 2 LB LOAF

INGREDIENTS

» 1 1/4 cups semi-skimmed milk or soya milk
» 1/2 cup ml water
» 2 cup strong wholemeal flour
» 1 1/2 cups strong white flour
» 2 tablespoons vegetable oil
» 1 dessertspoon malt extract
» 1 dessertspoon black treacle
» 1 cup + 1 tablespoon sultanas
» 1 teaspoon fast-acting dried yeast

INSTRUCTIONS

In the bread machine pan, combine all ingredients except the sultanas. Select the basic setting, then light/medium crust, and push the start button. Just before the final kneading cycle, add the sultanas. When the baking is finished, take the bread pan from the machine and place it on a wire cooling rack on

its side. Allow for a few minutes in the pan before turning it upside down and sliding the loaf onto the wire rack. Allow the bread to cool before slicing it upside down.

26. BRIOCHE LOAF

READY IN ABOUT: 2 1/2 HOURS
YIELDS: 1 1/2 LB LOAF

INGREDIENTS

» 2 teaspoons active dry yeast
» 4 cups Light Flour Blend
» 1/3 cup granulated cane sugar
» 1/4 cup milk powder
» 2 1/2 teaspoons salt
» 1 teaspoon baking powder
» 1 teaspoon xanthan gum
» 1/2 teaspoon dough enhancer
» 12 tablespoons unsalted European-style butter (melted)
» 4 large eggs (beaten)
» 2/3 cup 1% milk/water (warm)
» 2 teaspoons apple cider vinegar
» 1/8 teaspoon ascorbic acid (optional)

INSTRUCTIONS

Place the bread pan on the counter with the beater paddle inside. Add the water first in the pan, then the dry ingredients except for the yeast. In the center of these ingredients, make a well with a spoon and add the yeast. Insert the bread pan into the machine, center it, and lock it in place. Close the lid and choose from the following option: Cycle gluten-free with 1 12 pound/750 g Loaf size: pick Medium crust, and then hit Start. When the baking is finished, take the bread pan from the machine and place it on a wire cooling rack on its side. Allow for a few minutes in the pan before turning it upside down and sliding the loaf onto the wire rack. Allow the bread to cool before slicing it upside down.

27. ALMOST WHEAT SANDWICH BREAD

READY IN ABOUT: 3 1/2 HOURS
YIELDS: 1 1/2 LB LOAF

INGREDIENTS

» 2 cups Light Flour Blend
» 1 cup sorghum flour
» 1/2 cup milk powder
» 1/4 cup flaxseed meal/ground flaxseed
» 2 tablespoons active dry yeast
» 3 tablespoons granulated cane sugar
» 2 teaspoons baking powder
» 2 teaspoons xanthan gum
» 1 1/2 teaspoons salt
» 1/8 teaspoon ascorbic acid (optional)
» 3 large eggs (beaten)
» 1 cup+2 tablespoon warm Water
» 3 tablespoons olive oil
» 2 teaspoons apple cider vinegar

INSTRUCTIONS

Place the bread pan on the counter with the beater paddle inside. Add the water first in the pan, then the dry ingredients except for the yeast. In the center of these ingredients, make a well with a spoon and add the yeast. Insert the bread pan into the machine, center it, and lock it in place. Close the lid and choose from the following option: Cycle gluten-free with 1 12 pound/750 g Loaf size: pick Medium crust, and then hit Start. When the baking is finished, take the bread pan from the machine and place it on a wire cooling rack on its side. Allow for a few minutes in the pan before turning it upside down and sliding the loaf onto the wire rack. Allow the bread to cool before slicing it upside down.

28. BASIC WHITE BREAD

READY IN ABOUT: 3 1/2 HOURS
YIELDS: 2 LB LOAF

INGREDIENTS

- » 1 cup water
- » 3/4 cup milk
- » 2 tablespoons butter
- » 1/4 cup sugar
- » 2 teaspoons salt
- » 4 cups bread flour
- » 2 teaspoons active dry yeast

INSTRUCTIONS

In a bread pan, combine all ingredients with the least amount of liquid indicated in the recipe. Press Start after selecting the standard and medium Crust settings for the baking cycle. Keep checking your dough as it kneads. If the dough appears dry and stiff after 5 to 10 minutes, or if your machine sounds like it's straining to knead it, add more liquid 1 tablespoon at a time until it forms a smooth, soft, malleable ball that is slightly tacky to the touch. When the baking is finished, remove the bread from the pan and lay it to cool for 1 hour before slicing.

29. BROWN BEGGER'S WHITE BREAD

READY IN ABOUT: 3 HOURS
YIELDS: 2 LB LOAF

INGREDIENTS

- » 3/4 cup water
- » 5/8 cup milk
- » 2 eggs
- » 2 tablespoons oil
- » 1/4 cup sugar
- » 2 teaspoons salt
- » 4 cups bread flour
- » 1/4 cup white germ
- » 2 tablespoons instant potato flakes
- » 2 teaspoons active dry yeast

INSTRUCTIONS

In a bread pan, combine all ingredients with the least amount of liquid indicated in the recipe. Select the regular Bake cycle

and the Medium Crust setting, then push Start. Keep checking your dough as it kneads. If the dough appears dry and stiff after 5 to 10 minutes, or if your machine sounds like it's straining to knead it, add more liquid 1 tablespoon at a time until it forms a smooth, soft, malleable ball that is slightly tacky to the touch. When the baking is finished, remove the bread from the pan and lay it to cool for 1 hour before slicing.

30. DEDE'S BUTTERMILK BREAD

READY IN ABOUT: 2 1/2 HOURS
YIELDS: 2 LB LOAF

INGREDIENTS

- » 1 1/2 cups buttermilk
- » 1/4 cup honey
- » 2 teaspoons salt
- » 2 tablespoons butter
- » 4 cups bread flour
- » 2 1/2 teaspoons active dry yeast

INSTRUCTIONS

In a bread pan, combine all ingredients with the least amount of liquid indicated in the recipe. Press Start after selecting the Light Crust setting and bake cycle standard. Keep checking your dough as it kneads. If the dough appears dry and stiff after 5 to 10 minutes, or if your machine sounds like it's straining to knead it, add more liquid 1 tablespoon at a time until it forms a smooth, soft, malleable ball that is slightly tacky to the touch. When the baking is finished, remove the bread from the pan and lay it to cool for 1 hour before slicing.

31. IRISH POTATO BREAD

READY IN ABOUT: 2 1/2 HOURS
YIELDS: 2 LB LOAF

INGREDIENTS

- » 7/8 cup milk
- » 1/4 cup potato water
- » 2 tablespoons butter
- » 2 tablespoons sugar
- » 2 teaspoons salt
- » 4 cups all-purpose flour
- » 1/2 cup plain mashed potato
- » 2 teaspoons active dry yeast

INSTRUCTIONS

In a bread pan, combine all ingredients with the least amount of liquid indicated in the

recipe. Choose the Medium Crust setting and the conventional or rapid bread bake cycle, then push Start. Keep checking the dough while it kneads. If the dough appears dry and stiff after 5 to 10 minutes, or if your machine sounds like it's straining to knead it, add more liquid 1 tablespoon at a time until it forms a smooth, soft, malleable ball that's slightly tacky to the touch. When the baking is finished, remove the bread from the pan and lay it to cool for 1 hour before slicing.

32. MIDNIGHT SUN BREAD

READY IN ABOUT: 2 1/2 HOURS
YIELDS: 2 LB LOAF

INGREDIENTS

- » 1 1/2 cup buttermilk
- » 3 tablespoons butter
- » 3 tablespoons honey
- » 2 teaspoon salt
- » 4 cups bread flour
- » 4 teaspoons grated orange rind
- » 2 teaspoon caraway seeds
- » 2/3 cup raisins
- » 3 teaspoon active dry yeast

INSTRUCTIONS

In a bread pan, combine all ingredients with the least amount of liquid indicated in the recipe. Select Light Crust, standard or sweet, raisin or nut bake cycle, and then push Start. Keep checking your dough as it kneads. If the dough appears dry and stiff after 5 to 10 minutes, or if your machine sounds like it's straining to knead it, add more liquid 1 tablespoon at a time until it forms a smooth, soft, malleable ball that is slightly tacky to the touch. After the baking cycle is completed, remove the bread from the pan and lay it to cool for 1 hour before slicing.

33. LOW CARB BREAD

READY IN ABOUT: 2 1/2 HOURS
YIELDS: 1 1/2 LB LOAF

INGREDIENTS

- » 1 cup Water Warm Water
- » 1 1/2 tbsp Sugar
- » 3 cups All-Purpose Low Carb Flour
- » 3 tsp Vital Wheat Gluten
- » 1 1/2 tsp Bread Machine Yeast
- » 1/4 cup Vegetable Oil

INSTRUCTIONS

In a bread pan, combine all ingredients with the least amount of liquid indicated in the recipe. Select the basic bake cycle, the delayed timer, and the Medium Crust setting, then push Start. Keep checking your dough as it kneads. If the dough appears dry and stiff after 5 to 10 minutes, or if your machine sounds like it's straining to knead it, add more liquid 1 tablespoon at a time until it forms a smooth, soft, malleable ball that is slightly tacky to the touch. When the baking is finished, remove the bread from the pan and lay it to cool for 1 hour before slicing.

34. BRITISH MUFFIN BREAD

READY IN ABOUT: 3 HOURS
YIELDS: 1 LB LOAF

INGREDIENTS

- » 2/3 cup buttermilk at 80 degrees F
- » 1 tablespoon melted butter
- » 1 tablespoon sugar
- » 3/4 teaspoon salt
- » 1/4 teaspoon baking powder
- » 1 3/4 cups white bread flour
- » 1 1/8 teaspoons instant yeast

INSTRUCTIONS

Fill your bread machine halfway with all of the ingredients and follow the manufacturer's directions carefully. Set your bread machine's program to Basic/White Bread and the crust type to Medium. Start by pressing the START button. Wait till the cycle is finished. When the loaf is done (when the bake cycle ends), remove it from the bucket and set it aside to cool down for a few minutes. To remove the bread, gently shake the pan the Put it on a wire rack to cool before slicing and serving.

35. ANADAMA BREAD

READY IN ABOUT: 3 HOURS
YIELDS: 2 LB LOAF

INGREDIENTS

- » 1 1/2 cup water
- » 1/4 cup molasses
- » 2 teaspoons salt
- » 2 tablespoons butter
- » 4 cups bread flour
- » 1/2 cup cornmeal
- » 3 teaspoons active dry yeast

INSTRUCTIONS

In a bread pan, combine all ingredients with the least amount of liquid indicated in the recipe. Select the normal or sweet bake cycle, the delayed timer, and the Medium Crust setting, then push Start. Keep checking your dough as it kneads. If the dough appears dry and stiff after 5 to 10 minutes, or if your machine sounds like it's straining to knead it, add more liquid 1 tablespoon at a time until it forms a smooth, soft, malleable ball that is slightly tacky to the touch. When the baking is finished, remove the bread from the pan and lay it to cool for 1 hour before slicing.

36. L & L BAKERS DRILL BREAD

READY IN ABOUT: 2 1/2 HOURS
YIELDS: 1 LB LOAF

INGREDIENTS

- » 3 tablespoons milk
- » 3 to 4 tablespoons water
- » 1 egg
- » 1 teaspoon salt
- » 1 tablespoon butter
- » 2 tablespoons sugar
- » 1/3 cup low fat cottage cheese
- » 2 cups bread flour
- » 1 tablespoon dried minced
- » 2 teaspoons dried dill

» 2 teaspoons dried parsley

» 1 1/2 teaspoon active dry yeast

INSTRUCTIONS

In a bread pan, combine all ingredients with the least amount of liquid indicated in the recipe. Press Start after selecting the Light Crust setting. Keep checking your dough as it kneads. If the dough appears dry and stiff after 5 to 10 minutes, or if your machine sounds like it's straining to knead it, add more liquid 1 tablespoon at a time until it forms a smooth, soft, malleable ball that is slightly tacky to the touch. When the baking is finished, remove the bread from the pan and cool for 1 hour before slicing.

37. IRISH SODA BREAD

READY IN ABOUT: 3 HOURS
YIELDS: 2 LB LOAF

INGREDIENTS

» 1 1/2 cups warm Water

» 2 tablespoons margarine/butter

» 2 tablespoons white sugar

» 1 teaspoon salt

» 4 1/4 cups bread flour

» 2 tablespoons dry milk powder

» 2 teaspoons active dry yeast

» 2/3 cup raisins

» 3 teaspoons caraway seed

INSTRUCTIONS

In the bread machine's baking pan, place all ingredients (save the raisins) in the order advised by the manufacturer. Close the cover on the bread maker and place the baking pan inside. Choose the Fruit Bread option. To begin, press the start button. Before adding the raisins, wait for the bread machine to beep. Remove the baking pan carefully from the machine, and invert the bread loaf onto a wire rack to cool entirely before slicing. Cut the bread loaf into desired-sized slices with a sharp knife and serve.

38. ALL-PURPOSE WHITE BREAD

READY IN ABOUT: 3 HOURS
YIELDS: 1 LB LOAF

INGREDIENTS

» 3/4 cup water

» 1 tablespoon melted butter

» 1 tablespoon sugar

» 3/4 teaspoon salt

» 2 tablespoons skim milk powder

» 2 cups white bread flour

» 3/4 teaspoon instant yeast

INSTRUCTIONS

Fill your bread machine halfway with all of the ingredients and follow the manufacturer's directions carefully. Set your bread machine's program to Basic/White Bread and the crust type to Medium. Start by pressing the START button. Wait till the cycle is finished. When the loaf is done (when the bake

cycle ends), remove it from the bucket and set it aside to cool down for a few minutes. To remove the bread, gently shake the pan. Place the baked bread on a wire rack (to cool) before you slice it and serve.

39. MUSTARD FLAVORED BREAD

READY IN ABOUT: 3 HOURS
YIELDS: 2 LB LOAF

INGREDIENTS

» 1 1/4 cups milk

» 3 tablespoons sunflower milk

» 3 tablespoons sour cream

» 2 tablespoons dry mustard

» 1 whole egg, beaten

» 1/2 sachet sugar vanilla

» 4 cups flour

» 1 teaspoon dry yeast

» 2 tablespoons sugar

» 2 teaspoon salt

INSTRUCTIONS

Remove the bread machine pan and pour in the milk and sunflower milk; stir, then add the sour cream and beaten egg. Combine flour, salt, sugar, mustard powder, and vanilla sugar in a large mixing bowl. Sprinkle the yeast into a small groove in the flour. Cover the bucket and place it in your bread maker. Set your bread machine's program to Basic/White Bread and the crust type to Medium. Start by pressing the START button. Wait till the cycle is finished. When the loaf is done (when the bake cycle ends), remove it from the pan, set it aside and let it rest for a few minutes. To remove the bread, gently shake the pan. Put it (the pan) on a wire rack to cool before slicing and serving.

40. ITALIAN SEMOLINA BREAD

READY IN ABOUT: 3 1/2 HOURS
YIELDS: 1 1/2 LB LOAF

INGREDIENTS

» 1 cup water

» 1 teaspoon salt

» 2 1/2 tablespoons butter

» 2 1/2 teaspoons sugar

» 2 1/4 cups flour

» 1/3 cups semolina

» 1 1/2 teaspoons dry yeast

INSTRUCTIONS

Fill your bread machine halfway with all of the ingredients and follow the manufacturer's directions carefully. Set your bread machine's program to Italian Bread/Sandwich mode and medium crust type. Start by pressing the START button. Wait till the cycle is finished. When the loaf is done (when the bake cycle ends), remove it from the bucket and set it aside to cool down for a few minutes. To remove the bread, gently shake the bucket. Placed the bread on a wire rack to cool before slicing and serving.

41. CRISPY FRENCH BREAD DELIGHT

READY IN ABOUT: 4 HOURS
YIELDS: 1 LB LOAF

INGREDIENTS

» 2/3 cup water

» 2 teaspoons olive oil

» 1 tablespoon sugar

» 2/3 teaspoon salt

» 2 cups white bread flour

» 1 teaspoon instant yeast

INSTRUCTIONS

Fill your bread machine halfway with all of the ingredients and follow the manufacturer's directions carefully. Set your bread machine's program to French bread and the crust type to light. Start by pressing the START button. Wait till the cycle is finished. When the loaf is done (when the bake cycle ends, remove it from the bucket and set it aside to cool down for a few minutes. To remove the bread, gently shake the bucket. Put it (the pan) on a wire rack to cool before slicing and serving.

42. ALMOND FLOUR BREAD

READY IN ABOUT: 3 HOURS
YIELDS: 1 LB LOAF

INGREDIENTS

» 4 egg whites

» 2 egg yolks

» 2 cups almond flour

» 1/4 cup butter (melted)

» 1 1/2 tablespoon baking powder

» 1/2 teaspoon xanthan gum

» 1 teaspoon salt

» 1/2 cup + 2 tablespoons warm Water

» 2 1/4 teaspoon yeast

INSTRUCTIONS

Except for the yeast, put the dry ingredients in a small mixing dish. Combine all of the wet ingredients in the bread machine pan. Toss all of the dry ingredients into the bread machine pan from the lower mixing bowl. Add the yeast on top. Select the basic bread option on the bread maker. Remove the bread machine pan from the bread machine once the bread is done. Let it cool before transferring to a cooling rack. The bread can be kept on the counter for up to four days and frozen for three months.

43. COCONUT FLOUR BREAD

READY IN ABOUT: 3 1/2 HOURS
YIELDS: 1 LB LOAF

INGREDIENTS

» 3/4 cup warm water

» 1 1/2 cups coconut flour

» 1 1/2 cups bread flour

» 2 eggs

» 1 teaspoon salt

» 1 teaspoon baking powder

» 1/3 cup honey

» 1/3 cup vegetable oil

» 1/4 cup oats (optional)

» 1/4 cup coconut shredded (optional)

» 2 1/2 teaspoons granulated yeast

INSTRUCTIONS

Except for the yeast, put the dry ingredients in a small mixing dish. Combine all of the wet ingredients in the bread machine pan. Toss all of the dry ingredients into the bread machine pan from the small mixing dish. Add the yeast on top. Select the basic bread option on the bread maker. Remove the bread machine pan from the bread machine once the bread is done. Let it cool before transferring to a wire rack to cool completely. The bread can be kept on the counter for up to four days and frozen for three months.

44. BLACK OLIVE BREAD

READY IN ABOUT: 2 HOURS 35 MINUTES
YIELDS: 1 LB LOAF

INGREDIENTS

» 2/3 cup milk

» 1 tablespoon melted butter

» 2/3 teaspoon minced garlic

» 1 tablespoon sugar

» 2/3 teaspoon salt

» 2 cups white bread flour

» 3/4 teaspoon bread machine yeast

» 1/4 cup chopped black olives

INSTRUCTIONS

In your bread machine, combine the ingredients according to the manufacturer's instructions. Select light or medium crust and press Start to program the machine for Basic/White bread. Remove the bucket from the machine once the loaf is completed. Allow for a 5-minute cooling period. To remove the loaf, gently shake the bucket and place it on a cooling rack.

45. BEST BREAD MACHINE LOAF

READY IN ABOUT: 2 1/2 HOURS
YIELDS: 1 1/2 LB LOAF

INGREDIENTS

» 1 cup warm water (at 45 C)

» 2 tablespoons caster sugar

» 1 teaspoon quick yeast

» 4 tablespoons vegetable oil

» 3 1/8 cup bread flour

» 1 teaspoon salt

INSTRUCTIONS

In the bread machine's pan, combine the water, sugar, and yeast. Allow 10 minutes for the yeast to dissolve and foam. Toss the yeast with the oil, flour, and salt. Press Start after selecting the Basic or White Bread setting. When the bake cycle ends, the bread is ready. Take the bread out from the machine pan and let it cool before serving.

46. CORN, POPPY SEEDS & SOUR CREAM BREAD

READY IN ABOUT: 4 HOURS
YIELDS: 2 LB LOAF

INGREDIENTS

» 3 1/2 cups wheat flour
» 1 3/4 cups cornflour
» 2/3 cup sour cream
» 2 tablespoons corn oil
» 2 teaspoons active dried yeast
» 2 teaspoons salt
» 2 cup water
» poppy seeds for sprinkling

INSTRUCTIONS

Fill the bread maker bucket with water and corn oil. Add flour, sour cream, sugar, and salt. Make a groove in the flour and sprinkle the yeast on top. Set your bread machine's program to Basic/White Bread and the crust type to Medium. Start by pressing the START button. Wait till the cycle is finished. When the loaf is done, take it from the bucket and set it aside to cool for 5 minutes. To remove the bread, gently shake the bucket. Wet the surface and sprinkle the poppy seeds on top. Let it cool before slicing and serving.

47. SIMPLE DARK RYE BREAD

READY IN ABOUT: 3 HOURS
YIELDS: 1 LB LOAF

INGREDIENTS

» 2/3 cup water
» 1 tablespoon melted butter
» 1/4 cup molasses
» 1/4 teaspoon salt
» 1 tablespoon unsweetened cocoa powder
» 1/2 cup rye flour
» 1 1/4 cups white bread flour
» 1 1/8 teaspoons instant yeast
» Pinch of ground nutmeg

INSTRUCTIONS

Fill your bread machine halfway with all of the ingredients and follow the manufacturer's directions carefully. Set your bread machine's program to Basic/White Bread and the crust type to Medium. Start by pressing the START button. Wait till the cycle is finished. When the loaf is done, take it from the bucket and set it aside to cool for 5 minutes. To remove the bread, gently shake the bucket. Let it cool before slicing and serving.

48. BRAN PACKED HEALTHY BREAD

READY IN ABOUT: 3 HOURS
YIELDS: 1 LB LOAF

INGREDIENTS

» 3/4 cup milk
» 1 1/2 tablespoons melted butter
» 2 tablespoons sugar
» 1 teaspoon salt
» 1/4 cup wheat bran
» 1 3/4 cups white bread flour
» 1 teaspoon instant yeast

INSTRUCTIONS

Fill your bread machine halfway with all of the ingredients and follow the manufacturer's directions carefully. Set your bread machine's program to Basic/White Bread and the crust type to Light. Start by pressing the START button. Wait till the cycle is finished. When the loaf is done, take it from the bucket and set it aside to cool for 5 minutes. To remove the bread, gently shake the bucket. Let it cool before slicing and serving.

49. AWESOME MULTIGRAIN BREAD

READY IN ABOUT: 3 HOURS
YIELDS: 1 LB LOAF

INGREDIENTS

» 3/4 cup water
» 1 tablespoon melted butter
» 1/2 tablespoon honey
» 1/2 teaspoon salt
» 3/4 cup multigrain flour
» 1 1/3 cups white bread flour
» 1 teaspoon active dry yeast

INSTRUCTIONS

Fill your bread machine halfway with all of the ingredients and follow the manufacturer's directions carefully. Set your bread machine's program to Basic/White Bread and the crust type to Medium. Start by pressing the START button. Wait till the cycle is finished. When the loaf is done, take it from the bucket and set it aside to cool for 5 minutes. To remove the bread, gently shake the bucket. Let it cool before slicing and serving.

50. MESMERIZING WALNUT BREAD

READY IN ABOUT: 3 1/2 HOURS
YIELDS: 2 LB LOAF

INGREDIENTS

» 4 cups wheat flour
» 1/2 cup water
» 1/2 cup milk
» 2 whole eggs (beaten)
» 1/2 cup walnut
» 1 tablespoon vegetable oil

- » 1 tablespoon sugar
- » 1 teaspoon salt
- » 1 teaspoon bread machine yeast

INSTRUCTIONS

Fill the bread machine bucket with milk, water, vegetable oil, and eggs. Sift in the wheat flour. Then add salt, sugar, and yeast. Set your bread machine's program to French bread and the crust type to Light. Start by pressing the START button. Allow for kneading to commence, and then close the cover. In a dry frying pan, lightly cook the walnuts until crispy, and then set aside to cool. Add the nuts to the bread maker once the bread maker has given the signal. Using a spatula, combine the ingredients. Allow the remaining cycle to finish. When the loaf is done, take it from the bucket and set it aside to cool for 5 minutes. To remove the bread, gently shake the bucket. Let it cool before slicing and serving.

Chapter 4
WHOLE WHEAT BREAD

51. WHOLE WHEAT BREAD

READY IN ABOUT: 2 1/2 HOURS
YIELDS: 2 LB LOAF

INGREDIENTS

» 2 tablespoons water + 1 1/2 cup
» 2 teaspoons salt
» 2 tablespoons vegetable oil
» 1/3 cup packed brown sugar
» 4 1/4 quarter cup of whole wheat flour
» 3 Tablespoon nonfat dry milk
» 2 teaspoons dry active yeast

INSTRUCTIONS

Collect the necessary components. Then Place the ingredients in the bread pan in the order mentioned or as directed by the manufacturer. Make a small well in ingredients with a spoon to add the yeast when adding it last. That will ensure that the yeast reaction occurs at the correct time. Follow the manufacturer's instructions or use Whole Wheat or Timed Cycle.

52. WHEAT CORNMEAL BREAD

READY IN ABOUT: 2 1/2 HOURS
YIELDS: 2 LB LOAF

INGREDIENTS

» 2 1/2 teaspoons active dry yeast
» 1 1/3 cups room temperature water
» 2 tablespoons dark brown or light brown sugar
» 1 large beaten egg
» 2 tablespoons softened Butter
» 1 1/2 teaspoons salt
» 3/4 cup cornmeal
» 3/4 cup whole wheat flour
» 2 3/4 cups bread flour

INSTRUCTIONS

Collect the necessary components. In the sequence advised by your bread machine manufacturer, add the ingredients to the bread maker. Bake at 350°F for about 20 minutes on the basic cycle, with a medium crust.

53. QUINOA OATMEAL BREAD

READY IN ABOUT: 4 HOURS
YIELDS: 2 LB LOAF

INGREDIENTS

- » 1/3 cup quinoa uncooked
- » Or 1/2 cup quinoa flakes
- » 2/3 cup water
- » 1 1/2 cups bread flour
- » 1/2 cup whole wheat flour
- » 4 tbsp unsalted melted and cooled Butter
- » 1 tbsp sugar
- » 1/2 cup quick-cooking oats
- » 1 cup buttermilk
- » 1 1/2 tsp yeast
- » 1 tbsp honey
- » 1 tsp salt

INSTRUCTIONS

Collect the necessary components. Fill a bowl with water halfway, and add the quinoa. (Omit this step if using quinoa flakes instead of raw quinoa.) Bring to a boil, then in low heat and cover for 5 minutes. Bring it to a boil, then reduce to low heat and simmer for 5 minutes, covered. Turn the heat off and cover the quinoa for 10 minutes. Check the bread machine's instructions to see what order to put the ingredients in. In the bread machine, combine bread flour, sugar, whole wheat flour, buttermilk, oats, butter, honey, salt, and yeast (in the sequence suggested by the manual), as well as the cooked quinoa. Allow the bread machine to cycle and bake a whole grain loaf after programming it. Allow at least 15 minutes for the bread to cool before slicing.

Note: Raw quinoa grains must be boiled before being added to the bread dough; however, you can skip this step by substituting quinoa flakes (a processed type of quinoa meant to be consumed as a hot cereal) mimics oatmeal) for the cooked quinoa.

54. WHOLE WHEAT BREAD WITH CHEESE

READY IN ABOUT: 2 1/2 HOURS
YIELDS: 1 1/2 LB LOAF

INGREDIENTS

- » 1/2 Cup milk
- » 1/4 Cup water
- » 1/4 Cup curd cottage Cheese
- » 3 tablespoon unsalted butter
- » 3 tablespoon Honey
- » 1 1/2 teaspoon Salt
- » 1 cup Whole Wheat Flour
- » 2 1/2 Cups Bread Flour
- » 1 3/4 Teaspoon Bread Machine Yeast

INSTRUCTIONS

In a bread pan, layer the ingredients in the order stated. Securely place the bread pan in the baking chamber and close the cover. Connect the unit to a wall outlet. Choose Whole Wheat. Choose the size of the loaf and the color of the crust. START/STOP by pressing the START/STOP button. When the bake cycle ends and the bread is done, the complete signal will sound. Take the bread pan from the baking chamber with potholders and carefully remove the bread from the pan. (If the kneading paddle is still in the bread, remove it once it has cooled.) Allow the bread to cool on a wire rack for at least 20 minutes before serving.

55. WHOLE WHEAT BREAD 100%

READY IN ABOUT: 2 1/2 HOURS
YIELDS: 1 1/2 LB LOAF

INGREDIENTS

- » 1/2 Cup Water
- » 1/2 Cup Milk
- » 1 tablespoon unsalted butter
- » 2 tablespoon Molasses
- » 1 teaspoon salt
- » 3 cups Whole Wheat Flour
- » 2 tablespoon Vital wheat gluten (optional)
- » 2 teaspoon Bread Machine Yeast

INSTRUCTIONS

In a bread pan, layer the ingredients in the order stated. Securely place the bread pan in

the device and close the top. Connect the device to a wall outlet. Choose Whole Wheat. Choose the size of the loaf and the color of the crust. START/STOP by pressing the START/STOP button. When the bake cycle ends, the bread is done, the complete signal will sound. Take out the bread pan from the baking chamber with potholders and carefully remove the bread. (If the kneading paddle is still in the bread, remove it once it has cooled.) Allow the bread to cool on a wire rack for at least 20 minutes before serving.

56. CARAWAY RYE BREAD

READY IN ABOUT: 2 1/2 HOURS
YIELDS: 1 1/2 LB LOAF

INGREDIENTS

- » 1 Egg
- » 1 1/4 Cup Water
- » 3 tablespoon Oil
- » 3 tablespoon Honey
- » 2 tablespoon dry skim milk powder
- » 1 1/4 teaspoon Salt
- » 1 1/2 Cup Bread Flour
- » 1 Cup Rye Flour
- » 3/4 Cup White Wheat Flour
- » 1 1/2 tablespoon Caraway Seeds
- » 1 1/4 teaspoon Bread machine Yeast

INSTRUCTIONS

Crack and blend an egg in a measuring cup and fill it halfway with water. Pour the batter into a bread pan. In the sequence specified, add the remaining ingredients to the bread pan.

Securely place the bread pan in the baking chamber and close the cover. Connect the unit to a wall outlet. Select WHOLE WHEAT from the drop-down menu. Choose the size of the loaf and the color of the crust. START/STOP by pressing the START/STOP button. When the bread is done, the entire signal will sound. Remove the bread pan from the baking chamber with potholders and carefully remove the bread from the pan. (If the kneading paddle is still in the bread, remove it once it has cooled.) Allow the bread to cool on a wire rack for at least 20 minutes before serving.

57. RUSSIAN BLACK BREAD

READY IN ABOUT: 2 1/2 HOURS
YIELDS: 1 1/2 LB LOAF

INGREDIENTS

» 2 Egg
» 3/4 cup Water
» 2 tablespoon Oil
» 2 tablespoon Honey
» 3 tablespoon dry skim milk powder
» 3 tablespoon Cocoa powder
» 2 teaspoon Caraway seeds
» 2 teaspoon Instant coffee granules
» 1 1/2 teaspoon Salt
» 3/4 Cup Whole wheat flour
» 3/4 Cup Rye flour
» 1 1/2 Cup Bread flour
» 1 3/4 teaspoon Bread machine yeast

INSTRUCTIONS

In a bread pan, layer the ingredients in the order stated. Securely place the bread pan in the baking chamber and close the cover. Connect the unit to a wall outlet. Choose Whole Wheat. Choose the size of the loaf and the color of the crust. START by pressing the START/STOP button. When the bake cycle ends, bread is done, the complete signal will sound. Take out the bread pan from the baking chamber with potholders and carefully remove the bread from the pan. (If the kneading paddle is still in the bread, remove it once it has cooled.) Allow the bread to cool on a wire rack for at least 20 minutes before serving.

58. HONEY WHEAT BREAD

READY IN ABOUT: 2 HOURS
YIELDS: 2 LB LOAF

INGREDIENTS

» 41/2 cups 100% whole wheat flour
» 1 1/2 cups warm water
» 1/3 cup olive oil
» 2 teaspoons salt
» 1/3 cup honey
» 1 tablespoon active dry yeast

INSTRUCTIONS

Fill the bread machine halfway with water. In the same measuring cup, measure and add the oil first, then the honey;

this will help the honey glide out more readily. After that, add the flour. Add the yeast to a small well in the flour. Set the cycle to Wheat Bread, select the crust color, then push the Start button. The bread is baked, removed from the machine, and cool on a wire rack before serving when the bake cycle ends.

59. OATMEAL PECAN BREAD

READY IN ABOUT: 2 1/2 HOURS
YIELDS: 1 1/2 LB LOAF

INGREDIENTS

» 1 1/4 cups water
» 1/4 cup molasses
» 1 tablespoon vegetable oil
» 1 1/2 teaspoon salt
» 1/2 cup dry oatmeal
» 1 cup whole wheat flour
» 2 1/2 cups bread flour
» 2 teaspoon bread machine yeast
» 1/2 cup dried apricots (chopped)
» 1/3 cup pecans (chopped and toasted)

INSTRUCTIONS

Add all ingredients in the bread pan in the order listed, except the apricots and pecans. Securely place the bread pan in the baking chamber and close the cover. Connect the item to a power source. Choose WHOLE WHEAT. Choose the size of the loaf and the color of the crust. START/STOP by pressing the START/STOP button. Add apricots and pecans at the "add ingredient" beep for larger loaves if adding ingredients directly to the bread pan. When the bread is done, the entire signal will sound. Remove the bread pan from the unit with potholders and carefully remove the bread from the pan. (If the kneading paddle is still in the bread, remove it once it has cooled.) Let the bread cool on a wire rack for at least 20 minutes before serving.

60. WHOLE WHEAT CRANBERRY BREAD

READY IN ABOUT: 2 1/2 HOURS
YIELDS: 2 LB LOAF

INGREDIENTS

» 1 1/4 cup warm water
» 2 1/2 tablespoon unsalted Butter
» 2 tablespoon honey
» 2 teaspoon grated orange peel
» 1 1/4 teaspoon salt
» 1 1/2 cups whole wheat flour
» 2 1/2 cups bread flour
» 2 tablespoon bread machine yeast
» 1 cup dried cranberries

INSTRUCTIONS

Add all of the ingredients in the bread pan in the order stated, except the cranberries.
Securely insert a bread pan into the device and close the cover. Connect the unit to a wall outlet. Choose WHOLE

WHEAT. Choose the size of the loaf and the color of the crust. START/STOP by pressing the START/STOP button. Add cranberries at the "add ingredient" beep for larger loaves if adding ingredients directly to the bread pan. When the bread is done, the entire signal will sound. Remove the bread pan from the baking chamber with potholders and carefully remove the bread. (If the kneading paddle is still in the bread, remove it once it has cooled.) Let the bread cool on a wire rack for at least 20 minutes before serving.

Note: For a 1-pound loaf, put the apricots and pecans to the automatic fruit and nut dispenser here; for a 2-pound loaf, wait until the "add ingredient" beep and add directly to the bread pan, as the full amount necessary for the recipe is more than the dispenser can hold.

61. YOGURT WHOLE WHEAT BREAD

READY IN ABOUT: 2 HOURS
YIELDS: 2 LB LOAF

INGREDIENTS

- » 1 cup plain nonfat yogurt
- » 1/2 cup water
- » 1 1/2 tablespoon vegetable oil
- » 2 tablespoon maple syrup
- » 2 teaspoon salt
- » 1 1/2 cups whole wheat flour
- » 2 1/2 bread flour
- » 2 tablespoon bulgur wheat
- » 2 1/4 bread machine yeast

INSTRUCTIONS

In the order specified, pour the ingredients into the bread pan. Close the cover and secure the bread pan in the baking chamber. Connect the unit to a wall outlet. CHOOSE WHOLE WHEAT. Choose the size of the loaf and the color of the crust. START/STOP by pressing the START/STOP button. When the bread is done, the entire signal will sound. Remove the bread pan from the baking chamber with potholders and carefully remove the bread from the pan. (If the kneading paddle is still in the bread, remove it once it has cooled.) Let the bread cool on a wire rack for at least 20 minutes before serving.

62. OLD FASHIONED SESAME WHOLE WHEAT BREAD

READY IN ABOUT: 3 1/2 HOURS
YIELDS: 1 1/2 LB LOAF

INGREDIENTS

- » 3/4 cup water
- » 1/4 cup + 2 tablespoon milk
- » 2 tablespoons butter, cut into pieces
- » 2 1/4 cups bread flour
- » 3/4 cup whole wheat flour
- » 2 tablespoons light or dark brown sugar
- » 1 tablespoon sesame seeds
- » 1 tablespoon + 1 teaspoon gluten
- » 1 1/2teaspoons salt
- » 2 1/2teaspoons bread machine yeast

INSTRUCTIONS

Place all of the ingredients in the pan in the sequence specified by the maker. Set the crust to medium and begin the Basic cycle by pressing the Start button. (The Delay Timer is not compatible with this recipe.) Take out the bread from the pan and place it on a rack when the baking cycle is finished. Before slicing, allow it cool to room temperature.

63. TECATE RANCH WHOLE WHEAT FLOUR

READY IN ABOUT: 2 1/2 HOURS
YIELDS: 1 1/2 LB LOAF

INGREDIENTS

- » 1 1/3 cups water
- » 3 tablespoons canola oil
- » 2 tablespoons honey
- » 2 tablespoons molasses
- » 3 1/4 cups whole wheat flour
- » 1/3 cup wheat bran
- » 1 tablespoon poppy seeds
- » 1 1/2 teaspoons salt
- » 1 tablespoon + active 1/2 teaspoon bread machine yeast

INSTRUCTIONS

Place all of the ingredients in the pan in the sequence specified by the maker. Set the crust too dark and begin the Whole Wheat cycle by pressing the Start button. (The Delay Timer in the machine can be used to make this dish.) Check the dough ball with your finger after 10 minutes. It'll be a sticky situation. 1 to 2 teaspoons more flour. Don't worry if the dough still appears sticky; it will absorb the liquid during the rising process. The bread will be dense rather than bouncy if you use too much flour. The top may collapse if you don't add the extra flour as needed. Take out the bread from the pan and place it on a rack when the baking cycle is finished. Before slicing, allow it cool to room temperature.

64. SCANDINAVIAN LIGHT RYE

READY IN ABOUT: 3 HOURS
YIELDS: 1 1/2 LB LOAF

INGREDIENTS

- » 1 1/8 cups water
- » 1 1/2 tablespoons canola oil
- » 1 7/8 cups bread flour
- » 1 1/8 cups medium rye flour
- » 2 tablespoons brown sugar
- » 1 tablespoon plus 1 teaspoon gluten
- » 1 1/2 tablespoons caraway seeds
- » 1 1/2 teaspoons salt
- » 1 tablespoon bread machine yeast

INSTRUCTIONS

Place all of the ingredients in the pan in the sequence specified by the maker. Set the crust to medium and begin the Basic cycle by pressing the Start button. (The Delay Timer can be used to make this dish.) The dough will be elastic and soft. Take out the bread from the pan and place it on a rack when the baking cycle is finished. Before slicing, allow it cool to room temperature.

65. BARLEY BREAD

READY IN ABOUT: 3 1/2 HOURS
YIELDS: 1 1/2 LB LOAF

INGREDIENTS

» 1 cup+3 tablespoons water
» 2 tablespoons light brown sugar
» 2 tablespoons vegetable oil
» 2 1/4 cups bread flour
» 1/2 cup barley flour
» 1/4 cup whole wheat flour
» 3 tablespoons dry buttermilk powder
» 1 tablespoon plus 2 teaspoons gluten
» 1 teaspoon ground cinnamon
» 1 1/2 teaspoons salt
» 2 3/4 teaspoons bread machine yeast

INSTRUCTIONS

Place all of the ingredients in the pan in the sequence specified by the maker. Set the crust
to medium and begin the Basic or Whole Wheat cycle by pressing the Start button. (The Delay Timer can be used to make this dish.) take out the bread from the pan and place it on a rack when the baking cycle is finished. Before slicing, allow it cool to room temperature.

66. BASIC WHOLE WHEAT BREAD

READY IN ABOUT: 3 1/2 HOURS
YIELDS: 1 1/2 LB LOAF

INGREDIENTS

» 1 1/8 cups lukewarm water
» 3 tablespoons honey
» 2 tablespoons vegetable oil
» 1 1/2 cups plain bread flour
» 1 1/2 cups whole wheat flour
» 1/3 teaspoon salt
» 1 1/2 teaspoons instant dry yeast

INSTRUCTIONS

Add all the ingredients in the bread machine pan in the sequence specified on the package. Alternatively, consult the instruction booklet for your bread maker. Choose the whole wheat option and the medium crust option. When the bake cycle ends, the bread is done, place it on a drying rack to cool before serving.

67. MULTIGRAIN SEED WHOLE WHEAT BREAD

READY IN ABOUT: 3 HOURS
YIELDS: 1 LB LOAF

INGREDIENTS

» 1 cup whole wheat flour
» 2/3 cups lukewarm water

» 3 tablespoons milk powder
» 1 tablespoon honey
» 1 tablespoon unsalted butter
» 1 cup plain bread flour
» 2 tablespoons poppy seeds
» 2 tablespoons sesame seeds
» 2 tablespoons sunflower seeds
» 3/4 teaspoon salt
» 2 teaspoons instant dry yeast

INSTRUCTIONS

Add all the bread machines with the ingredients in the sequence stated above or as directed
by your bread machine's instruction manual. Choose the basic crust function and the basic setting. When the bake cycle ends, the bread is done, place it on a drying rack to cool before serving.

68. HONEY AND OAT WHOLE WHEAT BREAD

READY IN ABOUT: 3 HOURS
YIELDS: 1 LB LOAF

INGREDIENTS

» 2/3 cup lukewarm water
» 1/2 tablespoon olive oil
» 8 teaspoons honey
» 1/2 cup rolled oats
» 3/4 cup whole wheat flour
» 3/4 cup white bread flour
» 1/2 teaspoon salt
» 1/2 teaspoon instant yeast

INSTRUCTIONS

Add all ingredients in the pa of your bread machine in the sequence mentioned or directed per the manufacturer's instructions. Choose the standard bread setting as well as the soft crust option. When the bake cycle ends, the bread is done, place it on a drying rack to cool before serving.

69. TANGY WHOLE WHEAT BREAD

READY IN ABOUT: 3HOURS
YIELDS: 2 LB LOAF

INGREDIENTS

» Zest of 2 oranges, cut into very thin strips
» 1 2/3 cups fat-free milk
» 3 tablespoons olive/walnut oil
» 3 tablespoons honey
» 2 1/4 cups whole wheat flour
» 2 cups bread flour
» 1 tablespoon + 1 teaspoon gluten
» 1 1/2 teaspoons salt
» 2 3/4 teaspoons bread machine yeast

INSTRUCTIONS

Finely cut the orange peel in a food processor, or chop it by hand. Place all of the ingredients in the pan in the sequence specified by the maker. Set the crust to medium and select the Whole Wheat cycle from the menu; hit Start. Take out the bread from the pan and place it on a rack when the baking cycle is finished. Before slicing, allow it cool to room temperature.

70. POTATO WHOLE WHEAT BREAD

READY IN ABOUT: 2 HOURS 45 MINUTES
YIELDS: 2 LB LOAF

INGREDIENTS

» 1 2/3 cups water
» 4 tablespoons butter
» 3 tablespoons honey
» 2 1/2 cups whole wheat flour
» 1 1/2 cups bread flour
» 1/3 cup instant potato flakes
» 2 tablespoons gluten
» 2 teaspoons salt
» 1 tablespoon bread machine yeast

INSTRUCTIONS

Place all of the ingredients in the pan in the sequence specified by the maker. Set the crust to medium and select the Whole Wheat cycle from the menu; hit Start. When the bake cycle ends, the bread is ready.
Please take the bread from the pan and place it on a rack when the baking cycle is finished. Before slicing, allow it cool to room temperature.

71. AUTHENTIC WHOLE WHEAT BREAD

READY IN ABOUT: 2 HOURS 45 MINUTES
YIELDS: 1 LB LOAF

INGREDIENTS

» 1 cup lukewarm water
» 1 1/4 tablespoons milk powder
» 1 1/4 tablespoons unsalted butter, diced
» 1 1/4 tablespoons honey
» 1 1/4 tablespoons molasses
» 1 teaspoon salt
» 2 1/4 cups whole wheat flour
» 1 teaspoon active dry yeast

INSTRUCTIONS

Add all the ingredients in a pan of the bread machine in the sequence stated above or as directed by your bread machine's instruction manual. Choose the whole wheat option and the medium crust option. When the bake cycle ends, the bread is done, place it on a drying rack to cool before serving.

72. BUTTERMILK WHOLE WHEAT BREAD

READY IN ABOUT: 2 HOURS 55 MINUTES
YIELDS: 2 LB LOAF

INGREDIENTS

» 1 1/2 cups buttermilk
» 3 tablespoons canola oil
» 2 1/2 tablespoons maple syrup
» 2 cups whole wheat flour
» 2 cups bread flour
» 1 tablespoon + 2 teaspoons gluten
» 2 teaspoons salt
» 2 3/4 teaspoons bread machine yeast

INSTRUCTIONS

Place all of the ingredients in the pan in the sequence specified by the maker. Set the crust to medium and begin the Basic or Whole Wheat cycle by pressing the Start button. Take out the bread from the pan and place it on a rack when the baking cycle is finished. Before slicing, allow it cool to room temperature.

73. FLAX SEED WHOLE WHEAT BREAD

READY IN ABOUT: 2 HOURS 20 MINUTES
YIELDS: 2 LB LOAF

INGREDIENTS

» 1 1/2 cups water
» 3 tablespoons canola oil
» 1/4 cup honey
» 2 2/3 cups bread flour
» 1 1/3 cups whole wheat flour
» 1/3 cup nonfat dry milk
» 2 1/2 tablespoons flaxseed
» 1 1/4 tablespoons gluten
» 1 1/2 teaspoons salt
» 2 3/4 teaspoons bread machine yeast

INSTRUCTIONS

Place all of the ingredients in the pan in the sequence specified by the maker. Set the crust to medium and begin the Basic or Whole Wheat cycle by pressing the Start button. (The Delay Timer can be used to make this dish.) Take out the bread from the pan and place it on a rack when the baking cycle is finished. Before slicing, allow it cool to room temperature.

74. GRAHAM BREAD

READY IN ABOUT: 3 HOURS AND 10 MINUTES
YIELDS: 2 LB LOAF

INGREDIENTS

» 1 1/3 cups water
» 1 large egg + 1 egg yolk
» 3 tablespoons butter, cut into pieces
» 3 cups bread flour
» 1 cup graham flour

- » 1/2 cup nonfat dry milk
- » 1/3 cup light brown sugar
- » 2 teaspoons salt
- » 2 3/4 teaspoons bread machine yeast

INSTRUCTIONS

Place all of the ingredients in the pan in the sequence specified by the maker. Set the crust to medium and begin the Basic or Whole Wheat cycle by pressing the Start button. Take out the bread from the pan and place it on a rack when the baking cycle is finished. Before slicing, allow it cool to room temperature.

75. WHOLE WHEAT MAPLE SEED BREAD

READY IN ABOUT: 3 HOURS
YIELDS: 1 LB LOAF

INGREDIENTS

- » 2/3 cup lukewarm water
- » 1 tablespoon olive oil
- » 2 tablespoons maple syrup
- » 1 3/4 cups white whole wheat flour
- » 6 teaspoons assorted seeds (an even mix of flax, sesame and sunflower seeds)
- » 3/4 teaspoon salt
- » 3/4 teaspoon instant yeast

INSTRUCTIONS

Fill your bread maker with all of the ingredients in the precise sequence provided. Select the whole-wheat setting and the medium crust function. When the bake cycle ends, the bread is done, place it on a drying rack to cool before serving.

76. LOW CARB WHOLE WHEAT BREAD

READY IN ABOUT: 3 HOURS
YIELDS: 2 LB LOAF

INGREDIENTS

- » 2 cups warm water
- » 1/4 cup unsalted butter/margarine (cut into pieces)
- » 2 large eggs
- » 2 teaspoon lemon juice
- » 1 3/4 teaspoon salt
- » 2 1/2 cups whole wheat flour
- » 1/2 cup whey protein powder
- » 1/2 cup vital wheat gluten
- » 1/2 cup psyllium husk powder
- » 1/4 cup flaxseed meal
- » 1/4 cup wheat bran
- » 3 tablespoon nutritional yeast powder
- » 3 tablespoon oat bran
- » 41/2 teaspoon bread machine yeast

INSTRUCTIONS

In the order specified, pour the ingredients into the bread pan. Close the cover and secure the bread pan in the baking chamber. Connect the unit to a wall outlet. LOW CARB is the option to choose. START/STOP by pressing the START/STOP button. When the bread is done, the entire signal will sound. Remove the bread pan from the baking chamber with potholders and carefully remove the bread from the pan. (If the kneading paddle is still in the bread, remove it once it has cooled.) Allow the bread to cool on a wire rack for at least 20 minutes before serving.

77. LIGHT WHOLE WHEAT BREAD

READY IN ABOUT: 3 HOURS
YIELDS: 1 1/2 LB LOAF

INGREDIENTS

- » 1 cups water
- » 1 large egg
- » 2 tablespoons vegetable/nut oil
- » 2 1/2 cups bread flour
- » 1/2 cup whole wheat flour
- » 3 tablespoons dry buttermilk powder
- » 2 tablespoons dark brown sugar
- » 1 tablespoon gluten
- » 1 1/2 teaspoons salt
- » 2 1/2 tablespoon bread machine yeast

INSTRUCTIONS

Place all of the ingredients in the pan in the sequence specified by the maker. Set the crust to medium or dark and begin the Basic cycle by pressing the Start button. It will be a moist dough ball. (The Delay Timer is not compatible with this recipe.) Take out the bread from the pan and place it on a rack when the baking cycle is finished. Before slicing, allow it cool to room temperature.

78. THREE SEED WHOLE WHEAT BREAD

READY IN ABOUT: 3 1/2 HOURS
YIELDS: 1 1/2 LB LOAF

INGREDIENTS

- » 1 1/4 cups water
- » 2 tablespoons sunflower seed oil
- » 1 1/2 cups bread flour
- » 1 1/2 cups whole wheat flour
- » 3 tablespoons nonfat dry milk
- » 2 tablespoons brown sugar
- » 1 tablespoon gluten
- » 1 teaspoon salt
- » 2 1/2 teaspoons bread machine yeast
- » 1/3 cup raw sunflower seeds
- » 2 tablespoons sesame seeds
- » 2 teaspoons poppy seeds

INSTRUCTIONS

Place all ingredients in the pan, except the seeds, in the sequence specified in the manufacturer's instructions. Set the crust to medium and begin the Basic or Whole Wheat cycle by pressing the Start button. (The Delay Timer is not compatible with this recipe.) Add all the seeds when the machine whistles or between Knead 1 and Knead 2. Take out the bread from the pan and place it on a rack when the baking cycle is finished. Before slicing, allow it cool to room temperature.

79. DAKOTA BREAD

READY IN ABOUT: 3 1/2 HOURS
YIELDS: 1 1/2 LB LOAF

INGREDIENTS

» 1 1/4 cups water
» 2 tablespoons canola oil
» 2 tablespoons honey
» 2 1/4 cups bread flour
» 1/2 cup whole wheat flour
» 1/4 cup raw bulgur cracked wheat
» 2 teaspoons gluten
» 1 1/2 teaspoons salt
» 1/4 cup raw sunflower seeds
» 1/4 cup raw pumpkin seeds, chopped
» 2 teaspoons sesame seeds
» 1 1/2 teaspoons poppy seeds
» 2 1/2 teaspoons bread machine yeast

INSTRUCTIONS

Place all of the ingredients in the pan in the sequence specified by the maker. Set the crust too dark and begin the Basic cycle by pressing the Start button. (The Delay Timer can be used to make this dish.) Remove the bread from the pan and place it on a rack when the baking cycle is finished. Before slicing, allow it cool to room temperature.

80. WHITE WHOLE WHEAT BREAD

READY IN ABOUT: 3 HOURS
YIELDS: 1 1/2 LB LOAF

INGREDIENTS

» 1 1/4 cups water
» 2 tablespoons nut oil or olive oil
» 1/4 cup maple syrup
» 3 1/4 cups white whole wheat flour
» 1 1/2 teaspoons salt
» 2 1/2 teaspoons bread machine yeast

INSTRUCTIONS

Place all of the ingredients in the pan in the sequence specified by the maker. Set the crust too dark and begin the Basic or Whole Wheat cycle by pressing the Start button. (The Delay Timer can be used to make this dish.) Remove the bread from the pan and place it on a rack when the baking cycle is finished. Before slicing, allow it cool to room temperature.

81. NUTRITIOUS 9-GRAIN BREAD

READY IN ABOUT: 2 1/2 HOURS
YIELDS: 1 LB LOAF

INGREDIENTS

» 3/4 cup+2 tablespoons warm water
» 1 cup whole wheat flour
» 1 cup bread flour
» 1/2 cup 9-grain cereal
» 1 teaspoon salt
» 1 tablespoon butter
» 2 tablespoons sugar
» 1 tablespoon milk powder
» 2 teaspoons active dry yeast

INSTRUCTIONS

In the bread machine, combine all of the ingredients. Start by selecting whole wheat and then light/medium crust. Remove the loaf pan from the machine after the loaf is done. Allow 10 minutes for cooling. Cut into slices and serve.

82. BROWN BAGGING IT LOAF

READY IN ABOUT: 4 HOURS
YIELDS: 2 LB LOAF

INGREDIENTS

» 1 3/8 cups water
» 1 1/2 tablespoons light olive oil
» 3 1/2 cups Strong brown, wholemeal bread flour
» 1 1/4 teaspoon salt
» 1 tablespoon Soft brown sugar
» 1 1/2 tablespoon Dried milk powder (skimmed)
» 2 teaspoon Active dry yeast

INSTRUCTIONS

Add all the ingredients (above mentioned) to the pan of your bread machine according to the manufacturer's instructions. Please make a small well in dry ingredients in the center of the flour and carefully place the yeast in it, ensuring it does not overlap or mix with any liquid. Select the Whole Wheat setting and adjust the crust setting to your preference according to your machine's manual. When the loaf is done, carefully remove the bowl from the machine and place it on a wire rack to cool. Remove the paddle once it has cooled. Finally, use a serrated bread knife to slice for the best results.

Chapter 5

SPICE, HERB & VEGETABLE BREAD

83. HERB AND PARMESAN BREAD

READY IN ABOUT: 3 1/2 HOURS
YIELDS: 2 LB LOAF

INGREDIENTS

- » 1 1/3 cups Water
- » 2 cloves crushed Garlic
- » 2 tablespoons Olive Oil
- » 1 teaspoon salt
- » 4 cups bread Flour
- » 3 tablespoons chopped fresh herbs (e.g., basil, chives, oregano, and rosemary)
- » 1 tablespoon Sugar
- » 4 tablespoons grated Parmesan cheese
- » 2 1/4 teaspoons Active Dry Yeast

INSTRUCTIONS

Collect the necessary components. In the sequence advised by the manufacturer, add all ingredients to your bread machine. Bake your bread at 350°F for 20 minutes on the basic cycle, with a medium crust. When the loaf is baking, remove it from the pan and cool thoroughly on a wire rack.

84. KALAMATA BREAD

READY IN ABOUT: 2 HOURS AND 10 MINUTES
YIELDS: 2 LB LOAF

INGREDIENTS

- » 1/3 Olive Brine
- » 1 cup warm water
- » 3 cups Bread Flour
- » 1 2/3 cups Whole Wheat Flour
- » 1 1/2 teaspoons salt
- » 2 tablespoons sugar
- » 2 teaspoons Dry Active Yeast
- » 2 tablespoons Olive Oil
- » 1 1/2 teaspoons Dried Basil
- » 1/2 - 2/3 cup Kalamata Olives (finely chopped, 2 dozen pitted olives)

INSTRUCTIONS

Collect the necessary components. Fill a 2-cup measure halfway with warm water and add at least 1/3 cup of olive brine to produce 1 1/2 cups total liquid. If you don't have enough brine to make a third of a cup, the flavor of the bread will be milder but still wonderful. Simply add enough water to equal the total amount required. In the bread machine, add all ingredients except the olives in the sequence recommended by your manufacturer. On your bread machine, select the basic or wheat preset. When the beep indicates that it's time to add the mix-in ingredients, add the olives. Take your loaf from the machine and set it aside to cool somewhat before slicing.

85. GARLIC BREAD

READY IN ABOUT:: 2 HOURS
YIELDS: 1 LB LOAF

INGREDIENTS

- » 1 Bulb Roasted Garlic
- » 4 Cloves Garlic
- » 3 tablespoons Butter
- » 1/2 cup Water
- » 1/3 cup Milk
- » 2 3/4 cups Bread Flour

- » 1 teaspoon salt
- » 1/3 cup grated Parmesan Cheese
- » 2 tablespoons sugar
- » 1/2 teaspoon Garlic Powder
- » 1-1/2 teaspoons Bread Machine Yeast

INSTRUCTIONS

Collect the necessary components. Prepare the garlic that has been roasted. Squeeze the garlic cloves and crush them slightly before measuring 1/4 cup for the 1 1/2-pound batch. Mix butter with minced garlic in a small microwave-safe dish. Microwave for 1 to 2 minutes on high, or until garlic is aromatic. Place all components, save the roasted garlic, in the bread machine pan in the order specified by the manufacturer: butter and garlic mixture, water, milk, bread flour, Parmesan cheese, sugar, salt, garlic powder, and yeast. If the machine sounds rough or straining as it kneads, add more warm water. Add flour if the dough becomes too wet or soft. Add mashed garlic at the Raisin/Nut indication, or 5 to 10 minutes before the last kneading cycle concludes. Use Medium or Light Crust Color on the Basic/White cycle. Do not use Delay cycles in this recipe.

86. CAJUN BREAD

READY IN ABOUT: 2 HOURS 40 MINUTES
YIELDS: 1 LB LOAF

INGREDIENTS

- » 2 cups Bread Flour
- » 1/2 cup Water
- » 1/4 cup Chopped Onion
- » 1/2 teaspoon salt
- » 1/4 cup Chopped Green Bell Pepper
- » 1 tablespoon Granulated Sugar
- » 2 teaspoons Chopped Garlic
- » 2 teaspoons unsalted butter
- » 1 teaspoon Active Dry Yeast
- » 1 teaspoon Cajun or Creole

INSTRUCTIONS

Collect the necessary components. Add all ingredients into the machine according to the manufacturer's instructions for doing so. Choose the basic or white bread cycle. Use a crust color that is medium or dark. (Avoid using delay cycles.) Remove from pan and cool for 30 minutes on wire rack.

87. HERB BREAD

READY IN ABOUT: 2 HOURS
YIELDS: 1 LB LOAF

INGREDIENTS

- » 3/4 to 7/8 cup milk
- » 1 tablespoon Sugar
- » 1 teaspoon salt
- » 1 tablespoon butter or margarine
- » 1/3 cup chopped onion
- » 2 cups bread flour
- » 1/2 teaspoon dried dill

- » 1/2 teaspoon dried basil
- » 1/2 teaspoon dried rosemary
- » 1 1/2 teaspoon Active dry yeast

INSTRUCTIONS

In a bread pan, combine all of the ingredients. Use the rapid baking cycle with medium crust. The press begins to work. If you hear straining sounds in your machine or if the dough appears stiff and dry after 5-10 minutes, add 1 tablespoon Liquid at a time until the dough becomes smooth, flexible, soft, and slightly tacky to the touch. After baking, take the bread from the pan. Leave to cool for 1 hour before slicing on a rack.

88. ROSEMARY BREAD

READY IN ABOUT: 3 HOURS
YIELDS: 1 LB LOAF

INGREDIENTS

- » 3/4 cup + 1 tablespoon water
- » 1 2/3 tablespoons butter (melted and cooled)
- » 1 teaspoon sugar
- » 1 teaspoon salt
- » 1 tablespoon fresh rosemary (chopped)
- » 2 cups white bread flour
- » 1 1/3 teaspoons instant yeast

INSTRUCTIONS

Fill your bread machine halfway with all of the ingredients and follow the manufacturer's directions carefully. Set your bread machine's program to Basic/White Bread and the crust type to Medium. Start by pressing the START button. Wait till the cycle is finished. When the loaf is done, take it from the bucket or pan and set it aside to cool for 5 minutes. To remove the bread, gently shake the bucket. Place it on a cooling rack to let it cool before slicing and serving

89. ORIGINAL ITALIAN HERB BREAD

READY IN ABOUT: 3 1/2 HOURS
YIELDS: 2 LB LOAF

INGREDIENTS

- » 1 1/2 C. Milk (lukewarm)
- » 6 tbsp Unsalted Butter (sliced & softened)
- » 1 1/2 tsp salt
- » 1 tsp Onion Powder (if you like it)
- » 1 1/2 tsp Bread Machine Yeast
- » 4 cups Bread Flour
- » 2 tbsp White Granulated Sugar
- » 1 1/2 tbsp Italian Herbs Seasoning

INSTRUCTIONS

2-pound loaf, light color, and "basic" set these bread settings in the bread machine. Pull the bread pan from the bread machine and ensure that it is unplugged. Pour the milk into the bread pan first, followed by the remaining ingredients (including the Italian herb seasoning). Last, add the bread machine yeast, making sure it does not contact the liquid.

Replace the bread pan in the bread machine, turn on the machine and press start. Unplug the bread machine after it has completed baking the bread. Place the bread on a cooling rack after removing it from the bread pan.

90. GARLIC, HERB AND CHEESE BREAD

READY IN ABOUT: 2 HOURS
YIELDS: 2 LB LOAF

INGREDIENTS

» 1/2 cup ghee
» 6 eggs
» 2 cups almond flour
» 1 teaspoon baking powder
» 1/2 teaspoon xanthan gum
» 1 cup cheddar cheese, shredded
» 1 tablespoon garlic powder
» 1 tablespoon parsley
» 1/2 tablespoon oregano
» 1/2 teaspoon salt

INSTRUCTIONS

Before pouring into the bread machine pan, lightly whisk eggs and ghee. Then toss the rest of the items in the pan. Make sure your bread maker is set to gluten-free mode. Remove the bread machine pan from the bread machine once the bread is done. Then allow cooling slightly before transferring to a wire rack to cool completely. You can keep the bread in the refrigerator for up to 5 days.

91. GARDEN HERB BREAD

READY IN ABOUT: 3 HOURS
YIELDS: 1 1/2 LB LOAF

INGREDIENTS

» 1 1/4 cups water
» 3 cups white bread flour
» 2 tablespoons dry milk
» 1 1/2 teaspoons salt
» 2 tablespoons sugar
» 2 tablespoons butter
» 2 teaspoons thyme
» 2 teaspoons marjoram
» 1 teaspoon basil
» 2 teaspoons chives
» 2 teaspoons active dry yeast

INSTRUCTIONS

To begin, combine all of the wet ingredients in a bread machine pan. Then combine all of the dry ingredients in a mixing bowl. Set the crust type to MEDIUM and the baking program to BASIC. Remove the bread machine pan from the bread machine once the bread is done. Allow cooling slightly before placing it to a wire rack to cool completely. You can keep your bread in the refrigerator for up to 5 days.
Tips: Use dried herbs that are flakes rather than ground for best results. If using fresh herbs, increase the amount by a factor of two.

92. CUMIN BREAD

READY IN ABOUT: 3 1/2 HOURS
YIELDS: 2 LB LOAF

INGREDIENTS

» 4 cups bread machine flour
» 1 1/2 teaspoon kosher salt
» 1 1/2 tablespoon sugar
» 1 tablespoon bread machine yeast
» 1 3/4 cups lukewarm water
» 1 tablespoon black cumin
» 1 tablespoon sunflower oil

INSTRUCTIONS

Place all dry and liquid ingredients in the pan and bake according to your bread machine's instructions. Then set the crust type to MEDIUM and the baking program to BASIC. Adjust the amount of flour and liquid in the recipe if the dough is too dense or too wet. Take the pan from the bread machine after the program has finished and set it aside to cool for 5 minutes. Remove the bread from the pan by shaking it. Use a spatula if required. Set the bread aside for an hour after wrapping it in a kitchen towel. You may also cool it on a wire rack.

93. SAFFRON BREAD

READY IN ABOUT: 2 1/2 HOURS
YIELDS: 1 1/2 LB LOAF

INGREDIENTS

» 1 cup milk
» 1/3 cup sugar
» 2 eggs
» 3 1/4 cups flour
» 1/8 teaspoon ground saffron (1 package)
» 1 tablespoon butter softened
» 1 teaspoon salt
» 1 package bread maker yeast
» 3/4 cup raisins

INSTRUCTIONS

Prepare the ingredients in your bread machine according to the manufacturer's instructions. Set the machine to make basic/white bread, Light or Medium Crust, and then select the Start button. When the bread maker beeps to indicate that more ingredients are needed, lift the top and add the raisins.

Remove the bucket from the machine after the bread is done. Allow 5 minutes for the bread to cool. Remove the bread from the bucket with a little shake and place it on a plate. Place on a cooling rack.

94. CRACKED BLACK PEPPER BREAD

READY IN ABOUT: 3 HOURS 45 MINUTES
YIELDS: 2 LB LOAF

INGREDIENTS

- » 1 1/2 cup water
- » 3 tablespoon olive oil
- » 3 tablespoon sugar
- » 2 teaspoon salt
- » 1 teaspoon garlic powder
- » 3 tablespoon minced chives
- » 2 minced garlic cloves
- » 1 teaspoon cracked black pepper
- » 1/4 cup parmesan cheese (grated)
- » 1 teaspoon dry basil
- » 4 cups white bread flour
- » 2 1/2 teaspoons active dry yeast

INSTRUCTIONS

Prepare the ingredients in your bread machine according to the manufacturer's instructions. Set the machine to make basic/white bread, Light or Medium. Crust, and then select the Start button. Remove the bucket from the machine after the bread is done. Allow 5 minutes for the bread to cool. Remove the bread from the bucket with a little shake and place it on a plate. Place on a cooling rack.

95. AN EASY LEMON BREAD

READY IN ABOUT: 2 HOURS AND 15 MINUTES
YIELDS: 1 1/2 LB LOAF

INGREDIENTS

- » 1/2 cup + 2 tablespoon water
- » 3 tablespoons lemon juice
- » 1 egg
- » 1 tablespoon grated lemon
- » 2 tablespoons poppy seeds
- » 3 tablespoons sugar
- » 3/4 teaspoon salt
- » 3 tablespoons butter
- » 1/4 teaspoon ground nutmeg
- » 3 cups bread flour
- » 2 teaspoons bread machine yeast

INSTRUCTIONS

Prepare the ingredients in your bread machine according to the manufacturer's instructions. Set the machine to Basic/White bread, choose light or medium crust, and start the machine. Remove the bucket from the machine after the bread is done. Remove the bread from the oven and set it aside to cool for 5 minutes. Remove the loaf from the bucket with a little shake and place it on a cooling rack.

96. CARDAMOM BREAD

Ready in about 2 1/2 hours
YIELDS: 1,5 LB LOAF

INGREDIENTS

- » 1/2 cup milk
- » 1 egg
- » 1 teaspoon melted butter
- » 1 teaspoon honey
- » 2/3 teaspoon salt
- » 1/2 teaspoon ground cardamom
- » 3 cups white bread flour
- » 3/4 teaspoon bread machine or instant yeast

INSTRUCTIONS

Add the ingredients to the pan of your bread machine according to the manufacturer's instructions. Set the machine to Basic/White bread, choose light or medium crust, and start the machine. Remove the bucket from the machine after the bread is done. Allow 5 minutes for the bread to cool. Remove the loaf from the bucket with a little shake and place it on a cooling rack.

97. LOVELY AROMATIC LAVENDER BREAD

READY IN ABOUT: 3 HOURS
YIELDS: 1 LB LOAF

INGREDIENTS

- » 3/4 cup milk
- » 1 tablespoon melted butter
- » 1 tablespoon sugar
- » 3/4 teaspoon salt
- » 1 teaspoon fresh lavender flower (chopped)
- » 1/4 teaspoon lemon zest
- » 1/4 teaspoon fresh thyme (chopped)
- » 2 cups white bread flour
- » 3/4 teaspoon instant yeast

INSTRUCTIONS

Fill your bread machine halfway with all of the ingredients and follow the manufacturer's directions carefully. Set your bread machine's program to Basic/White Bread and the crust type to Medium. Wait till the cycle is finished. When the loaf is ready, grab it from the bucket and set it aside to cool for 5 minutes. To remove the bread, gently shake the bucket.

98. HERBAL GARLIC CREAM CHEESE

READY IN ABOUT: 3 HOURS
YIELDS: 1 LB LOAF

INGREDIENTS

- » 1/3 cup water
- » 1/3 cup herb and garlic cream with cheese mix
- » 1 whole egg, beaten, at room temp
- » 4 teaspoons melted butter
- » 1 tablespoon sugar
- » 2/3 teaspoon salt
- » 2 cups white bread flour

» 1 teaspoon instant yeast

INSTRUCTIONS

Fill your bread machine halfway with all of the ingredients and follow the manufacturer's directions carefully. Set your bread machine's program to Basic/White Bread and the crust type to Medium. Wait till the cycle is finished. When the loaf is done, grab it from the bucket and set it aside to cool for 5 minutes. To remove the bread, gently shake the bucket.

99. CUMIN TOSSED FANCY BREAD

READY IN ABOUT: 3 1/2 HOURS
YIELDS: 2 LB LOAF

INGREDIENTS

» 5 1/3 cups wheat flour
» 1 1/2 teaspoons salt
» 1 1/2 tablespoons sugar
» 1 tablespoon dry yeast
» 1 3/4 cups water
» 2 tablespoons cumin
» 3 tablespoons sunflower oil

INSTRUCTIONS

Fill the bread machine bucket halfway with warm water. Combine the salt, sugar, and sunflower oil in a mixing bowl. Sift in the wheat flour and stir in the yeast. Set your bread machine's program to French Bread and the rust type to Medium. Add cumin when the maker beeps. Wait till the cycle is finished. When the loaf is done, pull it from the bucket and set it aside to cool for 5 minutes. To remove the bread, gently shake the bucket.

100. POTATO ROSEMARY LOAF BREAD

READY IN ABOUT: 3 1/2 HOURS
YIELDS: 2 POUNDS

INGREDIENTS

» 4 cups wheat flour
» 1 tablespoon sugar
» 1 tablespoon sunflower oil
» 1 1/2 teaspoons salt
» 1 1/2 cups water
» 1 teaspoon dry yeast
» 1 cup mashed potatoes, ground through a sieve
» crushed rosemary

INSTRUCTIONS

Combine the sunflower oil and water in a mixing bowl. Attach the mixing paddle to the bread maker bucket and add flour, salt, sugar and the water mixture. As suggested, add the yeast. Set your bread machine's program to Bread with Filling and the crust type to Medium. When the bread maker beeps to indicate that more ingredients are needed, lift the top and add the mashed potatoes and chopped rosemary. Wait till the cycle is finished. When the loaf has baked, take it out from the bucket and set it aside to cool for 5 minutes. To remove the bread, gently shake the bucket.

101. INSPIRING CINNAMON BREAD

READY IN ABOUT: 2 1/2 HOURS
YIELDS: 1LB LOAF

INGREDIENTS

» 2/3 cup milk
» 1 whole egg
» 3 tablespoons melted butter
» 1/3 cup sugar
» 1/3 teaspoon salt
» 1 teaspoon ground cinnamon
» 2 cups white bread flour
» 1 1/3 teaspoons active dry yeast

INSTRUCTIONS

Fill your bread machine halfway with all of the ingredients and follow the manufacturer's directions carefully. Set your bread machine's program to Basic/White Bread and the crust type to Medium. Wait till the cycle is finished. When the loaf is done, pull it from the bucket and set it aside to cool for 5 minutes. Remove the loaf from the oven.

102. LAVENDER BUTTER MILK BREAD

READY IN ABOUT: 3 HOURS
YIELDS: 1 1/2 POUND LOAF

INGREDIENTS

» 1/2 cup water
» 7/8 cup buttermilk
» 1/4 cup olive oil
» 3 tablespoons finely chopped fresh lavender leaves
» 1 1/4 teaspoon finely chopped fresh lavender flowers
» Grated zest of 1 lemon
» 4 cups bread flour
» 2 teaspoon salt
» 2 3/4 teaspoon bread machine yeast

INSTRUCTIONS

In the order advised by your bread machine manufacturer, add each ingredient to the bread machine and at the temperature indicated by your bread machine manufacturer. Close the cover and start your bread maker on the basic bread, medium crust setting. Take the bread from the bread machine and place it on a cooling rack once it has done baking.

103. TURMERIC BREAD

READY IN ABOUT: 3 HOURS
YIELDS: 1,5 LB LOAF

INGREDIENTS

» 1 teaspoon dried yeast
» 4 cups strong white flour
» 1 teaspoon turmeric powder
» 2 teaspoon beetroot powder
» 2 tablespoon olive oil
» 1.5 teaspoon salt

- » 1 teaspoon chili flakes
- » 1 3/8 water

INSTRUCTIONS

In the order advised by your bread machine manufacturer, add each ingredient to the bread machine and at the temperature indicated by your bread machine manufacturer. Close the cover and start your bread maker on the basic bread, medium crust setting. Take the bread from the bread machine and place it on a cooling rack once it has done baking.

104. ROSEMARY CRANBERRY BREAD

READY IN ABOUT: 3 1/2 HOURS
YIELDS: 2 LB LOAF

INGREDIENTS

- » 1 1/3 cups water
- » 2 tablespoon water
- » 2 tablespoon butter
- » 2 teaspoon salt
- » 4 cups bread flour
- » 3/4 cup dried sweetened cranberries
- » 3/4 cup toasted chopped pecans
- » 2 tablespoon non-fat powdered milk
- » 1/4 cup sugar 2 teaspoon yeasts

INSTRUCTIONS

Combine all ingredients in the order advised by your bread machine manufacturer. Close the cover and start your bread maker with the basic bread, medium crust setting. Add cranberries and pecans when the maker beeps. Wait till the cycle is finished. Take the bread from the bread machine and place it on a cooling rack once it has done baking.

105. SESAME FRENCH BREAD

Ready in about 3 1/2 hours
YIELDS: 1 LB LOAF

INGREDIENTS

- » 7/8 cup water
- » 1 tablespoon butter
- » 2 teaspoon sugar
- » 1 teaspoon salt
- » 2 teaspoon yeast
- » 2 3/4 cups bread flour
- » 2 Tablespoon sesame seeds toasted

INSTRUCTIONS

In the order advised by your bread machine manufacturer, add each ingredient to the bread machine and at the temperature indicated by your bread machine manufacturer. Close the cover and start your bread maker with the French Bread, medium crust setting. Take the bread from the bread machine and place it on a cooling rack once it has done baking.

106. SUNFLOWER & FLAX SEED BREAD

Rady in about: 3 hours
YIELDS: 2 LB LOAF

INGREDIENTS

- » 1 1/3 cups water
- » 2 tablespoons butter
- » 3 tablespoons honey
- » 1 1/2 cups bread flour
- » 1 1/3 cups whole wheat flour
- » 1 teaspoon salt
- » 1 teaspoon active dry yeast
- » 1/2 cup flax seeds
- » 1/2 cup sunflower seeds

INSTRUCTIONS

In the bread machine pan, combine all ingredients except the sunflower seeds. Select the basic setting, then light/medium crust, and push the start button. Just before the final kneading cycle, add the sunflower seeds. Remove the loaf pan from the machine after the loaf is done. Allow 10 minutes for cooling. Cut into slices and serve.

107. OATMEAL SUNFLOWER BREAD

READY IN ABOUT: 3 HOURS 45 MINUTES
YIELDS: 1,5 LB LOAF

INGREDIENTS

- » 1 cup water
- » 1/4 cup honey
- » 2 tablespoons butter
- » 3 cups bread flour
- » 1/2 cup old fashioned oats
- » 2 tablespoons milk powder
- » 1 1/4 teaspoons salt
- » 2 1/4 teaspoons active dry yeast
- » 1/2 cup sunflower seeds

INSTRUCTIONS

In the bread machine pan, combine all ingredients except the sunflower seeds. Select the basic setting, then light/medium crust, and push the start button. Just before the final kneading cycle, add the sunflower seeds. Remove the loaf pan from the machine after the loaf is done. Allow 10 minutes for cooling. Cut into slices and serve.

108. CORNMEAL WHOLE WHEAT BREAD

READY IN ABOUT: 2 1/2 HOURS
YIELDS: 1,5 LB LOAF

INGREDIENTS

- » 2 1/2 teaspoons active dry yeast
- » 1 1/3 cups water
- » 2 tablespoons sugar
- » 1 egg
- » 2 tablespoons butter

- » 1 1/2 teaspoons salt
- » 3/4 cup Cornmeal
- » 3/4 cup Whole wheat flour
- » 2 3/4 cups bread flour

INSTRUCTIONS

Fill the bread machine pan with all of the ingredients and bake according to the manufacturer's directions. Start by selecting the basic bread setting, then medium crust. Remove the loaf pan from the machine after the loaf is done. Allow 10 minutes for cooling. Cut into slices and serve.

109. COFFEE RAISIN BREAD

READY IN ABOUT: 3 1/2 HOURS
YIELDS: 1,5 LB LOAF

INGREDIENTS

- » 2 1/2 teaspoons active dry yeast
- » 1/4 teaspoon ground cloves
- » 1/4 teaspoon Ground allspice
- » 1 teaspoon ground cinnamon
- » 3 tablespoons Sugar
- » 1 egg
- » 3 tablespoons Olive oil
- » 1 cup Strong brewed coffee
- » 3 cups bread flour
- » 3/4 cup Raisins
- » 1 1/2 teaspoons salt

INSTRUCTIONS

In the bread machine pan, combine all ingredients except the raisins. Select the basic setting, then light/medium crust, and push the start button. Just before the final kneading cycle, add the raisins. Remove the loaf pan from the machine after the loaf is done. Allow 10 minutes for cooling. Cut into slices and serve.

110. HEALTHY MULTIGRAIN BREAD

READY IN ABOUT: 2 1/2 HOURS
YIELDS: 2 LB LOAF

INGREDIENTS

- » 1 1/4 cups Water
- » 2 tablespoons Butter
- » 1 1/3 cups bread flour
- » 1 1/2 cups Whole wheat flour
- » 1 cup Multigrain cereal
- » 3 tablespoons Brown sugar
- » 1 1/4 teaspoons Salt
- » 2 1/2 teaspoon Yeast

INSTRUCTIONS

Fill the bread machine pan with the indicated ingredients. Start by selecting the basic bread setting, then light/medium crust. Remove the loaf pan from the machine after the loaf is done. Allow 10 minutes for cooling. Cut into slices and serve.

111. WHOLE WHEAT RAISIN BREAD

READY IN ABOUT: 2 1/2 HOURS
YIELDS: 1,5 LB LOAF

INGREDIENTS

- » 3 1/2 cups Whole wheat flour
- » 2 teaspoons dry yeast
- » 2 eggs
- » 1/4 cup Butter
- » 3/4 cup water
- » 1/3 cup Milk
- » 1 teaspoon salt
- » 1/3 cup Sugar
- » 4 teaspoons Cinnamon
- » 1 cup Raisins

INSTRUCTIONS

In a bread pan, combine the water, milk, butter, and eggs. Toss the other ingredients into the bread pan, excluding the yeast. With your finger, make a small hole in the flour and pour the yeast into it. Make certain that no liquids will come into contact with the yeast. Start by selecting whole wheat and then light/medium crust. Remove the loaf pan from the machine after the loaf is done. Allow 10 minutes for cooling. Cut into slices and serve.

112. HEALTHY SPELT BREAD

READY IN ABOUT: 2 1/2 HOURS
YIELDS: 2 LB LOAF

INGREDIENTS

- » 1 1/4 cups Milk
- » 2 tablespoons Sugar
- » 2 tablespoons Olive oil
- » 1 teaspoon salt
- » 4 cups Spelt flour
- » 2 1/2 teaspoons yeast

INSTRUCTIONS

In the bread machine, combine all ingredients according to the manufacturer's instructions. Start by selecting the basic bread setting, then light/medium crust. Remove the loaf pan from the machine after the loaf is done. Allow 10 minutes for cooling. Cut into slices and serve.

113. CORIANDER BREAD

READY IN ABOUT: 2 1/2 HOURS
YIELDS: 1 1/2 LB LOAF

INGREDIENTS

- » 1 cup milk
- » 3 cups bread flour unbleached
- » 1/4 cup all-purpose flour
- » 1/4 cup honey
- » 2 teaspoons yeast, active dry
- » 3 tablespoons margarine
- » 1 teaspoon salt

- » 1/8 teaspoon ginger (ground)
- » 1/8 teaspoon cloves (ground)
- » 1/4 teaspoon cinnamon (ground)
- » 2 teaspoons coriander (ground)
- » 1/2 tablespoon orange zest (grated)
- » 1 each egg

INSTRUCTIONS

Toss all of the ingredients into your bread machine and carefully follow the manufacturer's instructions. Set your bread machine's program to Basic/White Bread and the crust type to Medium. Start by pressing the START button. Wait till the cycle is finished. When the loaf is baked, grab it from the bucket/pan and set it aside to chill for 5 minutes. To get the bread out of the bucket, gently shake it.

114. PUMPKIN AND SUNFLOWER SEED BREAD

READY IN ABOUT: 2 1/2 HOURS
YIELDS: 1,5 LB LOAF

INGREDIENTS

- » 1 cup warm water
- » 3 cups whole wheat flour
- » 1/4 cup wheat bran (optional)
- » 1/4 cup honey
- » 4 tablespoons vegetable oil
- » 1 teaspoon salt
- » 1/3 cup sunflower seeds
- » 1/3 cup pumpkin seeds, shelled, toasted and chopped
- » .25 oz active dry yeast

INSTRUCTIONS

To begin, combine all of the wet ingredients in a bread machine pan. Mix in the dry ingredients and select the whole wheat setting. When the beep indicates that it's time to add the mix-in ingredients, add the sunflower and pumpkin seeds. Remove the bread machine pan from the bread machine after the bread is done. Transfer to a cooling rack after allowing it to cool slightly. You can keep your bread in the refrigerator for up to 5 days.

115. ANISE ALMOND BREAD

READY IN ABOUT: 3 HOURS
YIELDS: 1 1/2 LB LOAF

INGREDIENTS

- » 3/4 cup water (75°F)
- » 3 cups bread flour
- » 1/2 teaspoon salt
- » 1 egg
- » 1/4 cup butter (or margarine)
- » 1/4 cup sugar
- » 2 teaspoons active dry yeast
- » 1 teaspoon anise seed
- » 1/2 cup almonds (chopped)

INSTRUCTIONS

Place the first eight ingredients in the bread machine pan in the sequence recommended by the manufacturer.

Choose the basic bread setting, light crust color and 1 1/2 lb loaf size. Add almonds just before the final kneading. Remove the bread machine pan from the bread machine once the bread is done. Allow cooling slightly before placing it to a wire rack to cool completely. The bread can be kept on the counter for up to 5 days and frozen for 3 months.

116. ZUCCHINI BREAD

READY IN ABOUT: 3 1/2 HOURS
YIELDS: 1 1/2 LB LOAF

INGREDIENTS:

- » 2 cups bread flour
- » 1 cup whole wheat flour
- » 1 cup shredded zucchini
- » 3/4 cup nonfat milk
- » 2 tablespoons olive oil
- » 1 lemon, zest of
- » 1 tablespoon dark brown sugar
- » 1 1/2 teaspoons salt
- » 2 1/2 t. bread machine yeast

INSTRUCTIONS

Toss all of the ingredients into your bread machine and carefully follow the manufacturer's instructions. Set your bread machine's program to Basic/White Bread and the crust type to Medium. Start by pressing the START button. Wait till the cycle is finished. When the loaf is baked, grab it from the bucket/pan and set it aside to chill for 5 minutes. To get the bread out of the bucket, gently shake it.

117. BEETROOT BREAD

READY IN ABOUT: 3 1/2 HOURS
YIELDS: 1 1/2 LB LOAF

INGREDIENTS:

- » 2/3 cup lukewarm water
- » 1 tablespoon soft butter
- » 3 1/4 cups white bread flour
- » 1 cup grated raw beetroot
- » 1 teaspoon sugar
- » 1 1/2 teaspoons salt
- » 1 teaspoon easy-blend dried yeast

INSTRUCTIONS

Toss all of the ingredients into your bread machine and carefully follow the manufacturer's instructions. Set your bread machine's program to Basic/White Bread and the crust type to Medium. Start by pressing the START button. Wait till the cycle is finished. When the loaf is baked, grab it from the bucket/pan and set it aside to chill for 5 minutes. To get the bread out of the bucket, gently shake it.

118. ZUCCHINI OAT BREAD

READY IN ABOUT: 3 HOURS
YIELDS: 1 1/2 LB LOAF

INGREDIENTS

- » 2 tablespoons active dry yeast
- » 2 cups Light Flour Blend
- » 1 cup oat flour
- » 1/4 cup granulated cane sugar
- » 4 teaspoons baking powder
- » 1 tablespoon psyllium husk flakes or powder
- » 1 1/4 teaspoons salt
- » 1/8 teaspoon ascorbic acid (optional)
- » 1 1/4 cups grated zucchini
- » 3 large eggs (beaten)
- » 1 cup + 1 tablespoon warm water
- » 1/4 cup olive oil/vegetable oil
- » 2 teaspoons apple cider vinegar
- » Milk, for brushing
- » 1 tablespoon gluten-free oats for toppings

INSTRUCTIONS

In a small bowl, measure out the yeast and leave it aside. Whisk together the remaining dry ingredients (excluding the zucchini) in a large mixing bowl. Toss in the zucchini and season with salt and pepper. Whisk the wet ingredients in a 4-cup glass measuring cup and pour into the bread pan. Spread the dry ingredients evenly over the wet components using a spatula, totally covering them. Pour the yeast into a shallow well in the center. Insert the bread pan into the machine, center it, and lock it in place. Close the lid and choose from the following options: Gluten-free cycle; Loaf size: 1 1/2 pound; Medium crust; Press Start.
When the mix/knead cycle is finished, brush the top of the dough with milk and sprinkle the oats on top. During the rise and bake processes, keep the lid closed.
When the baking is finished take the bread pan from the machine and place it on a wire cooling rack on its side. Allow for a few minutes in the pan before turning it upside down and sliding the loaf onto the wire rack. Allow the bread to cool before slicing it upside down.

119. TOMATO BREAD

READY IN ABOUT: 2 1/2 HOURS
YIELDS: 2 LB LOAF

INGREDIENTS

- » 3/4 cup milk
- » 3/4 cup tomato paste
- » 2 eggs
- » 4 teaspoons olive oil
- » 2 tablespoon sugar
- » 1 teaspoon salt
- » 4 cups bread flour
- » 1 1/2 teaspoon Italian seasoning
- » 1 tablespoon dried minced onion
- » 1/2 teaspoon garlic powder
- » 1/2 teaspoon grated nutmeg
- » 2 1/2 teaspoons active dry yeast

INSTRUCTIONS

In a bread pan, combine all ingredients with the least amount of liquid indicated in the recipe. Press Start after selecting the Light Crust setting. Keep checking the dough as it kneads. If the dough appears dry and stiff after 5 to 10 minutes, or if your machine sounds like it's straining to knead it, add more liquid 1 tablespoon at a time until it forms a smooth, soft, malleable ball that's slightly tacky to the touch. After the baking cycle is finished, remove the bread from the pan and cool before slicing.

120. RED PEPPER BREAD

READY IN ABOUT: 2 1/2 HOURS
YIELDS: 2 LB LOAF

INGREDIENTS

- » 1 cup water
- » 5 tablespoons tomato juice
- » 2 tablespoon butter
- » 2 tablespoon molasses
- » 2 teaspoon salt
- » 3 1/3 cups bread flour
- » 2/3 cup whole wheat flour
- » 2/3 cup minced red bell pepper
- » 2 teaspoon dried tarragon
- » 2 teaspoons active dry yeast

INSTRUCTIONS

In a bread pan, combine all ingredients with the least amount of liquid indicated in the recipe. Select standard or whole wheat bake cycle, medium Crust setting, and start. Keep checking the dough as it kneads. If the dough appears dry and stiff after 10 minutes, or if your machine is straining to knead it, add more water 1 tablespoon until it forms a smooth, soft, malleable ball that is slightly tacky to the touch. After the baking cycle is completed, remove the bread from the pan and cool before slicing.

121. ONION SOUP BREAD

READY IN ABOUT: 2 1/2 HOURS
YIELDS: 2 LB LOAF

INGREDIENTS

- » 1/4 cup milk
- » 1/4 cup water
- » 2 eggs
- » 2/3 cup sour cream
- » 4 teaspoons butter
- » 4 teaspoons sugar
- » 4 cups bread flour
- » 4 tablespoons dry onion soup mix
- » 2 teaspoons active dry yeast

INSTRUCTIONS

In a bread pan, combine all ingredients with the least amount of liquid indicated in the recipe. Press Start after selecting the Medium Crust setting. Keep checking the dough as it kneads. If the dough appears dry and stiff after 5 to 10 minutes, or if your machine sounds like it's straining to knead it, add more liquid 1 tablespoon at a time until it forms a smooth, soft, malleable ball that's slightly tacky to the touch. At the fruit and nut signal, add the onion soup mix. After the baking cycle is finished, remove the bread from the pan and cool before slicing.

122. YAM BREAD

READY IN ABOUT: 2 1/2 HOURS
YIELDS: 2 LB LOAF

INGREDIENTS

- » 3/4 cup milk
- » 2 eggs
- » 1/4 cup drained and chopped canned yams
- » 2 tablespoon butter
- » 2 tablespoon dark brown sugar
- » 2 teaspoon salt
- » 4 cups bread flour
- » 1/2 cup mini marshmallows (optional)
- » 2 teaspoons active dry yeast

INSTRUCTIONS

In a bread pan, combine all ingredients with the least amount of liquid indicated in the recipe. Press Start after selecting the Medium Crust setting. Keep checking the dough as it kneads. If the dough appears dry and stiff after 5 to 10 minutes, or if your machine sounds like it's straining to knead it, add more liquid 1 tablespoon at a time until it forms a smooth, soft, malleable ball that's slightly tacky to the touch. After the baking cycle is finished, remove the bread from the pan and cool before slicing.

123. LAVENDER BREAD

READY IN ABOUT: 4 HOURS
YIELDS: 2 LB LOAF

INGREDIENTS

- » 1 1/2 cups white wheat flour
- » 2 1/3 cups wholemeal flour
- » 1 teaspoon fresh yeast
- » 1 1/2 cups lukewarm water
- » 1 teaspoon lavender
- » 1 1/2 tablespoon honey (liquid)
- » 1 teaspoon salt

INSTRUCTIONS

Prepare all of your bread components, as well as measurement tools (a cup, a spoon, and kitchen scales). Except for the lavender, carefully measure the ingredients into the pan. Place all ingredients in the bread bucket in the correct order, as directed by your bread machine's manual. Close the lid. Select BASIC for your bread machine's program and MEDIUM for the crust color. Start by pressing the START button. Add the lavender once the signal has been given.

Wait for the software to finish. Remove the bucket from the oven and set it aside to cool for 5-10 minutes. Take out the bread from the pan and cool on a cooling rack for 30 minutes. Slice, serve and savor the aroma of freshly baked bread.

124. ONION BREAD

READY IN ABOUT: 2 1/2 HOURS
YIELDS: 2 LB LOAF

INGREDIENTS

- » 1 1/5 cups Water
- » 4 cups Bread Flour
- » 2 tablespoons + 2 teaspoons Butter
- » 1-1/2 teaspoons salt
- » 1 tablespoon + 1-1/2 teaspoons Sugar
- » 2 tablespoons + 2 teaspoons Nonfat Dry Milk
- » 2 teaspoons Active Dry Yeast
- » 3-4 tablespoons Dry Onion Soup Mix

INSTRUCTIONS

Collect the necessary components. Add all dry and wet ingredients to the bread pan in the manufacturer's order mentioned or as directed. At the fruit and nut signal, add the onion soup mix. It could happen anywhere between 30 and 40 minutes into the cycle, depending on your machine. When the baking cycle ends, take the bread out and let it cool before serving.

125. CARROT BREAD

READY IN ABOUT: 3 HOURS
YIELDS: 1 1/2 LB LOAF

INGREDIENTS

- » 2 cups bread flour
- » 1 cup Wholemeal bread flour
- » 1 cup Carrot juice
- » 1/2 cup Carrot, finely grated
- » 2 tablespoon butter
- » 1 1/2 teaspoon salt
- » 1 tablespoon Brown sugar
- » 1 1/2 teaspoon Ground nutmeg (optional)
- » 2 teaspoon Bread machine yeast

INSTRUCTIONS

Fill the bread maker with the ingredients according to the manufacturer's instructions. Please make a small well or dent in the flour and carefully pour the yeast into it, making sure it does not contact any of the liquid. According to your machine's manual, select Basic/White loaf and Medium crust. After five minutes, look at how the dough is kneading; it should have turned into a smooth ball. Depending on the consistency you want, you may need to add one tablespoon of liquid or one tablespoon of flour. When the loaf is done, carefully remove the bowl from the machine and place it on a wire rack to cool. Remove the paddle once it has cooled, then slice using a serrated bread knife for the best results.

126. TOMATO ONION BREAD

READY IN ABOUT: 4 HOURS
YIELDS: 1 1/2 LB LOAF

INGREDIENTS

» 2 cups all-purpose flour

» 1 cup wholemeal flour

» 1/2 cup warm water

» 1/2 cup milk

» 3 tablespoons olive oil

» 2 tablespoons sugar

» 1 teaspoon salt

» 2 teaspoons dry yeast

» 1/2 teaspoon baking powder

» 5 sun-dried tomatoes

» 1 onion

» 1/4 teaspoon black pepper

INSTRUCTIONS

In a frying pan, finely chop the onion and sauté it. Cut the sun-dried tomatoes into small pieces (10 halves). Fill the bowl halfway with liquid ingredients, then fill with flour and add the tomatoes and onions. Without touching the liquid, add the yeast and baking powder. Start by selecting the baking mode. When you select the Bread with Additives mode, the bread maker will knead the dough at low speeds.

Chapter 6

FRUIT BREAD

127. CINNAMON RAISIN BREAD

READY IN ABOUT: 3 1/2 HOURS
YIELDS: 2 LB LOAF

INGREDIENTS

- » 2 tsp Ground Cinnamon
- » 3 tbsp Unsalted Butter
- » 2 tsp Sea Salt
- » 3 tbsp Sugar
- » 4 1/4 C. Bread Flour
- » 1 1/4 C. Water
- » 2 tbsp Dry Milk (Nonfat)
- » 2 tsp Active Dry Yeast
- » 1 C. raisins
- » Unsalted Butter for Serving

INSTRUCTIONS

Collect the necessary components. In the bread machine pan, combine the water, butter, salt, sugar, bread flour, nonfat dry milk, and ground cinnamon in this order. Put your finger, make a small well in the ingredients. Fill the well with active dry yeast to ensure the optimum timing of the yeast reaction. In a bread machine, bake the bread on the sweet, quick, or timed cycle or according to the manufacturer's instructions. If the machine asks for the loaf size, choose 2 pounds. At the fruit and nut signal, add the raisins for about 30 to 40 minutes into the cycle, depending on the machine. The raisins will be pulverized if you add them at the beginning. Allow the bread maker to complete its cycle and finish baking the bread. Before serving, remove the bread from the pan and lay it on a cooling rack to cool it entirely. Enjoy with a dollop of room-temperature butter.

128. APPLE BACON QUINOA BREAD

READY IN ABOUT: 2 1/2 HOURS
YIELDS: 1 1/2 POUND LOAF

INGREDIENTS

- » 2 tablespoons active dry yeast
- » 2 cups Light Flour Blend
- » 1 cup quinoa flakes
- » 1/2 cup Better Than Milk soy powder
- » 2 /3 cup granulated cane sugar
- » 1 tablespoon baking powder
- » 1 tablespoon psyllium husk flakes or powder
- » 2 teaspoons kosher salt
- » 6 slices bacon (cooked, crumbled)

Wet Ingredients
- » 3 large eggs (beaten)
- » 3/4 cup water
- » 1/4 cup vegetable oil
- » 2 teaspoons apple cider vinegar
- » 2 cups finely grated peeled apple

INSTRUCTIONS

Place the bread pan on the counter with the beater paddle inside. Add the wet ingredient to the pan, then the dry ingredients except for the yeast. In the center of these ingredients, make a well with a spoon and add the yeast. Insert the bread pan into the machine, center it, and lock it in place. Close the lid and choose from the following option: Cycle gluten-free with 1 1/2 pound/750 g Loaf size, pick Medium crust and then hit Start. When the baking is finished, take the bread pan from the machine and place it on a wire cooling rack on its side. Allow for a few minutes in the pan before turning it upside down and sliding the loaf onto the wire rack. Allow the bread to cool before slicing it upside down.

129. CRANBERRY ORANGE BREAD

READY IN ABOUT: 2 1/2 HOURS
YIELDS: 1 1/2 POUND LOAF

INGREDIENTS

» 2 tablespoons active dry yeast
» 3 cups Light Flour Blend
» 3/4 cup granulated cane sugar
» 1 tablespoon psyllium husk flakes or powder
» 2 teaspoons baking powder
» 1 teaspoon kosher or fine sea salt
» 3 large eggs (beaten)
» 1/2 cup water
» 1/2 cup orange juice
» 1/4 cup vegetable or canola oil
» 2 teaspoons apple cider vinegar
» 2 cups fresh or frozen cranberries

INSTRUCTION

Place the bread pan on the counter with the beater paddle inside. Add the water first in the pan, then the dry ingredients except for the yeast. In the center of these ingredients, make a well with a spoon and add the yeast. Insert the bread pan into the machine, center it, and lock it in place. Close the lid and choose from the following option: Cycle gluten-free with 1 1/2 pound/750 g Loaf size: pick Medium crust, and then hit Start. When the baking is finished, take the bread pan from the machine and place it on a wire cooling rack on its side. Allow for a few minutes in the pan before turning it upside down and sliding the loaf onto the wire rack. Allow the bread to cool before slicing it upside down.

130. ALOHA BREAD

READY IN ABOUT: 2 1/2 HOURS
YIELDS: 2 LB LOAF

INGREDIENTS

» 3/4 to 7/8 cup buttermilk
» 8 ounce can crushed pineapple
» 2 tablespoons butter
» 1/4 cup sugar
» 1 teaspoon salt
» 2 2/3 cups whole wheat flour
» 1 1/3 cup bread flour
» 1/2 cup flaked sweetened coconut
» 2 teaspoons active dry yeast

INSTRUCTIONS

In a bread pan, combine all ingredients with the least amount of liquid indicated in the recipe. Press Start after selecting the Medium Crust option and the Whole Wheat cycle. If the dough appears dry and stiff after 5 to 10 minutes, or if your machine sounds like it's straining to knead it, add more liquid

1 tablespoon at a time until it forms a smooth, soft, malleable ball that's slightly tacky to the touch. When the baking is finished, remove the bread from the pan and cool for 1 hour before slicing.

131. SUNDAY MORNING APRICOT BREAD

READY IN ABOUT: 2 1/2 HOURS
YIELDS: 2 LB LOAF

INGREDIENTS

» 2/3 cup old fashioned rolled oats
» 1 3/8 cups buttermilk
» 1 egg
» 3 tablespoons butter
» 6 tablespoons apricot preserves
» 2 teaspoons salt
» 2 2/3 cups bread flour
» 1 1/3 cups whole wheat flour
» 2/3 cup chopped dried apricots
» 2 teaspoons active dry yeast

INSTRUCTIONS

In a bread pan, combine all ingredients with the least amount of liquid indicated in the recipe. Press Start after selecting the Medium Crust setting. If the dough appears dry and stiff after 5 to 10 minutes, or if your machine sounds like it's straining to knead it, add more liquid 1 tablespoon at a time until it forms a smooth, soft, malleable ball that's slightly tacky to the touch. When the baking is finished, remove the bread from the pan and cool for 1 hour before slicing.

132. CRUNCHY MUNCHY BREAD

READY IN ABOUT: 2 1/2 HOURS
YIELDS: 2 LB LOAF

INGREDIENTS

» 1 3/4 to 1 7/8 cups milk
» 6 tablespoons chunky peanut butter
» 2 tablespoons honey
» 1 teaspoon salt
» 2 1/2 cups whole wheat flour
» 1 1/2 cups bread flour
» 1 cup (cored unpeeled chopped) granny smith apple
» 1/4 cup unsalted peanuts
» 2 teaspoons active dry yeast

INSTRUCTIONS

In a bread pan, combine all ingredients with the least amount of liquid indicated in the recipe. Press Start after selecting the Medium Crust option and the Whole Wheat cycle. (Optional bake cycles: Standard; Sweet Bread; Raisin/Nut). If the dough appears dry and stiff after 5 to 10 minutes, or if your machine sounds like it's straining to knead it, add more liquid 1 tablespoon at a time until it forms a smooth, soft, malleable ball that's slightly tacky to the touch. When the baking is finished, remove the bread from the pan and cool for 1 hour before slicing.

133. APPLESEED BREAD

READY IN ABOUT: 2 1/2 HOURS
YIELDS: 2 LB LOAF

INGREDIENTS

- » 3/4 to 7/8 cup apple juice
- » 2/3 cup unsweetened applesauce
- » 2 tablespoons butter
- » 1/4 cup dark brown sugar
- » 2 teaspoons salt
- » 4 cups bread flour
- » 1 teaspoon ground cinnamon
- » 1/4 teaspoon grated nutmeg
- » 2/3 cup chopped apple
- » 6 tablespoons raisins (optional)
- » 2 teaspoons active dry yeast

INSTRUCTIONS

In a bread pan, combine all ingredients with the least amount of liquid indicated in the recipe. Press Start after selecting the Medium Crust setting. (Optional bake cycles: Standard; Whole Wheat; Sweet Bread; Raisin/Nut; Delayed. Time If the dough appears dry and stiff after 5 to 10 minutes, or if your machine sounds like it's straining to knead it, add more liquid 1 tablespoon at a time until it forms a smooth, soft, malleable ball that's slightly tacky to the touch. When the baking is finished, remove the bread from the pan and let cool for 1 hour before slicing.

134. BANANA OATMEAL BREAD

READY IN ABOUT: 2 1/2 HOURS
YIELDS: 2 LB LOAF

INGREDIENTS

- » 1 cup old fashioned rolled oats
- » 2 eggs
- » 3 to 4 tablespoons water
- » 1/2 cup sour cream
- » 2 cups sliced ripe banana (about 3 medium)
- » 1 tablespoon butter
- » 3 tablespoons honey
- » 1 teaspoon salt
- » 3 cups bread flour
- » 1 cup whole wheat flour
- » 1 teaspoon ground cinnamon
- » 1/2 teaspoon grated nutmeg
- » 4 teaspoons nonfat dry milk powder
- » 2 1/2 teaspoons active dry yeast

INSTRUCTIONS

In a bread pan, combine all ingredients with the least amount of liquid indicated in the recipe. Select the usual bake cycle and the Medium Crust setting, then push Start. If the dough appears dry and stiff after 5 to 10 minutes, or if your machine sounds like it's straining to knead it, add more liquid 1 tablespoon at a time until it forms a smooth, soft, malleable ball that's slightly tacky to the touch. When the baking is finished, remove the bread from the pan and cool for 1 hour before slicing.

135. APPLE OATMEAL BREAD WITH RAISINS

READY IN ABOUT: 2 1/2 HOURS
YIELDS: 2 LB LOAF

INGREDIENTS

- » 2/3 cup old fashioned rolled oats
- » 1 cup water
- » 2/3 cup unsweetened applesauce
- » 1 1/2 teaspoons salt
- » 2 tablespoons butter
- » 2 tablespoons dark brown sugar
- » 3 1/2 cups bread flour
- » 2 tablespoons nonfat dry milk powder
- » 1/2 cup raisins
- » 2 teaspoons ground cinnamon
- » 2 1/2 teaspoons active dry yeast

INSTRUCTIONS

In a bread pan, combine all ingredients with the least amount of liquid indicated in the recipe. Press Start after selecting the Light Crust setting and bake cycle standard. If the dough appears dry and stiff after 5 to 10 minutes, or if your machine sounds like it's straining to knead it, add more liquid 1 tablespoon at a time until it forms a smooth, soft, malleable ball that's slightly tacky to the touch. When the baking is finished, remove the bread from the pan and cool for 1 hour before slicing.

136. GRANOLA DATE BREAD

READY IN ABOUT: 2 1/2 HOURS
YIELDS: 2 LB LOAF

INGREDIENTS

- » 2/3 cup granola
- » 1 cup buttermilk
- » 3/4 water
- » 2 tablespoons butter
- » 3 tablespoons honey
- » 2 teaspoons salt
- » 2 cups bread flour
- » 2 cups whole wheat flour
- » 1/2 cup chopped dates
- » 2 teaspoons active dry yeast

INSTRUCTIONS

In a bread pan, combine all ingredients with the least amount of liquid indicated in the recipe. Select the Medium Crust setting, the regular bake cycle, and hit Start. If the dough appears dry and stiff after 5 to 10 minutes, or if your machine sounds like it's straining to knead it, add more liquid 1 tablespoon at a time until it forms a smooth, soft, malleable ball that is slightly tacky to the touch. When the baking cycle is finished, remove the bread from the pan and cool for 1 hour before slicing.

137. MIXED FRUIT BREAD

READY IN ABOUT: 2 1/2 HOURS
YIELDS: 2 LB LOAF

INGREDIENTS

» 2/3 cup bran cereal
» 1 1/4 to 1 3/8 cups buttermilk
» 2 eggs
» 2 tablespoons butter
» 2 tablespoons honey
» 1 teaspoon salt
» 4 cups bread flour
» 1/2 teaspoon ground cinnamon
» 1 cup mixed dried fruits (chopped)
» 2 1/2 teaspoons active dry yeast

INSTRUCTIONS

In a bread pan, combine all ingredients with the least amount of liquid indicated in the recipe. Press Start after selecting the Medium Crust setting. If the dough appears dry and stiff after 5 to 10 minutes, or if your machine sounds like it's straining to knead it, add more liquid 1 tablespoon at a time until it forms a smooth, soft, malleable ball that's slightly tacky to the touch. When the baking cycle is finished, remove the bread from the pan and cool for 1 hour before slicing.

138. ORANGE BREAD

READY IN ABOUT: 2 1/2 HOURS
YIELDS: 2 LB LOAF

INGREDIENTS

» 1 1/2 cups navel orange (peeled and chopped)
» 4 to 6 tablespoons orange juice
» 1 egg
» 2 tablespoons butter
» 6 tablespoons orange marmalade
» 2 teaspoons salt
» 4 cups bread flour
» 1/4 cup grated orange rind
» 1/2 cup slivered almonds
» 2 1/2 teaspoons active dry yeast

INSTRUCTIONS

In a bread pan, combine all ingredients with the least amount of liquid indicated in the recipe. Press Start after selecting the Medium Crust setting. If the dough appears dry and stiff after 5 to 10 minutes, or if your machine sounds like it's straining to knead it, add more liquid 1 tablespoon at a time until it forms a smooth, soft, malleable ball that's slightly tacky to the touch. When the baking is finished, remove the bread from the pan and let cool for 1 hour before slicing.

139. MARMALADE AND OATS BREAD

READY IN ABOUT: 2 1/2 HOURS
YIELDS: 2 LB LOAF

INGREDIENTS

» 1 cup old fashioned rolled oats
» 1 1/2 cups milk
» 2/3 cup orange marmalade
» 2 tablespoons butter
» 2 teaspoons salt
» 4 cups bread flour
» 2 teaspoons active dry yeast

INSTRUCTIONS

In a bread pan, combine all ingredients with the least amount of liquid indicated in the recipe. Press Start after selecting the Medium Crust setting. If the dough appears dry and stiff after 5 to 10 minutes, or if your machine sounds like it's straining to knead it, add more liquid 1 tablespoon at a time until it forms a smooth, soft, malleable ball that's slightly tacky to the touch. When the baking is finished, remove the bread from the pan and cool for 1 hour before slicing.

140. POPPYSEED PEACH BREAD

READY IN ABOUT: 2 1/2 HOURS
YIELDS: 2 LB LOAF

INGREDIENTS

» 5 to 7 tablespoons buttermilk
» 2 cups peeled and chopped peaches
» 2 tablespoons butter
» 1/4 cup sugar
» 1/4 cup dark brown sugar
» 2 teaspoons salt
» 3 cups bread flour
» 1 1/3 cups whole wheat flour
» 4 teaspoons poppy seeds
» 2 teaspoons active dry yeast

INSTRUCTIONS

In a bread pan, combine all ingredients with the least amount of liquid indicated in the recipe. Press Start after selecting the Medium Crust setting. If the dough appears dry and stiff after 5 to 10 minutes, or if your machine sounds like it's straining to knead it, add more liquid 1 tablespoon at a time until it forms a smooth, soft, malleable ball that's slightly tacky to the touch. When the baking is finished, remove the bread from the pan and let it cool for 1 hour before slicing.

141. PEACHES AND SPICE BREAD

READY IN ABOUT: 2 1/2 HOURS
YIELDS: 2 LB LOAF

INGREDIENTS

» 1 cup old fashioned rolled oats
» 6 tablespoons miller's bran
» 4 to 6 tablespoons apple juice

- » 2 eggs
- » 2 cups peeled and chopped peaches
- » 2 tablespoons butter
- » 2 tablespoons honey
- » 2 teaspoons salt
- » 2 cups whole wheat flour
- » 2 cups bread flour
- » 1 1/2 teaspoon ground cinnamon
- » 1 1/2 teaspoons ground ginger
- » 1 1/2 teaspoons grated nutmeg
- » 2 1/2 active dry yeast

INSTRUCTIONS

In a bread pan, combine all ingredients with the least amount of liquid indicated in the recipe. Press Start after selecting the Medium Crust option and the Whole Wheat cycle. If the dough appears dry and stiff after 5 to 10 minutes, or if your machine sounds like it's straining to knead it, add more liquid 1 tablespoon at a time until it forms a smooth, soft, malleable ball that's slightly tacky to the touch. When the baking is finished, remove the bread from the pan and cool for 1 hour before slicing.

142. SWEET LEILANI BREAD

READY IN ABOUT: 2 1/2 HOURS
YIELDS: 2 LB LOAF

INGREDIENTS

- » 2/3 cup canned pineapple chunks
- » 1/2 cup buttermilk
- » 1/4 cup reserved pineapple juice
- » 2 eggs
- » 2/3 cup sliced ripe banana
- » 2 teaspoons salt
- » 1/4 cup butter
- » 2 tablespoons sugar
- » 4 cups bread flour
- » 6 tablespoons whole wheat flour
- » 2/3 cup flaked sweetened coconut
- » 1/2 cup chopped macadamia nuts
- » 2 1/2 teaspoons active dry yeast

INSTRUCTIONS

In a bread pan, combine all ingredients with the least amount of liquid indicated in the recipe.

Press Start after selecting the Light Crust setting. If the dough appears dry and stiff after 5 to 10 minutes, or if your machine sounds like it's straining to knead it, add more liquid 1 tablespoon at a time until it forms a smooth, soft, malleable ball that's slightly tacky to the touch. When the baking is finished, remove the bread from the pan and let it cool for 1 hour before slicing.

143. LEMON BLUEBERRY BREAD

READY IN ABOUT: 2 1/2 HOURS
YIELDS: 1 1/2 LB LOAF

INGREDIENTS

- » 2 tablespoons active dry yeast
- » 3 cups Light Flour Blend
- » 1/2 cup Better Than Milk soy powder
- » 3/4 cup granulated cane sugar
- » 1 tablespoon psyllium husk flakes or powder
- » 2 teaspoons baking powder
- » 1 teaspoon kosher or fine sea salt
- » 3 large eggs (beaten)
- » 3/4 cup water
- » 1/4 cup vegetable or canola oil
- » 2 teaspoons ume plum vinegar
- » 2 teaspoons lemon extract
- » 2 cups fresh or frozen blueberries (thawed first if frozen)

INSTRUCTIONS

In a small bowl, measure out the yeast and leave it aside. Combine the remaining dry ingredients in a large mixing bowl. Whisk the wet ingredients (excluding the blueberries) in a 4-cup glass measuring cup. Add the blueberries and pour the mixture into the bread pan. Spread the dry ingredients evenly over the wet components using a spatula, totally covering them. Pour the yeast into a shallow well in the center. Insert the bread pan into the machine, center it, and lock it in place. Close the lid and choose from the following options: Cycle gluten-free with 1 12 pound/750 g Loaf size: pick Medium crust, and then hit Start. When the baking is finished, take the bread pan from the machine and place it on a wire cooling rack on its side. Allow for a few minutes in the pan before turning it upside down and sliding the loaf onto the wire rack. Allow the bread to cool before slicing it upside down.

144. TRAIL MIX BREAD

READY IN ABOUT: 2 1/2 HOURS
YIELDS: 1 1/2 LB LOAF

INGREDIENTS

- » 2 tablespoons active dry yeast
- » 3 cups Light Flour Blend
- » 1/2 cup Better Than Milk soy powder
- » 1/2 cup granulated cane sugar
- » 1 tablespoon psyllium husk flakes or powder
- » 2 teaspoons baking powder
- » 1 teaspoon kosher or fine sea salt
- » 1/8 teaspoon ascorbic acid (optional)
- » 3 large eggs (beaten)
- » 1 cup water (at 27°C)
- » 1/4 cup vegetable or canola oil
- » 2 teaspoons ume plum vinegar
- » 2 teaspoons pure vanilla extract

Add-Ins

» 2 cups gluten-free, dairy-free trail mix

INSTRUCTIONS

Place the bread pan on the counter with the beater paddle inside. Add the water first in the pan, then the dry ingredients except for the yeast. In the center of these ingredients, make a well with a spoon and add the yeast. Insert the bread pan into the machine, center it, and lock it in place. Close the lid and choose from the following option: Cycle gluten-free with 1 12 pound/750 g Loaf size: pick Medium crust, and then hit Start. Add the trail mix after the first kneading cycle. Keep the lid closed during the rise and bake cycles once the mix/knead cycle is completed.

When the baking is finished, take the bread pan from the machine and place it on a wire cooling rack on its side. Allow for a few minutes in the pan before turning it upside down and sliding the loaf onto the wire rack. Allow the bread to cool before slicing it upside down.

Note: Choose a trail mix that is high in nutrients, such as nuts, seeds, dried fruits, and whole-grain cereals, and is free of high-fructose corn syrup, starches, and gums. Also, be sure the brand you purchase is gluten-free certified.

145. PINEAPPLE JUICE BREAD

READY IN ABOUT: 2 HOURS
YIELDS: 1 1/2 LB LOAF

INGREDIENTS

» 3/4 cup fresh pineapple juice
» 1 egg
» 2 tablespoons vegetable oil
» 2 1/2 tablespoons honey
» 3/4 teaspoon salt
» 3 cups bread flour
» 2 tablespoons dry milk powder
» 2 teaspoons quick-rising yeast

INSTRUCTIONS

Place all ingredients in the bread machine's baking pan in the manufacturer's recommended order. Close the cover on the bread maker and place the baking pan inside. Select the Sweet Bread option, followed by Light Crust. To begin, press the start button. The bread is done when the bake cycle is finished. Remove the baking pan carefully from the machine, and invert the bread loaf onto a wire rack to cool entirely before slicing. Cut the bread loaf into desired-sized slices with a sharp knife and serve.

146. SPICE APPLE BREAD

READY IN ABOUT: 2 1/2 HOURS
YIELDS: 1 LB LOAF

INGREDIENTS

» 2/3 cup warm milk
» 1 2/3 tablespoons (melted) butter
» 4 teaspoons sugar
» 1 teaspoon salt

» 2/3 teaspoon ground cinnamon
» Pinch ground cloves
» 2 cups white bread flour
» 1 1/2 teaspoon active dry yeast
» 2/3 cup finely diced peeled apple

INSTRUCTIONS

According to the manufacturer's instructions, place all of the ingredients in your bread machine, except the apple. Press Start after programming the machine for Basic/White bread and selecting light or medium crust. Add the apple to the bucket when the machine signals or immediately before the conclusion of the second kneading cycle if your machine doesn't have a signal. Remove the bucket from the machine after the loaf is done. Allow 5 minutes for the bread to cool. Remove the loaf from the bucket with a little shake and place it on a cooling rack.

147. MORNING OAT APPLE BREAD

READY IN ABOUT: 2 1/2 HOURS
YIELDS: 1 LB LOAF

INGREDIENTS

» 1/2 cup warm milk
» 2/3 teaspoon salt
» 2 3/4 tablespoons unsweetened applesauce
» 1/4 teaspoon ground cinnamon
» 2 teaspoons melted butter
» 1 1/2 cups white bread flour
» 2 teaspoons sugar
» 2 and 3/4 tablespoons quick oats
» Pinch ground nutmeg
» 1 and 1/2 teaspoons active dry yeast

INSTRUCTIONS

Add the ingredients to your bread machine pan according to the manufacturer's instructions. Press Start after programming the machine for Basic/White bread and selecting light or medium crust. Remove the bucket from the machine after the loaf is done. Allow 5 minutes for the bread to cool. Remove the loaf from the bucket with a little shake and place it on a cooling rack.

148. PLUM BREAD

READY IN ABOUT: 2 1/2 HOURS
YIELDS: 1 LB LOAF

INGREDIENTS

» 3/4 cup water
» 1 1/2 tablespoons melted butter
» 1/2 teaspoon orange zest
» 1/4 teaspoon ground cinnamon
» Pinch ground nutmeg
» 1 1/4 cups whole-wheat flour
» 3/4 cup white bread flour
» 1/2 teaspoon salt
» 1 teaspoon bread machine/instant yeast

» 3/4 cup chopped fresh plums

» 2 tablespoons sugar

INSTRUCTIONS

Place all ingredients in your bread machine, except the plums, as directed by the manufacturer. Set the machine to Basic/White bread, choose light or medium crust, and click the Start button. Add the chopped plums when the machine beeps. Remove the bucket from the machine after the loaf is done. Allow 5 minutes for the bread to cool. Remove the loaf from the bucket with a little shake and place it on a cooling rack.

149. TANGY BLUEBERRY BREAD

READY IN ABOUT: 2 1/2 HOURS
YIELDS: 1 LB LOAF

INGREDIENTS

» 1/2 cup plain yogurt

» 1/3 cup water

» 2 tablespoons honey

» 2 teaspoons melted butter

» 1 teaspoon salt

» 1/3 teaspoon lemon extract

» 1 teaspoon lime zest

» 2/3 cup dried blueberries

» 2 cups white bread flour

» 1 1/2 teaspoons bread machine yeast

INSTRUCTIONS

Add the ingredients to your bread machine according to the manufacturer's instructions. Press Start after programming the machine for Basic/White bread and selecting light or medium crust. Remove the bucket from the machine after the loaf is done. Allow 5 minutes for the bread to cool. Remove the loaf from the bucket with a little shake and place it on a cooling rack.

150. PEACH BREAD

READY IN ABOUT: 2 1/2 HOURS
YIELDS: 1 LB LOAF

INGREDIENTS

» 1/2 cup canned peaches (drained and chopped)

» 1/4 cup heavy whipping cream

» 1 egg

» 3/4 tablespoon melted butter cooled

» 1 1/2 tablespoons sugar

» 3/4 teaspoon salt

» 1/8 teaspoon ground nutmeg

» 1/4 cup whole-wheat flour

» 1 3/4 cups white bread flour

» 3/4 teaspoons bread machine yeast

» 1/4 teaspoon ground cinnamon

INSTRUCTIONS

Add the ingredients to your bread machine according to the manufacturer's instructions. Press Start after programming

the machine for Basic/White bread and selecting light or medium crust. Remove the bucket from the machine after the loaf is done. Allow 5 minutes for the bread to cool. Remove the loaf from the bucket with a little shake and place it on a cooling rack.

151. FRUITY HARVEST BREAD

READY IN ABOUT: 3 HOURS
YIELDS: 1,5 LB LOAF

INGREDIENTS

» 1/2 cup egg

» 1/2 cup lukewarm water

» 2 tablespoons unsalted butter, softened

» 2 1/2 cups plain bread flour

» 1/6 cup sugar

» 1 teaspoon salt

» 1 pinch ground allspice

» 1 pinch ground nutmeg

» 1 1/8 cup active dry yeast

» 1/4 cup pecan nuts, diced

» 1/2 cup mixed dried fruit

INSTRUCTIONS

Fill the bread machine on with the ingredients in the sequence stated above or as directed by your bread machine's instruction manual. Do not add the nuts or fruit until the last minute. Choose the nut or raisin setting, as well as the medium crust option. When the machine sounds, it's time to add the dried fruit and nuts mixture. When the bread is done (when the bake cycle ends), place it on a drying rack to cool before serving.

152. BLUEBERRY OATMEAL BREAD

READY IN ABOUT: 3 HOURS
YIELDS: 1 LB LOAF

INGREDIENTS

» 1/3 cup milk

» 3/4 teaspoon salt

» 1 egg

» 1 1/2 tablespoons melted butter

» 1 tablespoon honey

» 2 cups white bread flour

» 1/3 cup rolled oats

» 1 teaspoon bread machine yeast

» 1/3 cup dried blueberries

INSTRUCTIONS

According to the manufacturer's instructions, place all of the ingredients in your bread machine, except the blueberries. Press Start after programming the machine for Basic/White bread and selecting light or medium crust. When the bread machine beeps or 5 minutes before the second kneading cycle ends, add the blueberries. Remove the bucket from the machine after the loaf is done. Allow 5 minutes for the bread to cool. Remove the loaf from the bucket with a little shake and place it on a cooling rack.

153. STRAWBERRY SHORTCAKE BREAD

READY IN ABOUT: 3 HOURS
YIELDS: 1,5 LB LOAF

INGREDIENTS

» 1/4 cup warm water
» 1/4 cup warm heavy whipping cream
» 1/8 teaspoon of baking powder
» 1 teaspoon of salt
» 3 cups of bread machine flour
» 2 1/2 teaspoons of bread machine yeast
» 1 tablespoon of sugar
» 1 teaspoon of vanilla extract
» 1 pound of fresh strawberries plus
» 1/4 cup of sugar for glazing the strawberries

INSTRUCTIONS

Allow 15 minutes for the yeast to proof in the water and milk in the bread pan with the sugar and yeast. Slice the strawberries and coat them in 1/4 cup of sugar while the yeast is proofing. Toss the strawberries in the dressing to evenly coat them. Reserve the strawberries and add the remaining ingredients to the bread pan. For a 1.5-pound loaf with a medium crust, use the basic white bread option. When the bread machine beeps or 5 minutes before the second kneading cycle ends, add the strawberries.

Remove the bucket from the machine after the loaf is done. Allow 5 minutes for the bread to cool. Remove the loaf from the bucket with a little shake and place it on a cooling rack.

154. PINEAPPLE AND CARROT BREAD

READY IN ABOUT: 3 HOURS
YIELDS: 2 LB LOAF

INGREDIENTS

» 1 cup crushed pineapple with juice
» 1/2 cup carrots (shredded)
» 2 eggs
» 2 tablespoons butter
» 4 cups bread flour
» 3 tablespoons sugar
» 1 teaspoon salt
» 3/4 teaspoon ground ginger
» 1 1/4 teaspoons active dry yeast

INSTRUCTIONS

In the bread maker pan, combine all ingredients (excluding the yeast) in the sequence
stated above. In the center of all the dry ingredients, make a well and add the yeast. Press Start after selecting the Basic bread cycle. When the bake cycle ends, the bread is ready. Place the baked bread on a wire rack to cool for 15 minutes before slicing and serving.

155. CINNAMON & DRIED FRUITS BREAD

READY IN ABOUT: 3 HOURS
YIELDS: 1 LB LOAF

INGREDIENTS

» 2 3/4 cups flour
» 3/4 cup water
» 1 1/2 cups dried fruits
» 4 tablespoons sugar
» 2 1/2 tablespoons butter
» 1 tablespoon milk powder
» 1 teaspoon cinnamon
» 1/2 teaspoon ground nutmeg
» 1/4 teaspoon vanillin
» 1/2 cup peanuts powdered sugar (for sprinkling)
» 1 teaspoon salt
» 1 1/2 bread machine yeast

INSTRUCTIONS

Follow the manufacturer's instructions for adding all ingredients to your bread machine (except the peanuts and powdered sugar). Set your bread machine's program to Basic/White Bread and the crust type to Medium. When the bread maker beeps, wet the dough with a little water and sprinkle in the dried fruits. Wait till the cycle is finished. When the loaf is done, take it from the bucket and set it aside to cool for 5 minutes. To remove the bread, gently shake the bucket. Sprinkle with sugar powder.

156. ORANGE WALNUT CANDIED LOAF

READY IN ABOUT: 3 HOURS
YIELDS: 1 1/2 POUND LOAF

INGREDIENTS

» 1/2 cup warm water
» 1 tablespoon bread machine yeast
» 4 tablespoons sugar
» 2 orange juice
» 4 cups flour
» 2 teaspoon salt
» 3 teaspoons orange zest
» 1/3 teaspoon vanilla
» 3 tablespoons (walnut + almonds)
» 1/2 cup candied fruit

INSTRUCTIONS

Fill your bread machine halfway with all of the ingredients (excluding walnut, almonds and candied fruit) and follow the manufacturer's directions carefully. Set your bread machine's program to Basic/White Bread and the crust type to Medium. Start by pressing the START button. Add the walnut, almonds and candied fruit after the first kneading cycle. Wait till the cycle is finished. When the loaf is done, take it from the bucket and set it aside to cool for 5 minutes. To remove the bread, gently shake the bucket. Let it cool before slicing and serving.

Chapter 7

CHEESE BREAD

157. FRENCH CHEESE BREAD

READY IN ABOUT: 4 HOURS
YIELDS: 2 LB LOAF

INGREDIENTS

- » 1 teaspoon sugar
- » 2 1/4 teaspoon yeast
- » 1 1/4 cup water
- » 3 cups bread flour
- » 2 tablespoon parmesan cheese
- » 1 teaspoon garlic powder
- » 1 1/2 teaspoon salt

INSTRUCTIONS

In the order advised by your bread machine manufacturer, add each ingredient to the bread machine and at the temperature indicated by your bread machine manufacturer. Close the cover and start your bread maker with the basic bread, medium crust setting. Take the bread from the bread machine and place it on a cooling rack once it has completed baking.

158. BEER CHEESE BREAD

READY IN ABOUT: 2 1/2 HOURS
YIELDS: 2 LB LOAF

INGREDIENTS

- » 1 package active dry yeast
- » 3 cups bread flour
- » 1 tablespoon sugar
- » 1 1/2 teaspoon salt
- » 1 tablespoon room temperature butter
- » 1 1/4 cup room temperature beer
- » 1/2 cup shredded or diced American cheese
- » 1/2 cup shredded or diced Monterey jack cheese

INSTRUCTIONS

In a bowl, combine the beer and American cheese and heat until barely warm. In the order advised by your bread machine manufacturer, add each ingredient to the bread machine and at the temperature indicated by your bread machine manufacturer. Close the cover and start your bread maker with the basic bread, medium crust setting. Remove the bread and place it on a cooling rack once the bread machine has completed baking.

159. JALAPENO CHEESE BREAD

READY IN ABOUT: 3 HOURS
YIELDS: A 2 LB LOAF

INGREDIENTS

- » 3 cups bread flour
- » 1 1/2 teaspoon active dry yeast
- » 1 cup water
- » 2 tablespoon sugar
- » 1 teaspoon salt
- » 1/2 cup shredded cheddar cheese
- » 1/4 cup diced jalapeno peppers

INSTRUCTIONS

Place each ingredient in the bread machine in the order listed and at the time specified. Select the temperature that your bread machine recommends manufacturer. Close the lid and pick the basic bread setting with a medium crust. Start your bread maker by pressing the start button. Remove the bread and place it on a cooling rack once the bread machine has done baking.

160. CHEDDAR CHEESE BREAD

READY IN ABOUT: 3 1/2 HOURS
YIELDS: 2 LB LOAF

INGREDIENTS

» 1 cup lukewarm milk
» 3 cups all-purpose flour
» 1 1/4 teaspoon salt
» 1 teaspoon tabasco sauce, optional
» 1/4 cup Vermont cheese powder
» 1 Tablespoon sugar
» 1 cup grated cheddar cheese (firmly packed)
» 1 1/2 teaspoon instant yeast

INSTRUCTIONS

In the order advised by your bread machine manufacturer, add each ingredient to the bread machine and at the temperature indicated by your bread machine manufacturer. Close the cover and start your bread maker with the basic bread, medium crust setting. Take the bread from the bread machine and place it on a cooling rack once it has done baking.

161. COTTAGE CHEESE AND CHIVE BREAD

READY IN ABOUT: 3 HOURS
YIELDS: 2 LB LOAF

INGREDIENTS

» 3/8 cup water
» 1 cup cottage cheese
» 1 large egg
» 2 tablespoon butter
» 1 1/2 teaspoon salt
» 3 3/4 cups white bread flour
» 3 tablespoon dried chives
» 2 1/2 tablespoon granulated sugar
» 2 1/4 teaspoon active dry yeast

INSTRUCTIONS

In the order advised by your bread machine manufacturer, add each ingredient to the bread machine and at the temperature indicated by your bread machine manufacturer. Close the cover and start your bread maker with the basic bread, medium crust setting. Take the bread from the bread machine and place it on a cooling rack once it has completed baking.

162. RICOTTA BREAD

READY IN ABOUT: 3 1/2 HOURS
YIELDS: 2 LB LOAF

INGREDIENTS

» 3 tablespoon skim milk
» 2/3 cup ricotta cheese
» 4 teaspoon unsalted butter
» 1 large egg
» 2 tablespoon granulated sugar

» 1/2 teaspoon salt 1 1/2 cups bread flour + more flour
» 1 teaspoon active dry yeast

INSTRUCTIONS

In the order advised by your bread machine manufacturer, add each ingredient to the bread machine and at the temperature indicated by your bread machine manufacturer. Close the cover and start your bread maker with the basic bread, medium crust setting. Take the bread from the bread machine and place it on a cooling rack once it has done baking.

163. OREGANO CHEESE BREAD

READY IN ABOUT: 2 1/2 HOURS
YIELDS: A 2 LB LOAF

INGREDIENTS

» 3 cups bread flour
» 1 cup water
» 1/2 cup freshly grated parmesan cheese
» 3 tablespoon sugar
» 1 tablespoon dried leaf oregano
» 1 1/2 tablespoon olive oil
» 1 teaspoon salt
» 2 teaspoon active dry yeast

INSTRUCTIONS

In the order advised by your bread machine manufacturer, add each ingredient to the bread machine and at the temperature indicated by your bread machine manufacturer. Close the cover and start your bread maker with the basic bread, medium crust setting. Take the bread from the bread machine and place it on a cooling rack once it has done baking.

164. ITALIAN CHEESE BREAD

READY IN ABOUT: 2 1/2 HOURS
YIELDS: 2 LB LOAF

INGREDIENTS

» 1 1/4 cups water
» 3 cups bread flour
» 1/2 shredded pepper jack cheese
» 2 teaspoon Italian seasoning
» 2 tablespoon brown sugar
» 1 1/2 teaspoon salt
» 2 teaspoon active dry yeast

INSTRUCTIONS

In the order advised by your bread machine manufacturer, add each ingredient to the bread machine and at the temperature indicated by your bread machine manufacturer. Close the cover and start your bread maker with the basic bread, medium crust setting. Take the bread from the bread machine and place it on a cooling rack once it has done baking.

165. ONION, GARLIC, CHEESE BREAD

Cooking Time: 2 1/2 hours
YIELDS: 1,5 LB LOAF
INGREDIENTS

» 2 tablespoon dried minced onion
» 2 cups bread flour
» 2 teaspoon Garlic powder
» 1 teaspoon Active dry yeast
» 1 tablespoon White sugar
» 2 tablespoon Margarine
» 2 tablespoon Dry milk powder
» 1 cup shredded sharp cheddar cheese
» 1 1/8 cups warm water
» 1 1/2 teaspoon salt

INSTRUCTIONS

In the bread pan, combine the flour, water, powdered milk, margarine or butter, salt, and yeast in the order recommended by the manufacturer. With a light crust, run the basic cycle. Add 2 teaspoon onion flakes, garlic powder, and shredded cheese when the sound alerts or as specified by the maker. Sprinkle the remaining onion flakes over the dough after the final kneed.

166. MOZZARELLA CHEESE AND SALAMI LOAF

READY IN ABOUT: 3 1/2 HOURS
YIELDS: 1 LB LOAF
INGREDIENTS

» 3/4 cup water
» 1/3 cup mozzarella cheese (shredded)
» 1 teaspoon sugar
» 2/3 teaspoon salt
» 2/3 teaspoon dried basil
» Pinch of garlic powder
» 2 cups + 2 tablespoons white bread flour
» 1 teaspoon instant yeast
» 1/2 cup hot salami, finely diced

INSTRUCTIONS

Follow the manufacturer's directions when adding the stated ingredients to your bread machine (excluding the salami). Set the program to Basic/White Bread and the crust type to Light in the bread machine. Start by pressing the Start button. Allow the bread machine to work for a few minutes, and then add the remaining ingredients when it beeps. Add the salami at this point. Wait till the last bake cycle is finished.

167. OLIVE AND CHEDDAR LOAF

READY IN ABOUT: 3 1/2 HOURS
YIELDS: 1,5 LB LOAF
INGREDIENTS

» 1 cup water
» 1 teaspoon sugar
» 3/4 teaspoon salt
» 1/2 cups sharp cheddar cheese, shredded
» 3 cups bread flour
» 1 teaspoon active dry yeast
» 3/4 cup pimiento olives (drained and sliced)

INSTRUCTIONS

Follow the manufacturer's directions when adding the stated ingredients to your bread machine (excluding the salami). Set the program to Basic/White Bread and the crust type to Light in the bread machine. Start by pressing the Start button. Allow the bread machine to work for a few minutes, and then add the salami. Wait till the last bake cycle is finished. Remove the bucket from the bread machine once the loaf is done and set it aside to rest for 5 minutes. Remove the loaf from the bucket with a little shake, then place it on a cooling rack to cool before slicing.

168. COTTAGE CHEESE BREAD

READY IN ABOUT: 3 1/2 HOURS
YIELDS: 1,5 LB LOAF
INGREDIENTS

» 1/2 cup water
» 1 cup cottage cheese
» 2 tablespoons margarine
» 1 egg
» 1 tablespoon white sugar
» 1/4 teaspoon baking soda
» 1 teaspoon salt
» 3 cups bread flour
» 1/2 teaspoons active dry yeast

INSTRUCTIONS

Place the bread machine ingredients in the manufacturer's sequence specified, then press the start button. If the dough appears overly sticky, add up to a half cup of extra bread flour. When the bake cycle ends, the bread is ready. Take it out of the pan of the machine and let it rest for a few minutes. Let the bread cool down after taking it out of the pan before serving.

169. GREEN CHEESE BREAD

READY IN ABOUT: 3 1/2 HOURS
YIELDS: 1 LB LOAF
INGREDIENTS

» 3/4 cup lukewarm water
» 1 tablespoon sugar
» 1 teaspoon kosher salt
» 1 tablespoon green cheese
» 1 cup wheat bread machine flour
» 9/10 cup whole-grain flour, finely ground
» 1 teaspoon bread machine yeast
» 1 teaspoon ground paprika

INSTRUCTIONS

Place all dry and wet ingredients in the pan, except the paprika, and follow the bread machine's directions. In a saucepan, dissolve yeast in warm milk and add in the last turn. After the buzzer, add the paprika or place it in the bread machine's dispenser. Set the crust type to DARK and the baking program to BASIC. Adjust the amount of flour and liquid in the recipe if the dough is too dense or too wet. Take the pan from the bread machine after the program has finished and set it aside to cool for 5 minutes. Remove the bread from the pan by shaking it. Use a spatula if required. Set the bread aside for an hour after wrapping it in a kitchen towel. Otherwise, you can place it on a wire rack to cool.

170. CHEESE CHIPOTLE BREAD

READY IN ABOUT: 2 1/2 HOURS
YIELDS: 2 LB LOAF

INGREDIENTS

- » 1 1/4 cups water (80-90°F)
- » 4 cups bread flour
- » 1/4 cup sugar
- » 1 teaspoon bread machine yeast
- » 3 tablespoons dry milk
- » 1 1/2 teaspoons salt
- » 1 cup shredded sharp Cheddar cheese
- » 1 teaspoon Chipotle Chili powder

INSTRUCTIONS

Add all the ingredients to the pan of the bread machine according to the manufacturer's instructions. Press Start after programming the machine for Basic/White bread and selecting Light or medium crust. Remove the bucket from the machine after the loaf is done. Allow 5 minutes for the bread to cool. Remove the loaf from the bucket with a little shake and place it on a cooling rack.

171. CHEDDAR CHEESE BASIL BREAD

READY IN ABOUT: 2 1/2 HOURS
YIELDS: 1 LB LOAF

INGREDIENTS

- » 2/3 cup milk
- » 2 teaspoons melted butter
- » 2 teaspoons sugar
- » 2/3 teaspoon dried basil
- » 1/2 cup (shredded sharp) Cheddar cheese
- » 1/2 teaspoon salt
- » 2 cups white bread flour
- » 1 teaspoon bread machine/active dry yeast

INSTRUCTIONS

Add the ingredients to the pan of the bread machine according to the manufacturer's instructions. Press Start after programming the machine for Basic/White bread and selecting Light or medium crust. Remove the bucket from the machine after the loaf is done. Allow 5 minutes for the bread to cool. Remove the loaf from the bucket with a little shake

and place it on a cooling rack.

172. OLIVE CHEESE BREAD

READY IN ABOUT: 2 1/2 HOURS
YIELDS: 1 LB LOAF

INGREDIENTS

- » 2/3 cup milk
- » 1 tablespoon melted butter
- » 2/3 Teaspoon minced garlic
- » 1 tablespoon sugar
- » 2/3 teaspoon salt
- » 2 cups white bread flour
- » 1/2 cup (2 ounces) shredded Swiss cheese
- » 3/4 teaspoon bread machine or instant yeast
- » 1/4 cup chopped black olives

INSTRUCTIONS

Add all the ingredients in the pan to your bread machine according to the manufacturer's instructions. Press Start after programming the machine for Basic/White bread and selecting Light or medium crust. Remove the bucket from the machine after the loaf is done. Allow 5 minutes for the bread to cool. Remove the loaf from the bucket with a little shake and place it on a cooling rack.

173. DOUBLE CHEESE BREAD

READY IN ABOUT: 2 1/2 HOURS
YIELDS: 1 LB LOAF

INGREDIENTS

- » 3/4 cup plus 1 tablespoon milk
- » 2 cups white bread flour
- » 2/3 teaspoon salt
- » 2 teaspoons sugar
- » 1/3 teaspoon freshly ground black pepper
- » 1 teaspoons butter
- » 1 cup shredded aged sharp Cheddar cheese
- » 1/3 cup grated Parmesan cheese
- » 3/4 teaspoon bread machine/instant yeast
- » Pinch cayenne pepper

INSTRUCTIONS

Add all the ingredients to the pan of the bread machine according to the manufacturer's instructions. Press Start after programming the machine for Basic/White bread and selecting Light or medium crust. Remove the bucket from the machine after the loaf is done. Allow 5 minutes for the bread to cool. Remove the loaf from the bucket with a little shake and place it on a rack to cool.

174. CHILE CHEESE BACON BREAD

READY IN ABOUT: 2 1/2 HOURS
YIELDS: 1 POUND

INGREDIENTS

» 1/3 cup milk
» 1 teaspoon melted butter
» 1 tablespoon honey
» 1 teaspoon salt
» 1/3 cup chopped and drained green Chile
» 1/3 cup grated Cheddar cheese
» 1/3 cup chopped cooked bacon
» 2 cups white bread flour
» 1 1/3 teaspoons bread machine yeast

INSTRUCTIONS

Add all the ingredients to the pan of the bread machine according to the manufacturer's instructions. Press Start after programming the machine for Basic/White bread and selecting Light or medium crust. Remove the bucket from the machine after the loaf is done. Allow 5 minutes for the bread to cool. Remove the loaf from the bucket with a little shake and place it on a rack to cool.

175. ITALIAN PARMESAN BREAD

READY IN ABOUT: 2 1/2 HOURS
YIELDS: 1 LB LOAF

INGREDIENTS

» 3/4 cup water
» 2 tablespoons melted butter
» 1 teaspoon sugar
» 2/3 teaspoon salt
» 1 1/3 teaspoons chopped fresh basil
» 2 2/3 tablespoons grated Parmesan cheese
» 2 1/3 cups white bread flour
» 1 teaspoon bread machine/instant yeast

INSTRUCTIONS

Add the ingredients to the pan of the bread machine according to the manufacturer's instructions. Press Start after programming the machine for Basic/White bread and selecting Light or medium crust. Remove the bucket from the machine after the loaf is done. Allow 5 minutes for the bread to cool. Remove the loaf from the bucket with a little shake and place it on a rack to cool.

176. FETA OREGANO BREAD

READY IN ABOUT: 2 1/2 HOURS
YIELDS: 1 LB LOAF

INGREDIENTS

» 2/3 cup milk
» 1 teaspoon melted butter
» 1 teaspoon sugar
» 2/3 teaspoon salt
» 2 teaspoons dried oregano
» 2 cups white bread flour
» 1 1/2 teaspoon bread machine or instant yeast
» 2/3 cup (2 1/2 ounces) crumbled feta cheese

INSTRUCTIONS

Add the ingredients to the pan of the bread machine according to the manufacturer's instructions. Press Start after programming the machine for Basic/White bread and selecting Light or medium crust. Remove the bucket from the machine after the loaf is done. Allow 5 minutes for the bread to cool. Remove the loaf from the bucket with a little shake and place it on a rack to cool.

177. GARLICKY ASIAGO CHEESE BREAD

READY IN ABOUT: 2 1/2 HOURS
YIELDS: 1 LB LOAF

INGREDIENTS

» 1/2 cup + 1 tablespoon milk
» 2 2/3 tablespoons melted butter
» 2/3 teaspoon minced garlic
» 4 teaspoons sugar
» 2/3 teaspoon salt
» 1/3 cup grated Asiago cheese
» 1 3/4 cups + 1 tablespoon white bread flour
» 1 teaspoon bread machine/ instant yeast
» 1/3 cup mashed roasted garlic

INSTRUCTIONS

According to the manufacturer's instructions, place all of the ingredients in your bread machine, except the roasted garlic. Press Start after programming the machine for Basic/White bread and selecting Light or medium crust. When your machine beeps or 5 minutes before the last kneading, add the roasted garlic. Remove the bucket from the machine after the loaf is done. Allow 5 minutes for the bread to cool. Remove the loaf from the bucket with a little shake and place it on a rack to cool.

178. BLUE CHEESE ONION BREAD

READY IN ABOUT: 2 1/2 HOURS
YIELDS: 1 LB LOAF

INGREDIENTS

» 3/4 cup + 1 tablespoon water
» 1 egg
» 2 teaspoons melted butter
» 3 tablespoons powdered skim milk
» 2 teaspoons sugar
» 1/2 teaspoon salt
» 1/3 cup crumbled blue cheese
» 2 teaspoons dried onion flakes
» 2 cups white bread flour
» 3 tablespoons instant mashed potato flakes
» 3/4 teaspoon bread machine/active dry yeast

INSTRUCTIONS

Add all the ingredients to the pan of the bread machine according to the manufacturer's instructions. Press Start after programming the machine for Basic/White bread and selecting Light or medium crust. Remove the bucket from the machine after the loaf is done. Allow 5 minutes for the bread to cool. Remove the loaf from the bucket with a little shake and place it on a rack to cool.

179. SWISS CHEESE BREAD

READY IN ABOUT: 2 1/2 HOURS
YIELDS: 1 LB LOAF

INGREDIENTS

» 1 1/4 cups buttermilk
» 2/3 cup water
» 2 1/2 cups bread flour
» 1 1/4 cups shredded Swiss cheese
» 2 tablespoons sugar
» 1 1/2 teaspoons baking powder
» 2 teaspoons salt
» 1 tablespoon bread machine yeast

INSTRUCTIONS

Place all of the ingredients in the pan in the sequence specified by the maker. Set the crust to medium and begin the Basic cycle by pressing the Start button. (The Delay Timer is not compatible with this recipe.) Take the bread from the pan and place it on a rack when the baking cycle is finished. Before slicing, allow it cool to room temperature.

180. BLACK OLIVE CHEESE BREAD

READY IN ABOUT: 2 1/2 HOURS
YIELDS: 1 LB LOAF

INGREDIENTS

» 2/3 cup milk
» 1 tablespoon melted butter
» 2/3 teaspoon minced garlic
» 1 tablespoon sugar
» 2/3 teaspoon salt
» 2 cups white bread flour
» 1/2 cup shredded Swiss cheese
» 3/4 teaspoon bread machine/ instant yeast
» 1/4 cup chopped black olives

INSTRUCTIONS

Add all the ingredients to the pan of the bread machine according to the manufacturer's instructions. Press Start after programming the machine for Basic/White bread and selecting Light or medium crust. Remove the bucket from the machine after the loaf is done. Allow 5 minutes for the bread to cool. Remove the loaf from the bucket with a little shake and place it on a rack to cool.

181. CHILE-BACON CHEDDAR BREAD

READY IN ABOUT: 2 1/2 HOURS
YIELDS: 1 LB LOAF

INGREDIENTS

» 1/3 cup milk
» 1 teaspoon melted butter
» 1 tablespoon honey
» 1 teaspoon salt
» 1/3 cup chopped and drained green chiles
» 1/3 cup grated Cheddar cheese
» 1/3 cup chopped cooked bacon
» 2 cups white bread flour
» 1 1/3 teaspoons bread machine / instant yeast

INSTRUCTIONS

Add all the ingredients to the pan of the bread machine according to the manufacturer's instructions. Press Start after programming the machine for Basic/White bread and selecting Light or medium crust. Remove the bucket from the machine after the loaf is done. Allow 5 minutes for the bread to cool. Remove the loaf from the bucket with a little shake and place it on a rack to cool.

182. CHEDDAR CHIPOTLE BREAD

READY IN ABOUT: 2 1/2 HOURS
YIELDS: 1 LB LOAF

INGREDIENTS

» 2/3 cup water
» 1 1/2 tablespoons sugar
» 1 1/2 tablespoons powdered skim milk
» 3/4 teaspoon salt
» 1/2 teaspoon chipotle chili powder
» 2 cups white bread flour
» 1/2 cup shredded sharp Cheddar cheese
» 3/4 teaspoon bread machine/ instant yeast

INSTRUCTIONS

Add all the ingredients to the pan of your bread machine according to the manufacturer's

instructions. Press Start after programming the machine for Basic/White bread and selecting Light or medium crust. Remove the bucket from the machine after the loaf is done. Allow 5 minutes for the bread to cool. Remove the loaf from the bucket with a little shake and place it on a rack to cool.

183. EASY COTTAGE CHEESE BREAD

READY IN ABOUT: 2 1/2 HOURS
YIELDS: 1 LB LOAF

INGREDIENTS

» 1/3 cup water
» 1/2 cup low-fat cottage cheese
» 1 egg
» 4 teaspoons butter
» 2 teaspoons sugar
» 2/3 teaspoon salt
» 1/8 teaspoon baking soda
» 2 cups white bread flour
» 1 1/3 teaspoons bread machine/ instant yeast

INSTRUCTIONS

Add all the ingredients to the pan of your bread machine according to the manufacturer's instructions. Press Start after programming the machine for Basic/White bread and selecting Light or medium crust. Remove the bucket from the machine after the loaf is done. Allow 5 minutes for the bread to cool. Remove the loaf from the bucket with a little shake and place it on a rack to cool.

184. COTTAGE CHEESE DILL BREAD

READY IN ABOUT: 2 1/2 HOURS
YIELDS: 2 LB LOAF

INGREDIENTS

» 3 tablespoons olive oil
» 1 large shallot (chopped)
» 1 1/3 cups cottage cheese
» 1/3 cup fat-free milk
» 1 large egg plus
» 1 egg yolk
» 3 1/3 cups bread flour
» 2 tablespoons sugar
» 1 tablespoon plus 1 teaspoon gluten
» 2 1/2 tablespoons dried dill weed
» 1 3/4 teaspoons salt
» 2 3/4 teaspoons bread machine yeast

INSTRUCTIONS

Heat the oil in a small skillet, cook the shallot until it is translucent. Allow cooling to room temperature before using. Place the ingredients in the pan in the sequence specified by the manufacturer, including the shallot with the liquid ingredients. Set the crust too dark and select the Basic cycle; hit the Start button. (The Delay Timer is not compatible with this recipe.) At first, the dough ball will appear dry and will take a few minutes to come together. Refrain from adding extra liquid. Take the bread from the pan and place it on a rack when the baking cycle is finished. Before slicing, allow it cool to room temperature.

185. FARM-STYLE COTTAGE CHEESE BREAD

READY IN ABOUT: 2 1/2 HOURS
YIELDS: 2 LB LOAF

INGREDIENTS

» 1 1/8 cups water
» 1 cup small-curd low-fat cottage cheese
» 3 tablespoons olive oil
» 3 1/4 cups bread flour
» 3/4 cup whole wheat flour
» 1 tablespoon + 1 teaspoon gluten
» 3 tablespoons sugar
» 2 teaspoons salt
» 1 tablespoon bread machine yeast

INSTRUCTIONS

Place all of the ingredients in the pan in the sequence specified by the maker. Set the crust

to medium and hit Start on the Basic cycle. (The Delay Timer is not compatible with this recipe.) The dough ball will be wet to the touch. Take the bread from the pan and place it on a rack when the baking cycle is finished. Before slicing, allow it cool to room temperature.

186. GOAT CHEESE BREAD

READY IN ABOUT: 2 1/2 HOURS
YIELDS: 1 LB LOAF

INGREDIENTS

» 2/3 cup milk
» 2 2/3 tablespoons goat cheese
» 1 tablespoon honey
» 2/3 teaspoon salt
» 2/3 teaspoon freshly cracked black pepper
» 2 cups white bread flour
» 1 teaspoon bread machine or instant yeast

INSTRUCTIONS

Add all the ingredients in the pan to your bread machine according to the manufacturer's instructions. Press Start after programming the machine for Basic/White bread and selecting Light or medium crust. Remove the bucket from the machine after the loaf is done. Allow 5 minutes for the bread to cool. Remove the loaf from the bucket with a little shake and place it on a rack to cool.

187. FRENCH ROQUEFORT CHEESE-WALNUT BREAD

READY IN ABOUT: 2 1/2 HOURS
YIELDS: 2 LB LOAF

INGREDIENTS

» 1 1/3 cups water
» 3 tablespoons cream sherry
» 5 ounces (142 g) Roquefort cheese (crumbled)
» 1 1/2 tablespoon walnut oil

- » 1 1/2 tablespoon unsalted butter (cut into pieces)
- » 3 2/3 cups bread flour
- » 1/3 cup medium or dark rye flour
- » 1 1/2 tablespoons light brown sugar
- » 1 tablespoon + 1 teaspoon gluten
- » 3/4 teaspoon salt
- » 2/3 cup chopped walnuts/ pecans
- » 2 3/4 teaspoons bread machine yeast

INSTRUCTIONS

Add all of the ingredients in the pan in the sequence specified by the maker. Set the crust to medium and hit Start on the Basic cycle. (The Delay Timer is not compatible with this recipe.) The dough ball will be wet to the touch. Take the bread from the pan and place it on a rack when the baking cycle is finished. Before slicing, allow it cool to room temperature.

188. MOZZARELLA HERB BREAD

READY IN ABOUT: 2 1/2 HOURS
YIELDS: 1 LB LOAF

INGREDIENTS

- » 3/4 cup + 1 tablespoon milk
- » 2 teaspoons butter (melted and cooled)
- » 4 teaspoons sugar
- » 2/3 teaspoon salt
- » 1 1/3 teaspoons dried basil
- » 2/3 teaspoon dried oregano
- » 1 cup shredded mozzarella cheese
- » 2 cups white bread flour
- » 1 1/2 teaspoon bread machine or instant yeast

INSTRUCTIONS

Add all the ingredients to the pan of your bread machine according to the manufacturer's instructions. Press Start after programming the machine for Basic/White bread and selecting Light or medium crust. Remove the bucket from the machine after the loaf is done. Allow 5 minutes for the bread to cool. Remove the loaf from the bucket with a little shake and place it on a rack to cool.

189. CRESCIA AL FORMAGGIO

READY IN ABOUT: 2 1/2 HOURS
YIELDS: 1,5 LB LOAF

INGREDIENTS

- » 1/2 cup + 1 tablespoon water
- » 3 large eggs
- » 3 tablespoons olive oil
- » 3 1/4 cups bread flour
- » 3/4 cup grated Asiago
- » 1 1/2 tablespoons nonfat dry milk
- » 1 tablespoon sugar
- » 2 teaspoons gluten
- » 1/2 teaspoon salt

- » 2 1/2 teaspoons bread machine yeast

INSTRUCTIONS

Place all of the ingredients in the pan in the sequence specified by the maker. Set the crust to medium and hit Start on the Basic cycle. (The Delay Timer is not compatible with this recipe.) The dough ball will be wet to the touch. Take the bread from the pan and place it on a rack when the baking cycle is finished. Before slicing, allow it cool to room temperature.

190. RICOTTA CHIVE BREAD

READY IN ABOUT: 2 1/2 HOURS
YIELDS: 2 LB LOAF

INGREDIENTS

- » 1 1/3 cups water
- » 1/2 cup whole or part-skim ricotta cheese
- » 4 cups bread flour
- » 1 1/2 tablespoons light brown sugar
- » 1 tablespoon plus 1 teaspoon gluten
- » 2 teaspoons salt
- » 3/4 cup chopped fresh chives
- » Dash of ground black pepper
- » 1 tablespoon + 1/2 teaspoon bread machine yeast

INSTRUCTIONS

Place all of the ingredients in the pan in the sequence specified by the maker. Set the crust to medium and hit Start on the Basic cycle. (The Delay Timer is not compatible with this recipe.) The dough ball will be wet to the touch. Take the bread from the pan and place it on a rack when the baking cycle is finished. Before slicing, allow it cool to room temperature.

191. MOZZARELLA SALAMI BREAD

READY IN ABOUT: 2 1/2 HOURS
YIELDS: 1 LB LOAF

INGREDIENTS

- » 3/4 cup water
- » 1/3 cup shredded mozzarella cheese
- » 4 teaspoons sugar
- » 2/3 teaspoon salt
- » 2/3 teaspoon dried basil Pinch garlic powder
- » 2 cups + 2 tablespoons white bread flour
- » 1 teaspoon bread machine/ instant yeast
- » 1/2 cup finely diced hot German salami

INSTRUCTIONS

Add the ingredients to the pan of the bread machine according to the manufacturer's instructions. Press Start after programming the machine for Basic/White bread and selecting Light or medium crust. Remove the bucket from the machine after the loaf is done. Allow 5 minutes for the bread to cool. Remove the loaf from the bucket with a little shake and place it on a rack to cool.

192. PINE NUTS AND WALNUT CHEESE BREAD

READY IN ABOUT: 2 1/2 HOURS
YIELDS: 2 LB LOAF

INGREDIENTS

» 1 1/3 cups water
» 2 tablespoons olive oil
» 4 cups bread flour
» 3/4 cup grated Parmesan cheese
» 1 tablespoon + 1 teaspoon gluten
» Pinch of sugar
» 3/4 teaspoon salt
» 1 tablespoon bread machine yeast
» 1/2 cup pine nuts, coarsely chopped
» 2/3 cup walnuts, coarsely chopped

INSTRUCTIONS

Add all of the ingredients in the pan in the sequence specified by the maker. Set the crust to medium and hit Start on the Basic cycle. (The Delay Timer is not compatible with this recipe.) The dough ball will be wet to the touch. Take the bread from the pan and place it on a rack when the baking cycle is finished. Before slicing, allow it cool to room temperature.

193. FETA SPINACH BREAD

READY IN ABOUT: 2 1/2 HOURS
YIELDS: 2 LB LOAF

INGREDIENTS

» 1 1/8 cups water
» 1 cup frozen chopped spinach (defrosted plus squeezed dry)
» 3 tablespoons olive oil
» 4 cups bread flour
» 5 ounces (142 g) crumbled feta cheese
» 1 1/2 tablespoons sugar
» 1 teaspoon salt
» 2 3/4 teaspoons bread machine yeast

INSTRUCTIONS

Add all of the ingredients in the pan in the sequence specified by the maker. Set the crust to medium and hit Start on the Basic cycle. (The Delay Timer is not compatible with this recipe.) The dough ball will be wet to the touch. Take the bread from the pan and place it on a rack when the baking cycle is finished. Before slicing, allow it cool to room temperature.

194. TEX-MEX LONGHORN HOT JALAPEÑO BREAD

READY IN ABOUT: 2 1/2 HOURS
YIELDS: 2 LB LOAF

INGREDIENTS

» 1 1/3 cups water
» 4 cups bread flour
» 1 1/2 teaspoons salt
» 1 1/4 cups shredded longhorn cheddar cheese
» 4 tablespoons nonfat dry milk
» 4 canned jalapeño chiles, seeded and diced
» 1 1/2 tablespoons sugar
» 1 tablespoon bread machine yeast

INSTRUCTIONS

Add all of the ingredients in the pan in the sequence specified by the maker. Set the crust to medium and hit Start on the Basic cycle. (The Delay Timer is not compatible with this recipe.) The dough ball will be wet to the touch. Take the bread from the pan and place it on a rack when the baking cycle is finished. Before slicing, allow it cool to room temperature.

195. OREGANO MOZZA-CHEESE BREAD

READY IN ABOUT: 3 1/2 HOURS
YIELDS: 1,5 LB LOAF

INGREDIENTS

» 1 cup (milk + egg) mixture
» 1/2 cup mozzarella cheese
» 2 1/4 cups flour
» 3/4 cup whole grain flour
» 1 tablespoon sugar
» 1 teaspoon salt
» 1 teaspoons oregano
» 1 1/2 teaspoons dry yeast

INSTRUCTIONS

In your bread machine, combine all of the ingredients. Then set your bread machine's program to Basic/White Bread and the crust type to Dark. Then start the machine by pressing the start button. Wait till the cycle is finished. When the loaf is done, take it from the bucket and set it aside to cool for 5 minutes. To remove the bread, gently shake the bucket. Please put it on a rack to cool before slicing and serving.

196. TANGY BUTTERMILK CHEESE BREAD

READY IN ABOUT: 2 1/2 HOURS
YIELDS: 2 LB LOAF

INGREDIENTS (2 POUNDS)

» 1 3/4 cups buttermilk
» 2 tablespoons sugar
» 2 teaspoons salt
» 4 cups bread flour
» 1 cup grated extra-sharp cheddar cheese
» 3 teaspoons active dry yeast

INSTRUCTIONS

In a bread pan, combine all ingredients with the least amount of liquid indicated in the recipe. Press Start after selecting the Light Crust setting and the Bake cycle standard bread. Keep checking your dough as it kneads. If the dough appears dry and stiff after 5 to 10 minutes, or if your machine sounds like it's straining to knead it, add more liquid 1 tablespoon at a time until it forms a smooth, soft, malleable ball that is slightly tacky to the touch. When the baking is finished, remove the bread from the pan and lay it to cool for 1 hour before slicing.

197. BROCCOLI CHEESE BREAD

READY IN ABOUT: 2 1/2 HOURS
SERVINGS: 8-14
YIELDS: 2 LB LOAF

INGREDIENTS

» 10-ounce package frozen broccoli with cheese sauce

» 1/2 cup milk

» 2 eggs

» 6 tablespoons minced fresh onion

» 2 tablespoons butter

» 1 1/2 teaspoons salt

» 4 cups bread flour

» 2 teaspoons active dry yeast

INSTRUCTIONS

In a bread pan, combine all ingredients with the least amount of liquid indicated in the recipe. Press Start after selecting the Medium Crust setting. Keep checking the dough as it kneads. If the dough appears dry and stiff after 5 to 10 minutes, or if your machine sounds like it's straining to knead it, add more liquid 1 tablespoon at a time until it forms a smooth, soft, malleable ball that's slightly tacky to the touch. After the baking cycle is finished, remove the bread from the pan and cool for 1 hour before slicing.

Chapter 8

GLUTEN-FREE BREAD

198. GLUTEN-FREE CINNAMON RAISIN

READY IN ABOUT: 2 1/2 HOURS
YIELDS: 1 1/2 LB LOAF

INGREDIENTS

- » 1 1/4 cups water
- » 1 teaspoon apple cider vinegar/rice vinegar
- » 3 tablespoons vegetable or nut oil
- » 3 large eggs
- » 3/4 cup (add water if needed)
- » 1 3/4 cups white rice flour
- » 1 1/8 cups brown rice flour
- » 1/2 cup dry buttermilk powder/nonfat dry milk
- » 3 tablespoons sugar/powdered fructose
- » 2 teaspoons xanthan gum
- » 1 1/2 teaspoons ground cinnamon
- » 1 1/2 teaspoons salt
- » 2 3/4 teaspoons bread machine yeast
- » 3/4 cup golden raisins

INSTRUCTIONS

Place all ingredients in the pan, except the raisins, in the sequence specified in the manufacturer's directions. Set the crust to medium and click Start on the Non-Gluten or Quick Yeast Bread cycle. (The Delay Timer is not compatible with this recipe.) Set a timer for 5 minutes in the kitchen.

Open the cover and add the raisins when the timer goes off. Put the lid back on. Pull the pan from the machine and place it on a rack as soon as the baking cycle is through. Allow for a 10-minute cooling period before removing the loaf from the pan. Before slicing, allow the bread to cool to room temperature.

199. GLUTEN-FREE MOCK LIGHT RYE

READY IN ABOUT: 2 1/2 HOURS
YIELDS: 1 1/2 LB LOAF

INGREDIENTS

- » 1 1/4 cups water
- » 3 tablespoons dark molasses
- » 1 teaspoon apple cider or rice vinegar
- » 1/4 cup vegetable/ canola oil
- » 3 large eggs
- » 3/4 cup add water (if needed)
- » 2 1/4 cups white rice flour
- » 7/8 cup brown rice flour
- » 1/2 cup nonfat dry milk
- » 1/4 cup dark brown sugar
- » 1 tablespoon + 1 teaspoon caraway seeds
- » 1 Grated zest of orange/2 teaspoons dried orange peel
- » 1 1/2 teaspoons salt
- » 3/4 teaspoons bread machine yeast
- » 1 tablespoon xanthan gum

INSTRUCTIONS

Place all of the ingredients in the pan in the sequence specified by the maker. Set the crust too dark and click Start on the Non-Gluten or Quick Yeast Bread cycle. (The Delay Timer is not compatible with this recipe.) Pull the pan from the machine and place it on a rack as soon as the baking cycle is through. Allow for a 10-minute cooling period before transferring the loaf from the pan. Before slicing, allow the bread to cool to room temperature.

200. GLUTEN-FREE RICOTTA POTATO BREAD

READY IN ABOUT: 2 1/2 HOURS
YIELDS: 1 1/2 LB LOAF

INGREDIENTS

- » 1 1/3 cups water
- » 3/4 cup ricotta cheese
- » 1 teaspoon apple cider vinegar/rice vinegar
- » 3 tablespoons vegetable/canola oil
- » 3 large eggs
- » 1/3 cup tapioca flour
- » 1/2 cup instant potato flakes
- » 1/3 cup potato starch flour
- » 1/2 cup dry buttermilk powder/nonfat dry milk
- » 3 tablespoons sugar or powdered fructose
- » 2 teaspoons xanthan gum
- » 1 1/2 teaspoons salt
- » 3/4 teaspoon baking soda
- » 2 1/4 cups white rice flour
- » 2 3/4 teaspoons bread machine yeast

INSTRUCTIONS

In the machine's pan, combine all of the ingredients according to the manufacturer's directions. Set the crust to medium and start the bake cycle for Non-Gluten or Quick Yeast Bread. The Delay Timer is not compatible with this recipe. Pull the pan from the machine and place it on a rack as soon as the baking cycle is through. Allow for a 10-minute cooling period before removing the loaf from the pan. Before slicing, allow the bread to cool to room temperature.

201. GLUTEN-FREE BUTTERMILK WHITE BREAD

READY IN ABOUT: 2 1/2 HOURS
YIELDS: 2 LB LOAF

INGREDIENTS

- » 1 cup buttermilk
- » 4 tablespoons butter/margarine
- » 1/2 cup water
- » 1 teaspoon apple cider vinegar/rice vinegar
- » 4 large egg whites, beaten until foamy
- » 1 cup white rice flour
- » 1 cup brown rice flour
- » 3/4 cup potato starch flour
- » 1/4 cup tapioca flour
- » 3 tablespoons light or dark brown sugar
- » 1 tablespoon plus
- » 1/2 teaspoon xanthan gum
- » 1 1/2 teaspoons salt
- » 1 tablespoon + 1/2 teaspoon machine yeast

INSTRUCTIONS

Place all of the ingredients in the pan in the sequence specified by the maker. Set the crust to medium and click Start on the Non-Gluten or Quick Yeast Bread cycle. (The

Delay Timer is not compatible with this recipe.) Pull the pan from the machine and place it on a rack as soon as the baking cycle is through. Allow for a 10-minute cooling period before removing the loaf from the pan. Before slicing, allow the bread to cool to room temperature.

202. GLUTEN-FREE CHICKPEA RICE AND TAPIOCA FLOUR BREAD

READY IN ABOUT: 2 1/2 HOURS
YIELDS: 1 1/2 LB LOAF

INGREDIENTS

- » 1 1/4 cups water
- » 1 teaspoon apple cider vinegar/rice vinegar
- » 3 tablespoons maple syrup
- » 3 tablespoons olive oil
- » 3 large eggs
- » 1 cup chickpea flour
- » 1 cup brown rice flour
- » 1/2 cup cornstarch
- » 1/2 cup tapioca flour
- » 1/2 cup nonfat dry milk
- » 2 tablespoons light brown sugar
- » 1 tablespoon plus 1 teaspoon xanthan gum
- » 1 1/2 teaspoons salt
- » 2 3/4 teaspoons bread machine yeast

INSTRUCTIONS

Place all of the ingredients in the pan in the sequence specified by the maker. Set the crust too dark and click Start on the Non-Gluten or Quick Yeast Bread cycle. (The Delay Timer is not compatible with this recipe.)

Remove the pan from the machine and place it on a rack as soon as the baking cycle is through. Allow for a 10-minute cooling period before removing the loaf from the pan. Before slicing, allow the bread to cool to room temperature.

203. LOW GLUTEN WHITE SPELT BREAD

READY IN ABOUT: 2 1/2 HOURS
YIELDS: 1,5 LB LOAF

INGREDIENTS

- » 1 cup water
- » 1/4 cup apple juice concentrate, thawed
- » 1 1/2 tablespoons canola oil or soft butter
- » 3 cups white spelt flour
- » 1/4 cup oat bran or cornmeal
- » 1 tablespoon full-fat soy flour
- » 1 1/4 teaspoons salt
- » 1 tablespoon bread machine yeast

INSTRUCTIONS

Place all of the ingredients in the pan in the sequence specified by the maker. Set the crust to medium and begin the Basic cycle by pressing the Start button. (The Delay Timer is not compatible with this recipe.) If necessary, add 1 to 2 tablespoons of spelt flour or water to the dough ball, but keep it moist and somewhat tacky.

Pull the pan from the machine and place it on a rack as soon as the baking cycle is through. Allow for a 10-minute cooling period before removing the loaf from the pan. Before slicing, allow the bread to cool to room temperature.

204. GLUTEN-FREE ALMOND AND DRIED FRUIT HOLIDAY BREAD

READY IN ABOUT: 2 1/2 HOURS
YIELDS: 2 LB LOAF

INGREDIENTS

» 1 1/2 cups water
» 2 teaspoons almond extract
» 1 teaspoon apple cider vinegar/rice vinegar
» 3 large eggs
» 3/4 cup water (if needed)
» 2 cups white rice flour
» 1 tablespoon xanthan gum
» 1/2 cup potato starch flour
» 1/2 cup tapioca flour/arrowroot
» 1/2 cup dry buttermilk powder/nonfat dry milk
» 1/3 cup sugar/3 tablespoons powdered fructose
» 1 1/2 teaspoon ground cardamom
» 1/2 teaspoon ground mace or nutmeg
» 1 teaspoon dried lemon peel
» 1 1/2 teaspoons salt
» 1 tablespoon bread machine yeast
» 1/2 cup mix dried fruit bits + 2 tablespoons currants
» 1/3 cup toasted slivered almonds

INSTRUCTIONS

To create the dough, layer all ingredients in the pan, save the raisins in the sequence specified in the manufacturer's directions. Set the crust to medium and select the Non-Gluten or Quick Yeast Bread cycle from the menu; push Start. (The Delay Timer is not compatible with this recipe.) Set a timer for 5 minutes in the kitchen. Open the cover when the timer goes off and add the dried fruit and nuts. Put the lid back on.

Pull the pan from the machine and place it on a rack as soon as the baking cycle is through. Allow for a 10-minute cooling period before removing the loaf from the pan.

Place the bread on a rack with a plate underneath to catch any drips. Combine 1 cup confectioners' sugar, sifted; 1 tablespoon melted butter; 2–3 teaspoons freshly squeezed lemon juice, warmed in a separate bowl to make the lemon glaze. Pour over the top of the loaf right away, allowing it to drip down the edges. Before slicing, allow it cool to room temperature.

205. GLUTEN-FREE POTATO HONEY BREAD

READY IN ABOUT: 1 1/2 HOUR
YIELDS: 2 LB LOAF

INGREDIENTS

» 3 eggs
» 1 tablespoon cider vinegar
» 1/4 cup olive oil
» 1 1/2 cup buttermilk
» 1 tablespoon xanthan gum
» 1/3 cup cornstarch
» 1/2 cup potato starch
» 1/4 cup honey
» 1/2 cup soy flour
» 1 teaspoon salt
» 2 cup white rice flour
» 1 tablespoon active dry yeast

INSTRUCTIONS

Put all the ingredients (above mentioned) in the manufacturer's recommended order in the bread machine pan. Select the Sweet Dough cycle from the drop-down menu. Check the dough consistency five minutes into the cycle (if necessary, add more rice flour.) When the bake cycle ends, let the bread cool for about 10-15 minutes before removing it from the pan.

206. GRAIN-FREE CHIA BREAD

READY IN ABOUT: 3 HOURS
YIELDS: 1,5 LB LOAF

INGREDIENTS

» 1 cup warm water
» 3 large organic eggs, room temperature
» 1/4 cup olive oil
» 1 tablespoon apple cider vinegar
» 1 cup gluten-free chia seeds, ground to flour
» 1 cup almond meal flour
» 1/2 cup potato starch
» 3/4 cup millet flour
» 1 tablespoon xanthan gum
» 1 1/2 teaspoons salt
» 2 tablespoons sugar
» 1/4 cup coconut flour
» 3 tablespoons nonfat dry milk
» 6 teaspoons instant yeast

INSTRUCTIONS

Mix the wet ingredients in a bowl and pour into the bread machine pan. Combine all dry ingredients, except the yeast, in a mixing bowl and pour over the wet ingredients. Add the yeast to a well in the dry ingredients. Press Start after selecting Whole Wheat cycle and light crust color. When the bread is ready, allow it to cool before serving.

207. GLUTEN-FREE BROWN BREAD

READY IN ABOUT: 3 HOURS
YIELDS: 2 LB LOAF

INGREDIENTS

» 2 large eggs
» 1 3/4 cups warm water
» 3 tablespoons canola oil
» 1 cup brown rice flour
» 3/4 cup oat flour
» 1/4 cup tapioca starch
» 1 1/4 cups potato starch
» 1 1/2 teaspoons salt
» 2 tablespoons brown sugar
» 2 tablespoons gluten-free flaxseed meal
» 1/2 cup nonfat dry milk powder
» 2 1/2 teaspoons xanthan gum
» 3 tablespoons psyllium (whole husks)
» 2 1/2 teaspoons gluten-free yeast for bread machines

INSTRUCTIONS

In the bread maker pan, whisk together the eggs, water, and canola oil until smooth. In a large mixing basin, whisk together all of the dry ingredients except the yeast. On top of the wet components, layer the dry ingredients. In the center of all the dry ingredients, make a well with a finger or a spoon and add the yeast. Set the cycle to Gluten-Free with a medium crust color and push the Start button. When the bake cycle ends and the bread is ready, take it out and let it cool before serving.

208. EASY GLUTEN-FREE/DAIRY-FREE BREAD

READY IN ABOUT: 2 1/2 HOURS
YIELDS: 2 LB LOAF

INGREDIENTS

» 1 1/2 cups warm water
» 2 teaspoons active dry yeast
» 2 teaspoons sugar
» 2 eggs, room temperature
» 1 egg white, room temperature
» 1 1/2 tablespoons apple cider vinegar
» 4 1/2 tablespoons olive oil
» 3 1/3 cups multi-purpose gluten-free flour

INSTRUCTIONS

In a large bowl, mix the yeast and sugar with the warm water and stir to combine; set aside until frothy, about 8 to 10 minutes. In a separate mixing dish, whisk the 2 eggs and 1 egg white, then pour into the bread maker's baking pan. In a baking pan, combine the apple cider vinegar and the oil and pour the bubbly yeast/water mixture. On top, sprinkle the gluten-free multi-purpose flour. Start with the gluten-free bread setting. To take the bread from the baking pan, flip the pan onto a cooling rack. Allow for thorough cooling before slicing and serving.

209. GLUTEN-FREE SOURDOUGH BREAD

READY IN ABOUT: 2 1/2 HOURS
YIELDS: 2 LB LOAF

INGREDIENTS

» 1 cup water
» 3 eggs
» 3/4 cup ricotta cheese
» 1/4 cup honey
» 1/4 cup vegetable oil
» 1 teaspoon cider vinegar
» 3/4 cup gluten-free sourdough starter
» 2 cups white rice flour
» 2/3 cup potato starch
» 1/2 cup dry milk powder
» 3 1/2 teaspoons xanthan gum
» 1 1/2 teaspoons salt
» 1/3 cup tapioca flour

INSTRUCTIONS

Combine wet ingredients and pour into the bread maker pan. Mix dry ingredients in a large mixing bowl, and add on top of the wet ingredients. Select Gluten-Free cycle and press Start. Pull the pan from the machine and allow the bread to remain in the pan for approximately 10 minutes. Transfer to a cooling rack before slicing.

210. GLUTEN-FREE CRUSTY BOULE BREAD

READY IN ABOUT: 3 1/2 HOURS
YIELDS: 1,5 LB LOAF

INGREDIENTS

» 3 1/4 cups gluten-free flour mix
» 1 tablespoon active dry yeast
» 1 1/2 teaspoons kosher salt
» 1 tablespoon guar gum
» 1 1/3 cups warm water
» 2 large eggs, room temperature
» 2 tablespoons, plus 2 teaspoons olive oil
» 1 tablespoon honey

INSTRUCTIONS

Set aside in a large mixing bowl all of the dry ingredients, except the yeast. A separate mixing bowl is used to combine the water, eggs, oil, and honey. In a bread machine, combine the wet ingredients. On top of the wet components, add the dry ingredients. Toss the yeast into a well in the center of the dry ingredients. Press Start and select the Gluten-Free option. Pull the baked bread from the oven and set it aside to cool. Hollow out the center, fill with soup or dip, and slice to serve to make a boule.

211. GLUTEN-FREE POTATO BREAD

READY IN ABOUT: 3 HOURS
YIELDS: 1 1/2 LB LOAF

INGREDIENTS

» 1 medium russet potato (baked)
» 2 packets gluten-free quick yeast
» 3 tablespoons honey
» 3 2/3 cups almond flour
» 3/4 cup warm almond milk
» 2 eggs + 1 egg white
» 3/4 cup tapioca flour
» 1 teaspoon sea salt
» 1 teaspoon dried chives
» 1 tablespoon apple cider vinegar
» 1/4 cup olive oil

INSTRUCTIONS

In a large mixing basin, combine all dry ingredients, except the yeast, and set it aside. Mix the milk, eggs, oil, apple cider, and honey in another bowl. Put all of the wet ingredients in the bread maker. Sprinkle the dry ingredients on top of the wet. Add the yeast into a well in the dry ingredients. Select the Gluten-Free bread setting and the light crust color before pressing the Start button. When the bake cycle ends, the bread is ready. Remove it from the machine and cool completely before slicing.

212. PALEO BREAD

READY IN ABOUT: 3 1/2 HOURS
YIELDS: 2 LB LOAF

INGREDIENTS

» 4 tablespoons chia seeds
» 1/3 cup coconut flour
» 2 teaspoons cream of tartar
» 3/4 + plus 1 tablespoon water
» 1/4 cup coconut oil
» 3 eggs, room temperature
» 1/2 cup almond milk
» 1 tablespoon honey
» 1 tablespoon flax meal
» 2 cups almond flour
» 1 1/4 cups tapioca flour
» 1 teaspoon salt
» 1/4 cup flax meal
» 1 teaspoon baking soda
» 2 teaspoons active dry yeast

INSTRUCTIONS

Combine the chia seeds and 1 tablespoon flax meal; stir in the water and set aside. In a microwave-safe bowl, melt the coconut oil and set it aside to cool to lukewarm. Combine the eggs, almond milk, and honey in a mixing bowl. Pour the mixture into the bread machine pan after whisking in the chia seeds and flax meal gel. Combine the almond flour, tapioca

flour, coconut flour, salt, and 1/4 cup flax meal in a mixing bowl. In a separate basin, combine the tartar and baking soda cream, then combine with the remaining dry ingredients. Fill the bread maker halfway with dry ingredients. Make a well in the center of all the dry ingredients with a finger or spoon and pour in the yeast.

Press start and select wheat cycle with a light or medium crust color. When the baking is finished, remove the bread and allow it to cool completely before slicing to serve.

213. GLUTEN-FREE OAT AND HONEY BREAD

READY IN ABOUT: 3 HOURS
YIELDS: 1 1/2 LB LOAF

INGREDIENTS

» 1 1/4 cups warm water
» 3 tablespoons honey
» 2 eggs
» 3 tablespoons butter, melted
» 1 1/4 cups gluten-free oats
» 1 1/4 cups brown rice flour
» 1/2 cup potato starch
» 2 teaspoons xanthan gum
» 1 1/2 teaspoons sugar
» 3/4 teaspoon salt
» 1 1/2 tablespoons active dry yeast

INSTRUCTIONS

Except for the yeast, combine the dry ingredients stated above. In the center of the ingredients in a pan, make a well with a finger or spoon and then add the yeast. Mix all the wet ingredients make the dough in the bread machine. Press Start after selecting Gluten-Free cycle and light crust color. When the baking cycle ends and the bread is ready, remove it from the machine and let it cool for about 20 minutes on a cooling rack before serving.

214. GLUTEN-FREE PUMPKIN PIE BREAD

READY IN ABOUT: 3 HOURS
YIELDS: 1 1/2 LB LOAF

INGREDIENTS

» 1/4 cup olive oil
» 2 large eggs, beaten
» 1 tablespoon bourbon vanilla extract
» 1 cup canned pumpkin
» 4 tablespoons honey
» 1/4 teaspoon lemon juice
» 1/2 cup buckwheat flour
» 1/4 cup millet flour
» 1/4 cup sorghum flour
» 1/2 cup tapioca starch
» 1 cup light brown sugar
» 2 teaspoons baking powder
» 1 teaspoon baking soda
» 1/2 teaspoon sea salt

- » 1 teaspoon xanthan gum
- » 1 teaspoon ground cinnamon
- » 1 teaspoon allspice
- » 1-2 tablespoons peach juice

INSTRUCTIONS

In a bowl, combine the dry ingredients and set them aside. Pour the wet ingredients into the pan and combine the dry ingredients. Press Start on the Sweetbread cycle with a light or medium crust color. Scrape along the sides with a delicate silicone spatula as the ingredients begin to blend. If the batter is stiff, add one tablespoon of peach juice until it reaches the consistency of the muffin batter. Allow baking with the lid closed. Before slicing, chill for 20 minutes on a cooling rack.

215. GLUTEN-FREE PIZZA CRUST

READY IN ABOUT: 2 HOURS
YIELDS: 2 LB LOAF

INGREDIENTS

- » 3 large eggs (room temperature)
- » 1/2 cup olive oil
- » 1 cup milk
- » 1/2 cup water
- » 2 cups rice flour
- » 1 cup cornstarch (and extra for dusting)
- » 1/2 cup potato starch
- » 1/2 cup sugar
- » 2 tablespoons yeast
- » 3 teaspoons xanthan gum
- » 1 teaspoon salt

INSTRUCTIONS

In a bowl, combine the wet ingredients and pour them into the bread machine pan. Mix all dry ingredients in a separate bowl, except the yeast, and pour into the pan. Add the yeast to a well in the center of the dry ingredients. Choose the Dough cycle and hit the Start button. Roll the dough out on a surface lightly dusted with cornflour and form it into a pizza when the dough is ready. Use your favorite toppings and pizza recipe with this dough.

216. GLUTEN-FREE WHOLE GRAIN BREAD

READY IN ABOUT: 4 HOURS
YIELDS: 1,5 LB LOAF

INGREDIENTS

- » 2/3 cup sorghum flour
- » 1/2 cup buckwheat flour
- » 1/2 cup millet flour
- » 3/4 cup potato starch
- » 2 1/4 teaspoons xanthan gum
- » 1 1/4 teaspoons salt
- » 3/4 cup skim milk
- » 1/2 cup water
- » 1 tablespoon instant yeast
- » 5 teaspoons agave nectar (separated)

- » 1 large egg (lightly beaten)
- » 4 tablespoons extra virgin olive oil
- » 1/2 teaspoon cider vinegar
- » 1 tablespoon poppy seeds

INSTRUCTIONS

Set aside a bowl containing sorghum, buckwheat, millet, potato starch, xanthan gum, and sea salt. In a measuring cup, mix the milk and water. Heat to 110°F to 120°F, and then add 2 teaspoons agave nectar and yeast, stirring to mix. Set alone for a few minutes, covered.

Mix the egg, olive oil, remaining agave, and vinegar; then add the yeast and milk mixture. Pour the wet ingredients into the bread maker's bottom. Add the dry ingredients on top. Press Start after selecting Gluten-Free cycle and light color crust. Sprinkle poppy seeds on top after the second kneading cycle. Take the pan out of the bread maker. Let the bread rest for a few minutes before removing it to a cooling rack.

217. GLUTEN-FREE PULL-APART ROLLS

READY IN ABOUT: 2 HOURS
YIELDS: 1,5 LB LOAF

INGREDIENTS

- » 1 cup warm water
- » 2 tablespoons butter, unsalted
- » 1 egg, room temperature
- » 1 teaspoon apple cider vinegar
- » 2 3/4 cups gluten-free almond-blend flour
- » 1 1/2 teaspoons xanthan gum
- » 1/4 cup sugar
- » 1 teaspoon salt
- » 2 teaspoons active dry yeast

INSTRUCTIONS

In the bread maker pan, combine the wet ingredients. Place all of the dry ingredients in a pan, except the yeast. In the center of these ingredients, make a well with a finger or a spoon and add the yeast. Choose the Dough cycle and push the Start button. Using nonstick cooking spray, coat an 8-inch round cake pan. When the dough cycle is through, roll the dough into 9 balls, lay them in a cake pan, and baste them with warm water. Cover this dough with a cloth, and set it aside to rise for 1 hour in a warm location. Preheat your oven to 375 degrees F and bake for 26–28 minutes, or until golden brown. Serve with butter on top.

218. GLUTEN-FREE WHITE BREAD

READY IN ABOUT: 3 HOURS
YIELDS: 2 LB LOAF

INGREDIENTS

- » 2 cups white rice flour
- » 1 cup potato starch
- » 1/2 cup soy flour
- » 1/2 cup cornstarch
- » 1 teaspoon vinegar
- » 1 teaspoon xanthan gum

- » 1 tsp. instant yeast (bread yeast should be gluten-free, but always check)
- » 1 1/4 cup buttermilk
- » 3 eggs
- » 1/4 cup sugar or honey
- » 1/4 cup coconut or olive oil

INSTRUCTIONS

Place all ingredients in the bread pan. Choose the Bake option. Choose a gluten-free option. Start by pressing the Start button. Stop the machine five minutes into the kneading process to assess the dough's hardness. If required, add more flour. Return to the task at hand and wait until the bread is done. When the bread is done, the machine will switch to keep warm mode. Allow around 10 minutes for it to stay in that mode before unplugging it. After that, remove the pan from the bread machine and set it aside to cool for about 10 minutes.

219. GLUTEN-FREE BROWN RICE BREAD

READY IN ABOUT: 3 HOURS
YIELDS: 2 LB LOAF

INGREDIENTS

- » 1 1/2 cups milk
- » 2 Tablespoon honey
- » 3 large eggs, beaten
- » 1 Tablespoon xanthan gum
- » 1/8 cup vegetable oil
- » 3 1/4 cups brown rice flour
- » 1/4 cup potato starch
- » 1/2 cup corn starch
- » 1 Tablespoon active dry yeast
- » 1 Tablespoon apple cider vinegar
- » 1 teaspoon salt

INSTRUCTIONS

In the liquid-dry yeast layering, add all ingredients to the bread pan. In the Cuisinart bread machine, place the pan. Choose the Bake option. Choose a gluten-free option. Start by pressing the Start button. Stop the machine five minutes into the kneading process and check the dough consistency. If required, add more flour. Return to the task at hand and wait until the bread is done. When the bread is done, the machine will switch to keep warm mode. Before unplugging it, let it in that mode for around 10 minutes. Pull the pan from the machine and set it aside to cool for about 10 minutes.

220. GLUTEN-FREE BROWN RICE AND CRANBERRY BREAD

READY IN ABOUT: 3 HOURS
YIELDS: 2 LB LOAF

INGREDIENTS

- » 3 eggs (beaten)
- » 1 teaspoon white vinegar
- » 3 tablespoon gluten-free oil
- » 1 1/2 cup lukewarm water
- » 3 cups brown rice flour

- » 1 tablespoon xanthan gum
- » 1/4 cup flaxseed meal
- » 1 teaspoon salt
- » 1/4 cup sugar
- » 1/2 cup powdered milk
- » 2/3 cup cranberries (dried and cut into bits)
- » 2 1/4 teaspoon instant yeast

INSTRUCTIONS

Getting the Ingredients Ready Except for the yeast and cranberries, combine all wet and dry ingredients separately. In the liquid-dry yeast layering, place all ingredients in the Cuisinart bread pan. In the Cuisinart bread machine, place the pan. Fill the cranberry dispenser with cranberries. Choose the Bake option. Choose a gluten-free option. Start the machine and wait for the loaf to finish cooking. When the bread is done, the machine will switch to keep warm mode. Allow it to remain in that mode for approximately 10 minutes before unplugging it. Pull the pan from the machine and set it aside to cool for about 10 minutes. In the bread machine, layer them in the liquid-dry-yeast layering. Remove the cranberries before serving.

221. GLUTEN-FREE HAWAIIAN LOAF

READY IN ABOUT: 3 HOURS
YIELDS: 2 LB LOAF

INGREDIENTS

- » 4 cups gluten-free flour
- » 1 teaspoon xanthan gum
- » 2 1/2 teaspoon (bread yeast should be gluten-free, but always check)
- » 1/4 cup white sugar
- » 1/2 cup softened butter
- » One egg (beaten)
- » 1 cup fresh pineapple juice (warm)
- » 1/2 teaspoon salt
- » 1 teaspoon vanilla extract

INSTRUCTIONS

Combine all ingredients in the bread pan. In the bread machine, place the pan. Choose the Bake option. Choose a gluten-free option. Wait until the bread is done before pressing it open. When the bread is done, the machine will switch to keep warm mode. Allow 10 minutes for it to stay in that mode before unplugging it. Remove the pan from the oven and set it aside to cool for about 10 minutes.

222. GLUTEN-FREE SORGHUM BREAD

READY IN ABOUT: 2 1/2 HOURS
YIELDS: 1 1/2 LB LOAF

INGREDIENTS

- » 1 1/2 cups sorghum flour
- » 3 tablespoons sugar
- » 1 cup tapioca starch
- » 1/2 teaspoon salt
- » 1/2 cup brown or white sweet rice flour

- » 1 teaspoon xanthan gum
- » 1 teaspoon guar gum
- » 2 1/4 teaspoons instant yeast
- » 3 eggs (room temperature, lightly beaten)
- » 1/4 cup oil
- » 1 1/2 teaspoons vinegar
- » 3/4 to 1 cup milk warm

INSTRUCTIONS

Except for the yeast, combine the dry ingredients in a mixing dish. Place the liquid ingredients in the bread maker pan first, followed by the dry ingredients. In the center of all the dry ingredients, make a well with a finger or a spoon and add the yeast. Set the bread machine setting to the basic bread cycle with a light crust color and hit the Start button. When the bake cycle ends, the bread is ready. Take it out. Before serving, let it cool set it on a wire rack to cool.

223. GLUTEN-FREE SANDWICH BREAD

READY IN ABOUT: 2 HOURS
YIELDS: 1 1/2 LB LOAF

INGREDIENTS

- » 1 1/2 cups sorghum flour
- » 1 1/4 teaspoons salt
- » 1 cup tapioca starch/potato starch (not potato flour)
- » 1/2 cup gluten-free millet flour/gluten-free oat flour
- » 2 teaspoons xanthan gum
- » 2 1/2 teaspoons gluten-free yeast for bread machines
- » 1 1/4 cups warm water
- » 3 tablespoons extra virgin olive oil
- » 1 tablespoon honey or raw agave nectar
- » 1/2 teaspoon mild rice vinegar/lemon juice
- » 2 organic free-range eggs (beaten)
- » 1 1/4 teaspoons salt

INSTRUCTIONS

Set aside the dry ingredients (excluding the yeast) after whisking them together. Pour the liquid ingredients into the bread machine pan first, then slowly pour the dry ingredients on top. In the center of all the dry ingredients, make a well with a finger or spoon and add the yeast. Set the Rapid 1 hour 20 minutes with a medium crust color and push the Start button. When your bread becomes ready, take it out, then place it on a wire rack to cool for 15 minutes before serving.

224. GLUTEN-FREE HERB BREAD

READY IN ABOUT: 2 HOURS
YIELDS: 2 LB LOAF

INGREDIENTS

- » 1 1/2 cups warm water
- » 1 large egg (beaten)
- » 2 egg whites
- » 1 tablespoon cheese & chive egg substitute
- » 1 1/4 cups white rice flour
- » 1 cup brown rice flour

- » 3/4 cup tapioca flour
- » 1/4 cup potato starch
- » 1 1/4 teaspoon salt
- » 2/3 cup dry skim milk powder
- » 2 tablespoon sugar
- » 3 1/4 teaspoon xanthan gum
- » 1 teaspoon herbs de Provence
- » 5 teaspoon bread machine yeast

INSTRUCTIONS

In the order specified, pour the ingredients into the bread pan. Close the cover and secure the bread pan in the baking chamber. Connect the unit to a wall outlet. Choose GLUTEN-FREE. START/STOP by pressing the START/STOP button. When the bread is done, the entire signal will sound. Remove the bread pan from the baking chamber with potholders and carefully remove the bread from the pan. (If the kneading paddle is still in the bread, remove it once it has cooled.) Allow bread to cool on a wire rack for at least 20 minutes before serving.

225. SEEDED GLUTEN-FREE BREAD

READY IN ABOUT: 3 HOURS
YIELDS: 2 LB LOAF

INGREDIENTS

- » 1 2/3 cups warm water
- » 1 large egg, at room temperature + egg whites
- » 1/3 cup unsalted butter/margarine (melted)
- » 1 teaspoon cider vinegar
- » 1 package (16 oz.) gluten-free bread mix
- » 1 tablespoon golden flaxseeds
- » 1 tablespoon sesame seeds
- » 1 tablespoon black sesame seeds

INSTRUCTIONS

In the order specified, pour the ingredients into a bread pan. Close the lid after securing

the bread pan inside the baking chamber. Connect the outlet to the unit. GLUTEN-FREE is the option to go with. Press the START button and STOP button. When the bread is done, a full signal will sound. Remove the bread pan from the baking chamber using potholders, and carefully remove the bread. (If the kneading paddle is still in the bread after it has cooled, remove it.) Allow for at least 20 minutes of cooling on a wire rack before serving.

226. GLUTEN-FREE POTATO AND CHIVE BREAD

READY IN ABOUT: 3 HOURS
YIELDS: 2 LB LOAF

INGREDIENTS

- » 1 1/4 cups warm water
- » 3 large eggs
- » 3 tablespoon vegetable oil
- » 3/4 cup cottage cheese
- » 1 teaspoon cider vinegar

- » 1/2 cup cornstarch
- » 1/2 cup instant potato buds
- » 1/2 cup potato starch
- » 1/2 cup dry skim milk powder
- » 1/2 cup tapioca flour
- » 1/4 cup snipped fresh chives
- » 1/4 cup sugar
- » 2 cups white rice flour
- » 1 1/2 teaspoon salt
- » 2 1/4 teaspoon bread machine yeast

INSTRUCTIONS

In the order specified, pour the ingredients into the bread pan. Close the cover and secure the bread pan in the baking chamber. Connect to a wall outlet. Choose GLUTEN-FREE. START/STOP by pressing the START/STOP button. When the bread is done, the entire signal will sound. Remove the bread pan from the baking chamber with potholders and carefully remove the bread from the pan. (If the kneading paddle is still in the bread, remove it once it has cooled.) Allow bread to cool on a wire rack for at least 20 minutes before serving.

227. SIMPLE GLUTEN-FREE BREAD

READY IN ABOUT: 2 HOURS
YIELDS: 1,5 LB LOAF

INGREDIENTS

- » 1 1/2 cups warm water
- » 2 eggs
- » 1 1/2 tablespoon vegetable oil
- » 1 teaspoon cider vinegar
- » 3 cups gluten-free all-purpose baking flour
- » 2 teaspoon xanthan gum
- » 1 teaspoon salt
- » 1 tablespoon sugar
- » 1 tablespoon active dry yeast

INSTRUCTIONS

Combine the ingredients (salt, water, xanthan gum, eggs, oil, flour, sugar, vinegar, and yeast) in a bread machine in the order listed. Run the Basic cycle with the crust set to Light or Medium. The bread is ready when the bake cycle ends. Remove the pan from the machine and place it on a rack as soon as the baking cycle is through. Allow for a 10-minute cooling period before removing the loaf from the pan. Before slicing, allow the bread to cool to room temperature.

VEGAN BREAD

228. EASY BASIC VEGAN BREAD

READY IN ABOUT: 4 HOURS
YIELDS: 2 LB LOAF

INGREDIENTS

» 1 1/2 cups water
» 1/3 cup Silk Soy Original
» 2 tablespoon granulated sugar
» 2 tablespoon canola oil
» 1 1/2 tablespoon salt
» 3 1/2 cups all-purpose flour
» 1/4 cup ground flax seeds
» 1 1/2 tablespoon bread machine yeast

INSTRUCTIONS

In the sequence recommended by the manufacturer, add all of the ingredients to your bread machine. For a 2-pound loaf, place the insert into the machine and select "basic cycle." If your machine has the option of crust color, always go with "medium brown." Take out the pan from the machine and put the loaf onto a cooling rack once the machine is finished (mine takes around 3 hours). Then, before slicing, wait until the bread has completely cooled. Because the loaf is still hot, its structure will be damaged during slicing, resulting in a squished loaf. Slice your loaf lengthwise into two smaller loaves once it has cooled. Cut these loaves into bread slices now.

229. VEGAN PUMPKIN BREAD

READY IN ABOUT: 4 HOURS
YIELDS: 2 LB LOAF

INGREDIENTS

» 1/2 cup water
» 1/4 cup plant milk
» 1 cup canned pumpkin puree
» 1 1/2 tablespoon salt
» 1 cup whole wheat flour
» 1/3 cup packed brown sugar
» 1 cup canned pumpkin puree
» 2 tablespoon vegetable oil Canola
» 2 1/4 cups all-purpose flour
» 3/4 tablespoon allspice, ground clove/ pumpkin pie spice
» 1/2 cup pumpkin seeds toasted
» 1/2 tablespoon ground ginger
» 1/4 tablespoon ground nutmeg
» 1 1/2 tablespoon bread machine yeast

INSTRUCTIONS

Place a nonstick pan over medium heat to toast the pumpkin seeds. Pour in enough pumpkin seeds to fill the bottom of the pan evenly. Toast for approximately 5 minutes. Reduce the heat and continue to toast the pumpkin seeds for an additional 2-3 minutes, or until done. When you can smell them, and they're a golden-brown color, your seeds are ready.

To prepare the bread, place all ingredients in the bread pan in the sequence suggested by the bread maker's manufacturer. For a 2-pound loaf, choose the whole wheat cycle.

230. VEGAN SOURDOUGH BREAD

READY IN ABOUT: 3 HOURS
YIELDS: 2 LB LOAF

INGREDIENTS

» 1 1/2 cup water
» 1/2 teaspoon of coarse salt or to taste
» 2 tablespoon sugar
» 1 1/2 cup whole wheat flour
» 1 cup of organic raw flour
» 1/2 cup of rye/spelt/or cornflour
» 1 cup of sourdough bread starter
» 2 tablespoons of vegetable oil (sunflower oil)
» 2 tablespoons of sunflower seeds (optional)

INSTRUCTIONS

In the Bread machine pan, combine all of the ingredients in the sequence stated above.

Select the "French bread" setting or the "whole-wheat bread" setting if your Bread machine has one. Start by pressing the start button. Allow the bread to cool for 15 minutes on the rack before unmolding. Cool it on the rack for a while longer.

231. VEGAN CHOCOLATE CAKE BREAD

READY IN ABOUT: 2 HOURS
YIELDS: 1,5 LB LOAF

INGREDIENTS

» 1 1/3 cup Water
» 1/3 cup + 2 tablespoon Olive oil
» 1 teaspoon Vanilla extract
» 1 teaspoon Vinegar
» 2 cups all-purpose flour
» 1 1/3 cup organic cane sugar
» 1/2 teaspoon baking soda
» 1/2 teaspoon baking powder
» 1/2 teaspoon Salt
» 1/4 Cacao Powder (or cocoa powder)

INSTRUCTIONS

Sift the all-purpose flour and cacao powder together if possible. In the bread machine pan, combine the wet and dry materials according to the manufacturer's instructions (some require wet ingredients first, and some require dry). Select the "Quick Bread" cycle and start it. Using a silicone spatula, push any flour to the side as the machine mixes the ingredients for the first few minutes. Check the cake with a butter knife to see if it's done; if it comes out clean, it's done. Otherwise, bake it for a few minutes longer on the "baking cycle." Take the pan out of the bread machine and set it aside to cool for 40-45 minutes. Remove the cake from the bread machine pan by inverting it and shaking it. Allow the cake to cool completely before slicing or putting any frosting on it.

232. VEGAN CINNAMON RAISIN BREAD

READY IN ABOUT: 3 HOURS
YIELDS: 2 LB LOAF

INGREDIENTS

» 1 1/3 cup water
» 1/3 cup plant milk
» 1 1/2 tablespoon salt
» 1/4 cup granulated sugar
» 3 tablespoon vegetable oil
» 4 cups all-purpose flour
» 1 1/2 tablespoon ground cinnamon
» 2 tablespoon bread machine yeast
» 1 1/4 cup raisins

INSTRUCTIONS

In the bread maker, combine all ingredients, except the raisins, in the sequence specified in your bread machine's handbook. Select the "Sweet" cycle from the drop-down menu. Pour in the raisins when the machine beeps for the "add ingredient" indicator.

233. TUTTI FRUITY BREAD

READY IN ABOUT: 3 1/2 HOURS
YIELDS: 1 1/2 LB LOAF

INGREDIENTS

» 4 tablespoon Oil
» 1 cup water warm
» 1 teaspoon Vanilla extract optional
» 3 1/2 cups Bread flour
» 5 tablespoon organic cane sugar
» 1 tablespoon salt
» 2 1/4 tablespoon Bread machine yeast or instant yeast
» 1 cup Tutti Frutti

INSTRUCTIONS

In the sequence indicated by your bread machine, combine the wet and dry components (water, sugar, salt, oil, vanilla extract, bread flour, and yeast). While making bread in a bread machine, do not add tutti frutti to the container. If your bread machine has an extra ingredient slot, fill it with the tutti frutti. Start the cycle with the "Basic" cycle, 1.5-pound size, and medium crust (or your preference). Add the tutti fruity and close the lid when the machine beeps for extra ingredients in the middle of the cycle. Tutti frutti bread is ready when the cycle is finished. Place the bread on a cooling rack after removing it from the container. In the bread machine, make tutti frutti bread. Slice the loaf with a serrated or electric knife once it has cooled.

234. HEAVENLY WHOLE WHEAT BREAD

READY IN ABOUT: 2 1/2 HOURS
YIELDS: 1 LB LOAF

INGREDIENTS

» 3/4 to 7 /8 cup water
» 1 teaspoon salt
» 3 tablespoon butter
» 1 tablespoon sugar
» 1 1/3 cups whole wheat flour
» 2/3 cups bread flour
» 3 tablespoons instant potato flakes
» 1 1/2 teaspoons active dry yeast

INSTRUCTIONS

Place all ingredients in the bread pan, using the least amount of liquid listed in the recipe. Select Medium Crust setting, then the Whole Wheat cycle, and press Start. Keep checking the dough as it kneads. After 10 minutes, if it appears dry and stiff, or if your machine sounds as if it's straining to knead it, add more water 1 tablespoon at a time until dough forms a smooth, soft dough that is slightly tacky to the touch. After the baking cycle ends, the bread is ready to remove bread out of the pan, place on the rack, and let it cool 1 hour before slicing

235. SUN VEGETABLE BREAD

READY IN ABOUT: 3 1/2 HOURS
YIELDS: 2 LB LOAF

INGREDIENTS

» 2 cups wheat flour
» 2 cups whole-wheat flour
» 2 teaspoons pannarin
» 2 teaspoons yeast
» 1 1/2 teaspoons salt
» 1 tablespoon sugar
» 1 tablespoon paprika dried slices
» 2 tablespoons dried beets
» 1 tablespoon dried garlic
» 1 1/2 cups water
» 1 tablespoon vegetable oil

INSTRUCTIONS

Set the baking procedure for 4 hours; the crust color should be Medium. To create a smooth and velvety bum, pay attention to the kneading process of the dough. When the bake cycle ends, the bread is ready. Take the bread out of the pan and then let it cool for a few minutes before serving.

236. VEGAN TOMATO BREAD

READY IN ABOUT: 3 1/2 HOURS
YIELDS: 2 LB LOAF

INGREDIENTS

» 3 tablespoons tomato paste
» 1 1/2 cups water
» 4 1/3 cups flour
» 1 1/2 tablespoon vegetable oil
» 2 teaspoons sugar
» 2 teaspoons salt
» 1 1/2 teaspoons dry yeast
» 1/2 teaspoon oregano, dried
» 1/2 teaspoon ground sweet paprika

INSTRUCTIONS

Warm water is used to dilute the tomato paste. Reduce the amount of tomato paste if you don't like the flavor, but less than 1 tablespoon isn't a good idea because the color will fade. Get the spices ready. To the oregano and paprika, I added a little extra oregano and Provencal herbs (this bread begs for spices).To add oxygen to the flour, sieve it. Mix the spices into the flour thoroughly. Fill the bread maker container halfway with vegetable oil. Add the ingredients in this order: tomato/water mixture, sugar, salt, flour with spices, yeast, and turn on the bread machine. Turn off the bread machine when the baking cycle is finished. Remove the heated bread from the bread container. Place it on the grate for 1 hour to cool.

237. DELICIOUS CRANBERRY BREAD

READY IN ABOUT: 3 1/2 HOURS
YIELDS: 2 LB LOAF

INGREDIENTS

» 1 1/2 cups Warm water
» 2 tablespoons Brown sugar
» 1 1/2 teaspoons Salt
» 1 tablespoon Olive oil
» 4 cups flour
» 1 1/2 teaspoons cinnamon
» 1 1/2 teaspoons cardamon
» 1 cup dried cranberries
» 2 teaspoons yeast

INSTRUCTIONS

Add all of the ingredients in the bread machine in the sequence listed. Start by selecting the sweet bread setting, then light/medium crust. Remove the loaf pan from the machine after the loaf is done. Allow for a 20-minute cooling period. Cut into slices and serve.

238. ITALIAN PINE NUT BREAD

READY IN ABOUT: 3 1/2 HOURS
YIELDS: 1,5 LB LOAF

INGREDIENTS

» 1 cup+ 2 tablespoons water
» 3 cups bread flour
» 2 tablespoons sugar
» 1 teaspoon salt
» 1 1/4 teaspoons active dry yeast
» 1/3 cup basil pesto
» 2 tablespoons flour
» 1/3 cup pine nuts

INSTRUCTIONS

Combine basil pesto and 2 tablespoons flour in a small container and stir until thoroughly combined. Stir in the pine nuts thoroughly. Combine the water, bread flour, sugar, salt, and yeast in the bread machine pan. Select the basic setting, and then medium crust, and then press the start button. Just before the final kneading cycle, add the basil pesto mixture. Remove the loaf pan from the machine after the loaf is done. Allow 10 minutes for cooling. Cut into slices and serve.

239. MOM'S WHITE BREAD

READY IN ABOUT: 3 1/2 HOURS
YIELDS: 1,5 LB LOAF

INGREDIENTS

»   1 cup + 3 Tablespoon water
»   2 tablespoon vegetable oil
»   1 1/2 teaspoon salt
»   2 tablespoon sugar
»   3 1/4 cups white bread flour
»   2 teaspoon active dry yeast

INSTRUCTIONS

Add all the ingredients (above mentioned) to the pan of your bread machine. Close the lid and start your bread maker on the basic or white bread option with a medium crust. Take the bread from the bread machine when it is ready and place it on a cooling rack before serving.

240. SOFT WHITE BREAD

READY IN ABOUT: 3 1/2 HOURS
YIELDS: 1,5 LB LOAF

INGREDIENTS

»   1 cups water
»   4 teaspoon yeasts
»   3 Tablespoon sugar
»   1/2 cup vegetable oil
»   2 teaspoon salt
»   3 cups strong white flour

INSTRUCTIONS

The temperature advised by the manufacturer of your bread machine Close the cover and start your bread maker on the basic or white bread option with a medium crust. Please take the bread from the bread machine and place it on a cooling rack once it has done baking.

241. PEANUT BUTTER & JELLY BREAD

READY IN ABOUT: 3 1/2 HOURS
YIELDS: 1 1/2 POUND LOAF

INGREDIENTS

»   1 cup water
»   1 1/2 teaspoons active dry yeast
»   1 1/2 tablespoons vegetable oil
»   1/2 cup peanut butter
»   1/2 cup blackberry jelly
»   1 tablespoon white sugar
»   1 teaspoon salt
»   1 cup whole-wheat flour
»   2 cups bread flour

INSTRUCTIONS

Add all ingredients in the bread machine baking pan in the manufacturer's recommended order. Close the cover on the bread maker and place the baking pan inside. Choose the Sweet Bread option. To begin, press the start button. Remove the baking pan carefully from the machine, and invert the bread loaf onto a wire rack to cool entirely before slicing. Cut the bread loaf into desired-sized slices with a sharp knife and serve.

242. PUMPKIN BREAD

READY IN ABOUT: 3 1/2 HOURS
YIELDS: 2 LB LOAF

INGREDIENTS

»   1 cup mashed pumpkin
»   1/2 cup + 2 tablespoons of milk
»   2 tablespoons of vegetable oil
»   4 cups bread flour
»   1 1/4 teaspoons salt
»   2 tablespoons sugar
»   2 1/4 teaspoons active dry yeast

INSTRUCTIONS

Toss everything into the bread machine's pan. Choose the white bread option with a light crust. To begin, press the start button. When the pan is done, remove it and lay it aside for 10 minutes.

243. VEGAN CARROT BREAD

READY IN ABOUT: 3 1/2 HOURS
YIELDS: 2 LB LOAF

INGREDIENTS

»   1 1/3 cup water
»   2 teaspoons active dry yeast
»   1 cup grated carrot
»   4 cups bread flour
»   2 tablespoons margarine
»   1/2 tablespoon salt
»   2 tablespoons sugar

INSTRUCTIONS

Toss everything into the bread machine's pan. Choose the white bread option with a light crust. To begin, press the start button. When the pan is done, remove it and lay it aside for 10 minutes.

244. RAISIN BREAD

READY IN ABOUT: 3 1/2 HOURS
YIELDS: 1,5 LB LOAF

INGREDIENTS

» 1 cup water
» 3 cups bread flour
» 1 teaspoon salt
» 1 teaspoon ground cinnamon
» 2 tablespoons margarine
» 2 1/2 teaspoons active dry yeast
» 3/4 cup golden raisins
» 3 tablespoons white sugar

INSTRUCTIONS

In the bread machine's baking pan, place all ingredients (save the raisins) in the order advised by the manufacturer. Close the lid/cover of the bread machine and place the baking pan inside. Choose the Sweet Bread option. Start the game by pressing the start button. Before adding the raisins, wait for the bread machine to beep. Remove the baking pan carefully from the machine and invert the bread loaf onto a wire rack to cool thoroughly before slicing. Cut the bread loaf into desired-sized slices with a sharp knife and set aside.

245. OATS AND PICKLE BREAD

READY IN ABOUT: 3 1/2 HOURS
YIELDS: 3 LB LOAF

INGREDIENTS

» 1 and 1/2 cup pickle juice
» 3 tablespoon vegetable Oil
» 1/2 cup water
» 1/2 cup wheat Germ
» 1 + 1/4 cup Whole Wheat Flour
» 3/4 cup Rolled Oats
» 3/4 teaspoon salt
» 3 and 1/2 tablespoon White Sugar
» 3 cup all-purpose flour
» 1 teaspoon active Dry Yeast

INSTRUCTIONS

Place all the ingredients and yeast in the bread machine pan. Press Start after selecting the Sandwich and 3-lb. Loaf options. It should take around 3 hours and 10 minutes to finish the cycle. Take the loaf out from the pan and cool for 20 minutes on a wire rack before slicing.

Chapter 10

SWEET BREAD

246. MOLASSES AND HONEY OATMEAL BREAD

READY IN ABOUT: 2 HOURS AND 40 MINUTES
YIELDS: 1,5 LB LOAF

INGREDIENTS

» 1 Cup Water
» 2 tablespoons unsalted Butter
» 1 1/2 teaspoons salt
» 3 tablespoons Honey
» 1 tablespoon Dark Molasses
» 1/2 cup oats
» 1 Egg
» 3 cups Bread Flour
» 2 teaspoons Bread Machine Yeast

INSTRUCTIONS

In a mixing basin, combine the oats. 1 cup boiling water, poured over the oats and left aside. Transfer the oats to the bread machine pan once they have cooled but are still warm (approximately 105 F to 110 F). Make careful they don't get much hotter, or the yeast will die. Follow the manufacturer's instructions for adding the remaining ingredients to your bread maker.

247. MILK AND HONEY BREAD

READY IN ABOUT: 3 1/2 HOURS
YIELDS: 1,5 LB LOAF

INGREDIENTS

» 1 cup + 1 tablespoon Milk
» 3 tablespoons Honey
» 3 tablespoons melted butter
» 3 cups Bread Flour
» 1 1/2 teaspoons salt
» 2 teaspoons Active Dry Yeast

INSTRUCTIONS

Collect the necessary components. In the sequence advised by your bread machine manufacturer, add the ingredients to the bread machine pan. Select the basic or white bread option, as well as the medium crust option. Bake the bread in the bread maker. As soon as the hot bread is done, remove it from the oven. If you leave it in the machine for too long, it will become mushy. Allow cooling completely on a wire rack. Slice the bread and serve it immediately after it has cooled, or preserve it for later use.

248. PEANUT BUTTER BREAD

READY IN ABOUT: 1 HOUR
YIELDS: 1,5 LB LOAF

INGREDIENTS

» 1 cup + 1 tablespoon Water
» 1/2 cup Peanut Butter
» 3 cups Bread Flour
» 3 tablespoons Brown Sugar
» 1 teaspoon salt
» 2 teaspoons Bread Machine Yeast

INSTRUCTIONS

Collect the necessary components. In the bread machine, combine the water, salt, bread flour, peanut butter, brown sugar, and bread machine yeast in the sequence indicated by the manufacturer, carefully measuring each ingredient. Choose between the "Sweet" and "Basic/White" cycles. Turn the machine on and select "Medium" or "Light Crust Color." When the bread is done, it should be a dark gold color with a hollow sound when tapped with your fingers. Check the temperature of the bread, which should be around 210 degrees Fahrenheit. Let it cool on a wire rack before serving.

249. CARROT RAISIN BREAD

READY IN ABOUT: 2 1/2 HOURS
YIELDS: 1 1/2 LB LOAF

INGREDIENTS

» 2 tablespoons active dry yeast
» 3 cups Light Flour Blend
» 1/2 cup Better Than Milk soy powder
» 1/2 cup granulated cane sugar
» 2 tablespoons baking powder
» 1 tablespoon psyllium husk flakes or powder
» 1 teaspoon kosher or fine sea salt
» 1/8 teaspoon ascorbic acid (optional)

Wet Ingredients

» 3 large eggs (beaten)
» 3/4 cup carrot juice (at 27°C)
» 1/4 cup vegetable or canola oil
» 2 teaspoons ume plum vinegar
» 1 1/2 cups shredded peeled carrots
» 1 cup golden raisins

INSTRUCTIONS

Place the bread pan on the counter with the beater paddle inside. Blend the wet ingredients (save the carrots and raisins) in a 4-cup glass measuring cup. Pour the carrots and raisins into the bread pan after stirring them in. Spread the dry ingredients evenly over the wet components. Pour the yeast into a shallow well in the center. Insert the bread pan into the machine, center it, and lock it in place. Close the lid and choose from the following options: Gluten-free cycle; Loaf size: 1 1/2 pound; Medium crust; Press Start.

When the baking is finished, take the bread pan from the machine and place it on a wire cooling rack on its side. Allow for a few minutes in the pan before turning it upside down and sliding the loaf onto the wire rack. Allow the bread to cool before slicing it upside down.

250. CINNAMON BREAD

READY IN ABOUT: 2 1/2 HOURS
YIELDS: 1 1/2 LB LOAF

INGREDIENTS

» 2 tablespoons instant yeast
» 3 cups + 3 tablespoons Light Flour Blend or Whole-Grain Flour Blend
» 1/3 cup granulated cane sugar
» 1 tablespoon psyllium husk flakes or powder
» 1 teaspoon salt
» 3 teaspoons ground cinnamon
» 1 teaspoon dough enhancer
» 1 teaspoon ground allspice

Wet Ingredients

» 3 large eggs (beaten)
» 1 1/4 cups water (at 27°C)
» 4 tablespoons non-dairy butter substitute (melted)
» 2 teaspoons apple cider vinegar

INSTRUCTIONS

Place the bread pan on the counter with the beater paddle inside. Add the water first in the pan, then the dry ingredients except for the yeast. In the center of these ingredients, make a well with a spoon and add the yeast. Insert the bread pan into the machine, center it, and lock it in place. Close the lid and choose from the following option: Cycle gluten-free with 1 1/2 pound Loaf size, pick Medium crust and then hit Start. When the baking is finished, take the bread pan from the machine and place it on a wire cooling rack on its side. Allow for a few minutes in the pan before turning it upside down and sliding the loaf onto the wire rack. Allow the bread to cool before slicing it upside down.

251. CHAI LATTE BREAD

READY IN ABOUT: 2 HOURS
YIELDS: 1 1/2 LB LOAF

INGREDIENTS

» 2 cups Light Flour Blend or Whole-Grain Flour Blend
» 1 cup millet flour
» 1 1/4 cups granulated cane sugar
» 1/4 cup dairy-free chai powder
» 1 tablespoon baking powder
» 2 teaspoons psyllium husk flakes or powder
» 2 teaspoons instant espresso powder
» 1 teaspoon kosher salt

Wet Ingredients

» 1/2 cup unsweetened soy or coconut milk
» 1/3 cup vegetable oil
» 3 large eggs (beaten)
» 1 teaspoon pure vanilla extract

INSTRUCTIONS

Place the bread pan on the counter with the beater paddle inside. Add the water first in the pan, then the dry ingredients except for the yeast. In the center of these ingredients, make a well with a spoon and add the yeast. Insert the bread pan into the machine, center it, and lock it in place. Close the lid and choose from the following option: Quick bread/cake cycle with 1 1/2 pound Loaf size, pick Medium crust and then hit Start. When the baking is finished, take the bread pan from the machine and place it on a wire cooling rack on its side. Allow for a few minutes in the pan before turning it upside down and sliding the loaf onto the wire rack. Allow the bread to cool before slicing it upside down.

252. HOLIDAY EGGNOG BREAD

READY IN ABOUT: 2 1/2 HOURS
YIELDS: 1 1/2 LB LOAF

INGREDIENTS

- » 2 tablespoons active dry yeast
- » 3 cups Light Flour Blend
- » 1/4 cup granulated cane sugar
- » 1 tablespoon psyllium husk flakes or powder
- » 2 teaspoons baking powder
- » 1 teaspoon kosher salt
- » 3/4 teaspoon ground nutmeg

Wet Ingredients

- » 3 tablespoons mild honey
- » 1 cup eggnog, soy eggnog (at 27°C)
- » 3 tablespoons unsalted butter or non-dairy butter substitute (melted)
- » 3 large eggs (beaten)
- » 2 teaspoons water
- » 2 teaspoons apple cider vinegar
- » 1/4 teaspoon LorAnn eggnog flavoring, only if you are using half-and-half

INSTRUCTIONS

In a small bowl, measure out the yeast and leave it aside. Combine the remaining dry ingredients in a large mixing bowl. Whisk the honey into the eggnog in a 4-cup glass measuring cup to dissolve the honey. Return to the whisk and add the remaining wet ingredients. Pour the batter into the bread pan. Spread the dry ingredients evenly over the wet components using a spatula, totally covering them. Pour the yeast into a shallow well in the center. Insert the bread pan into the machine, center it, and lock it in place. Close the lid and choose from the following options: Gluten-free cycle; Loaf size: 1 1/2 pound; Medium crust; Press Start

When the baking is finished, take the bread pan from the machine and place it on a wire cooling rack on its side. Allow for a few minutes in the pan before turning it upside down and sliding the loaf onto the wire rack. Allow the bread to cool before slicing it upside down.

253. HONEY GRANOLA BREAD

READY IN ABOUT: 2 1/2 HOURS
YIELDS: 1 1/2 LB LOAF

INGREDIENTS

- » 2 tablespoons active dry yeast
- » 2 cups Light Flour Blend
- » 1 cup oat flour
- » 3/4 cup granulated cane sugar
- » 1/2 cup Better Than Milk soy powder
- » 1 tablespoon baking powder
- » 1 tablespoon psyllium husk flakes or powder
- » 1 teaspoon kosher salt
- » 1/8 teaspoon ascorbic acid (optional)

Wet Ingredients

- » 1/4 cup honey
- » 3/4 cup water (at 27°C)
- » 3 large eggs (beaten)
- » 1/4 cup vegetable or canola oil
- » 2 teaspoons apple cider vinegar
- » 2 teaspoons pure vanilla extract
- » 2 cups gluten-free granola

INSTRUCTIONS

In a small bowl, measure out the yeast and leave it aside. Combine the remaining dry ingredients in a large mixing bowl. Blend the honey and water in a 4-cup (1-liter) glass measuring cup to dissolve the honey. Whisk in the remaining wet ingredients, excluding the granola. Pour the mixture into the bread pan after stirring in the granola. Using a spatula, spread the dry ingredients evenly over the wet components, totally covering them. Pour the yeast into a shallow well in the center. Insert the bread pan into the machine, center it, and lock it in place. Close the lid and choose from the following options: Gluten-free cycle; Loaf size: 1 1/2 pound; Medium crust; Press Start.

When the baking is finished, take the bread pan from the machine and place it on a wire cooling rack on its side. Allow for a few minutes in the pan before turning it upside down and sliding the loaf onto the wire rack. Allow the bread to cool before slicing it upside down.

254. MARSHMALLOWS BREAD

READY IN ABOUT: 2 1/2 HOURS
YIELDS: 1 1/2 LB LOAF

INGREDIENTS

- » 2 tablespoons active dry yeast
- » 2 cups Light Flour Blend
- » 1/2 cup teff flour
- » 1/2 cup millet flour
- » 1/2 cup Better Than Milk soy powder
- » 1/3 cup granulated cane sugar
- » 1 tablespoon baking powder
- » 4 teaspoons psyllium husk flakes or powder
- » 1 teaspoon salt
- » 1/8 teaspoon ascorbic acid (optional)

Wet Ingredients

- » 3 large eggs (beaten)
- » 1 cups + 3 tablespoons water (at 27°C)
- » 1/4 cup vegetable oil
- » 2 teaspoons ume plum vinegar

Add-Ins

- » 2 cups mini marshmallows
- » 1 1/2 cups gluten-free, dairy-free semisweet chocolate chips

INSTRUCTIONS

In a small bowl, measure out the yeast and leave it aside. Combine the remaining dry ingredients in a large mixing bowl. Whisk the wet ingredients in a 4-cup glass measuring cup and pour into the bread pan. Spread the dry ingredients evenly over the wet components using a spatula, totally covering them. Pour the yeast into a shallow well in the center. Insert the bread pan into the machine, center it, and lock it in place. Close the lid and choose from the following options: Gluten-free cycle; Loaf size: 1 1/2 pound; Medium crust; Press Start.

Add the marshmallows and Chocolate after the first kneading cycle. Closed the lid during the rise and baked cycles once the mix/knead cycle is completed. When the baking is finished, take the bread pan from the machine and place it on a wire cooling rack on its side. Allow for a few minutes in the pan before turning it upside down and sliding the loaf onto the wire rack. Allow the bread to cool before slicing it upside down.

255. ITALIAN PANETTONE HOLIDAY BREAD

READY IN ABOUT: 2 1/2 HOURS
YIELDS: 1 1/2 LB LOAF

INGREDIENTS

» 2 tablespoons active dry yeast
» 3 cups + 2 tablespoons Light Flour Blend
» 1/4 cup granulated cane sugar
» 1 tablespoon baking powder
» 2 teaspoons xanthan gum
» 1 teaspoon kosher or fine sea salt
» 1/2 teaspoon dough enhancer
» 1/2 cup mixed candied fruit peels with citron or other candied fruits
» 1/4 cup golden raisins

Wet Ingredients

» 2 tablespoons honey
» 1 cup water (at 27°C)
» 4 tablespoons unsalted butter (melted)
» 3 large eggs (beaten)
» 2 teaspoons apple cider vinegar
» 3/4 teaspoon Fiori di Sicilia or 3/4 teaspoon pure vanilla extract plus several drops of orange oil

INSTRUCTIONS

In a small bowl, measure out the yeast and leave it aside. Whisk together the remaining dry ingredients (excluding the candied peel and raisins). Toss in the peel and raisins until they're uniformly distributed. Blend honey and water in a 4-cup glass measuring cup to dissolve the honey. Return to the whisk and add the remaining wet ingredients. Pour the batter into the bread pan. Spread the dry ingredients evenly over the wet components using a spatula, totally covering them. Pour the yeast into a shallow well in the center. Insert the bread pan into the machine, center it, and lock it in place. Close the lid and choose from the following options: Gluten-free cycle; Loaf size: 1 1/2 pound; Medium crust; Press Start.

If the fruits you're using are particularly wet, you'll probably need to add 1 tablespoon or more of the flour mixture. Keep the lid closed during the rise and bake cycles once the mix/knead cycle is completed.

When the baking is finished, take the bread pan from the machine and place it on a wire cooling rack on its side. Allow for a few minutes in the pan before turning it upside down and sliding the loaf onto the wire rack. Allow the bread to cool before slicing it upside down.

256. PAIN D' SPICES

READY IN ABOUT: 2 1/2 HOURS
YIELDS: 1 1/2 LB LOAF

INGREDIENTS

» 2 tablespoons instant yeast
» 3 cups Light Flour Blend or Whole-Grain Flour Blend
» 1/2 cup buckwheat flour
» 1 tablespoon baking powder
» 1 tablespoon psyllium husk flakes or powder
» 1 teaspoon salt
» 1 teaspoon ground cinnamon
» 1 teaspoon ground ginger
» 1 teaspoon ground nutmeg
» 1/2 teaspoon anise seeds
» 1/4 teaspoon ground cloves
» 1/4 teaspoon freshly ground black pepper

Wet Ingredients:

» 1 cup honey
» 3/4 cup water (at 27°C)
» 1 large egg (beaten)
» 4 tablespoons non-dairy butter substitute (melted)
» 2 teaspoons apple cider vinegar
» 1 tablespoon grated orange zest

INSTRUCTIONS

In a small bowl, measure out the yeast and leave it aside. Combine the remaining dry ingredients in a large mixing bowl. Blend the honey and water in a 4-cup glass measuring cup to dissolve the honey. Return to the whisk and add the remaining wet ingredients. Pour the batter into the bread pan. Spread the dry ingredients over the wet components with a spatula. Pour the yeast into a shallow well in the center. Insert the bread pan into the machine, center it, and lock it in place. Close the lid and choose from the following options: Gluten-free cycle; Loaf size: 1 1/2 pound; Medium crust; Press Start.

Scrape the lower half of the pan with the spatula after the first kneading cycle to ensure all the dry ingredients are integrated. Do not open the lid closed during the rise and bake cycles once the mix/knead cycle is completed. When the baking is finished, take the bread pan from the machine and place it on a wire cooling rack on its side. Allow for a few minutes in the pan before turning it upside down and sliding the loaf onto the wire rack. Allow the bread to cool before slicing it upside down.

257. SNICKERDOODLE BREAD

READY IN ABOUT: 2 1/2 HOURS
YIELDS: 1 1/2 LB LOAF

INGREDIENTS

- » 2 tablespoons active dry yeast
- » 3 cups Light Flour Blend
- » 1/2 cup Better Than Milk soy powder
- » 3/4 cup granulated cane sugar
- » 3 teaspoons ground cinnamon
- » 2 teaspoons baking powder
- » 2 teaspoons xanthan gum
- » 1 teaspoon kosher salt
- » 1/8 teaspoon ascorbic acid (optional)

Wet Ingredients
- » 3 large eggs (beaten)
- » 3/4 cup water (at 27°C)
- » 1/4 cup vegetable or canola oil
- » 2 teaspoons apple cider vinegar
- » 2 teaspoons pure vanilla extract

Toppings:
- » 1 tablespoon granulated cane sugar
- » 1/2 teaspoon ground cinnamon

INSTRUCTIONS

In a small bowl, measure out the yeast and leave it aside. Combine the remaining dry ingredients in a large mixing bowl. Whisk the wet ingredients in a 4-cup glass measuring cup and pour into the bread pan. Spread the dry ingredients evenly over the wet components using a spatula, totally covering them. Pour the yeast into a shallow well in the center. Insert the bread pan into the machine, center it, and lock it in place. Close the lid and choose from the following options: Gluten-free cycle; Loaf size: 1 1/2 pound; Medium crust; Press Start.
To prepare the topping, combine the sugar and cinnamon. Sprinkle the cinnamon sugar on top of the loaf after the second knead cycle, right before the rise and bake cycles begin. While it rises and bakes, close the lid and do not open it. When the baking is finished, take the bread pan from the machine and place it on a wire cooling rack on its side. Allow for a few minutes in the pan before turning it upside down and sliding the loaf onto the wire rack. Allow the bread to cool before slicing it upside down.

258. TOMATO JAM BREAD

READY IN ABOUT: 2 1/2 HOURS
YIELDS: 1 1/2 POUND LOAF

INGREDIENTS

- » 2 tablespoons active dry yeast
- » 3 cups Light Flour Blend
- » 3 tablespoons granulated cane sugar
- » 1 tablespoon baking powder
- » 2 teaspoons xanthan gum
- » 1 teaspoon kosher salt
- » 2 large eggs (beaten)
- » 1 cup water (at 27°C)
- » 1 cup Tomato Jam
- » 3 tablespoons olive oil
- » 2 teaspoons ume plum vinegar

INSTRUCTIONS

In a small bowl, measure out the yeast and leave it aside. Combine the other dry ingredients in a large mixing bowl. Whisk the wet ingredients in a 4-cup glass measuring cup and pour into the bread pan. Spread the dry ingredients evenly over the wet components using a spatula, totally covering them. Pour the yeast into a shallow well in the center. Insert the bread pan into the machine, center it, and lock it in place. Close the lid and choose from the following options: Gluten-free cycle; Loaf size: 1 1/2 pound; Medium crust; Press Start

When the baking is finished, take the bread pan from the machine and place it on a wire cooling rack on its side. Allow for a few minutes in the pan before turning it upside down and sliding the loaf onto the wire rack. Allow the bread to cool before slicing it upside down.

259. ALMOND OIL BREAD

READY IN ABOUT: 3 1/2 HOURS
YIELDS: 2 LB LOAF

INGREDIENTS

- » 1 1/4 cup water
- » 2 cup whole wheat flour
- » 4 teaspoon almond oil
- » 1 cup almond flour
- » 1/4 cup vital wheat gluten
- » 1/4 cup honey
- » 1 teaspoon xanthan gum
- » 0.25 oz package dry yeast
- » 1 teaspoon salt

INSTRUCTIONS

Place the water, almond flour, xanthan gum, almond oil, salt, whole wheat flour, honey, essential wheat gluten, and yeast in the bread machine pan in the manufacturer's recommended order. For a 2 pound loaf, follow the manufacturer's instructions. Scrape the sides of the pan with a spatula after the first kneading cycle to ensure all the dry ingredients are combined. Keep the lid closed during the rise and bake cycles once the mix/knead cycle is completed. Lift the lid and check the temperature at the end of the bake cycle. When the bread is ready, let it cool before serving.

260. CAKE BREAD

READY IN ABOUT: 4 HOURS
YIELDS: 1 LB LOAF

INGREDIENTS

» 1 (1.1 oz.) package chai tea powder
» 3/4 cup hot water
» 1/4 cup Chardonnay wine
» 1/2 teaspoon vanilla extract
» 1 egg yolk
» 1/2 cup frozen unsweetened raspberries
» 1 table butter
» 1/2 cup bread flour
» 1/4 cup rye flour
» 1 teaspoon coarse smoked salt flakes
» 1 cup all-purpose flour
» 1/2 cup wheat bran
» 0.25 oz. package active dry yeast
» 1/2 cup coarsely chopped walnuts
» 1/2 teaspoon caraway seed
» 1/4 cup white sugar

INSTRUCTIONS

Pour 3/4 cup hot water into a cup and mix in the chai tea powder box. Allow for a 10-minute cooling period. In the bread machine pan, combine the frozen raspberries, chai tea, vanilla essence, chardonnay, egg yolk, and butter. In a large mixing bowl, combine the rye flour, bread flour, yeast, sugar, all-purpose flour, wheat bran, walnuts, caraway seed, and salt. Press Start after selecting the Sweet option with a light crust. Let your bread cool down after baking the slice and serve.

261. BUTTERMILK MAPLE BREAD

READY IN ABOUT: 3 DAYS
YIELDS: 2 LB LOAF

INGREDIENTS

» 1/2 cup sprouted wheat berries
» 3/4 cup buttermilk
» 1 egg
» 2 tablespoon maple syrup
» 1/2 teaspoon salt
» 1/3 teaspoon baking soda
» 2 tablespoon vital wheat gluten
» 2 1/4 cup whole wheat flour
» 1 1/2 teaspoon active dry yeast

INSTRUCTIONS

Drain 1/2 cup raw wheat berries after rinsing them in lukewarm water. Add the berries to a large basin of water and soak for 12 hours or overnight, covered. Drain the berries

in a colander and store them in a dark area, covered. Rinse them three times a day, and they'll start sprouting soon. The sprouts will reach their ideal length of around l/4-inch in a few days. Drain the sprouts and crush them in a food processor. Place all of the ingredients in the bread machine pan in the sequence specified by the manufacturer. Press Start after selecting the Whole Wheat cycle and the Medium Crust setting.

262. COCOA BREAD

READY IN ABOUT: 3 1/2 HOURS
YIELDS: 1 1/2 LB LOAF

INGREDIENTS

» 1/4 cup water
» 1 cup milk
» 1 egg
» 1 tablespoon vanilla extract
» 3 1/3 cup bread flour
» 1/4 cup sucralose and brown sugar blend
» 1 teaspoon salt
» 1 teaspoon ground cinnamon
» 1 teaspoon cocoa powder
» 1 1/2 teaspoon active dry yeast
» 2 tablespoon margarine (softened)
» 1/2 cup peanut butter chips
» 1/4 cup semisweet chocolate chips

INSTRUCTIONS

Add the water, milk, egg, vanilla extract, bread flour, sucralose and brown sugar blend, salt, cinnamon, cocoa powder, yeast, and margarine in the bread machine pan according to the manufacturer's instructions. Press Start on a 1 1/2 pound loaf cycle with a Light Crust. When the final kneading cycle begins, add the peanut butter chips and semisweet chocolate chips. Before slicing the bread, let it cool for about 10-15 minutes.

263. DECEMBER'S ORANGE YOGURT BREAD

READY IN ABOUT: 3 HOURS
YIELDS: 1 1/2 LB LOAF

INGREDIENTS

» 3 cup all-purpose flour
» 1 cup dried cranberries
» 3/4 cup plain yogurt
» 1/2 cup warm water
» 3 tablespoon honey
» 1 tablespoon butter (melted)
» 2 teaspoon active dry yeast
» 1 1/2 teaspoon salt
» 1 teaspoon orange oil

INSTRUCTIONS

Put all the ingredients (above mentioned) in the pan of the bread machine pan in the manufacturer's recommended order. Press Start after selecting the Light Crust option. When the bake cycle ends, remove the pan from the machine and set it on a wire rack to cool. Allow 3 minutes for the bread to rise in the pan before turning it upside down and sliding the loaf onto the rack. If the paddle is stuck in the bottom of the bread, carefully remove it. Before slicing, turn the bread on its side and let it cool.

264. SUGARY WHEAT BREAD

READY IN ABOUT: 3 HOURS
YIELDS: 1 LB LOAF

INGREDIENTS

- » 1/2 cup water (at 27°C)
- » 1/4 cup milk (at 27°C)
- » 2 teaspoons butter (melted)
- » 1 tablespoon skim milk powder
- » 2 tablespoons honey
- » 1 cup white bread flour
- » 1 tablespoon molasses
- » 1 teaspoon sugar
- » 1/2 teaspoon salt
- » 1 teaspoon unsweetened cocoa powder
- » 1 1/4 cups whole-wheat flour
- » 1 teaspoon instant yeast

INSTRUCTIONS

Put all the ingredients (above mentioned) in the bread maker's pan according to the manufacturer's instructions. Press Start after programming the machine for Basic/White bread and selecting light or medium crust. Remove the bucket from the machine after the loaf is done. Allow 5 minutes for the bread to cool. Remove the loaf from the bucket with a little shake and place it on a cooling rack.

265. CHERRY CHOCOLATE BREAD

READY IN ABOUT: 3 1/2 HOURS
YIELDS: 2 LB LOAF

INGREDIENTS

- » 1 1/3 cups milk
- » 1 large egg
- » 3/4 teaspoon vanilla extract
- » 3/4 teaspoon almond extract
- » 4 tablespoons unsalted butter
- » 3 3/4 cups bread flour
- » 1/2 cup unsweetened Dutch-process cocoa powder
- » 1/3 cup light brown sugar
- » 1 tablespoon + 1 teaspoon gluten
- » 1 1/2 teaspoons salt
- » 1 tablespoon active dry yeast
- » 1 cup snipped glacéed tart dried cherries

INSTRUCTIONS

In the sequence specified in the manufacturer's directions, place all ingredients in the pan, except the cherries. Set the crust to medium and begin the Basic or Sweet Bread cycle by pressing the Start button. (The Delay Timer is not compatible

with this recipe.) Add the cherries when the machine whistles or between Knead 1 and Knead 2. Take out the bread from the pan and place it on a rack when the baking cycle is finished. Before slicing, allow it cool to room temperature.

266. CHOCOLATE HALLAH

READY IN ABOUT: 2 HOURS AND 45 MINUTES
YIELDS: 2 LB LOAF

INGREDIENTS

- » 1 1/4 cups water
- » 2 large eggs
- » 3 tablespoons vegetable oil
- » 1 tablespoon vanilla extract
- » 4 cups bread flour
- » 2/3 cup sugar
- » 1/3 cup unsweetened Dutch-process cocoa powder
- » 1 tablespoon + 1 teaspoon gluten
- » 2 teaspoons salt
- » 2 1/2 teaspoons bread machine yeast
- » 2/3 cup semisweet chocolate chips

INSTRUCTIONS

Place all of the ingredients in the pan, except the chocolate chips, in the sequence specified by the maker. Set the crust to medium and begin the Basic or Sweet Bread cycle by pressing the Start button. (The Delay Timer is not compatible with this recipe.) Add the chocolate chips when the beep goes off. Take out the bread from the pan and place it on a rack when the baking cycle is finished. Before slicing, allow it cool to room temperature.

267. CHOCOLATE BREAD WITH DATES AND PISTACHIO

READY IN ABOUT: 2 1/2 HOURS
YIELDS: 2 LB LOAF

INGREDIENTS

- » 1 1/8 cups water
- » 1 large egg + 1 egg yolk
- » 1/4 cup vegetable oil
- » 4 cups bread flour
- » 2/3 cup sugar
- » 1/3 cup unsweetened Dutch-process cocoa powder
- » 1 tablespoon + 1 teaspoon gluten
- » 1 1/2 teaspoons salt
- » 2 1/2 teaspoons SAF yeast / 1 tablespoon bread machine yeast
- » 1 cup snipped pitted dates
- » 1/3 cup chopped pistachios

INSTRUCTIONS

Put the ingredients, except the dates and pistachios, in the pan according to the order in the manufacturer's instructions. Set the crust to medium and begin the Basic or Sweet Bread cycle by pressing the Start button. (The Delay Timer is not compatible with this recipe.) Add the dates and pistachios when the machine whistles or between Knead 1 and Knead 2. Take out the bread from the pan and place it on a rack when the baking cycle is finished. Before slicing, allow it cool to room temperature.

268. MEXICAN FLAVORED CHOCOLATE BREAD

READY IN ABOUT: 2 1/2 HOURS
YIELDS: 2 LB LOAF

INGREDIENTS

» 1 cup milk
» 1/2 cup orange juice
» 4 tablespoons unsalted butter
» 2 large eggs
» 3 1/2 cups bread flour
» 1/3 cup light brown sugar
» 1/4 cup unsweetened Dutch-process cocoa powder
» 1 tablespoon + 1 teaspoon gluten
» 1 1/2 teaspoons salt
» 1 1/2 teaspoons instant espresso powder
» 1 teaspoon ground cinnamon
» 2/3 cup bittersweet chocolate chips
» 1 tablespoon bread machine yeast

INSTRUCTIONS

Place all of the ingredients in the pan, except the chocolate chips, in the sequence specified by the maker. Set the crust to medium and select the Sweet Bread cycle from the menu; push Start. (The Delay Timer is not compatible with this recipe). Add the chocolate chips when the machine whistles, or between Knead 1 and Knead 2. Take out the bread from the pan and place it on a rack when the baking cycle is finished. Before slicing, allow it cool to room temperature.

269. PISTACHIOS, MINT, AND CHOCOLATE BREAD

READY IN ABOUT: 2 1/2 HOURS
YIELDS: 2 LB LOAF

INGREDIENTS

» 3/4 cup milk
» 1/2 cup water
» 1 large egg + 1 egg yolk
» 4 tablespoons pistachio oil / melted unsalted butter
» 1 1/4 teaspoons mint extract
» 3 1/2 cups bread flour
» 1/3 cup sugar
» 4 tablespoons unsweetened Dutch-process cocoa powder
» 1 tablespoon + 2 teaspoons gluten
» 1 1/2 teaspoons salt
» 1 tablespoon bread machine yeast
» 2/3 cup bittersweet chocolate chips
» 1/2 cup chopped pistachios

INSTRUCTIONS

Place all of the ingredients in the pan, except the chocolate chips and pistachios, in the sequence specified by the maker. Set the crust to light and select the Sweet Bread cycle from the menu; press Start. (The Delay Timer is not compatible with this recipe.) Add the chocolate chips with pistachios when the machine whistles, or between Knead 1 and Knead 2. Take out the bread from the pan and place it on a rack when the baking cycle is finished. Before slicing, allow it cool to room temperature.

270. BUTTERY SWEET BREAD

Cook Time: 3 hours

YIELDS: 1,5 LB LOAF

INGREDIENTS

» 1/3 cup water
» 1/2 cup milk
» 1/4 cup sugar
» 1 beaten egg
» 1 teaspoon of salt
» 1/4 cup margarine/ 1/4 cup butter
» 2 teaspoons bread machine yeast
» 3 1/3 cups bread flour

INSTRUCTIONS

In your bread machine pan, combine all of the ingredients. Choose the white bread option, then the bake cycle. The bread is done when the bake cycle is finished. When the pan is finished, please remove it from the machine and lay it aside for 10 minutes. Before serving, remove the bread from the pan and allow it to cool.

271. CHOCOLATE BREAD

READY IN ABOUT: 2 HOURS
YIELDS: 1,5 LB LOAF

INGREDIENTS

» 1 pack active dry yeast
» 1/2 cup sugar
» 3 cups bread flour
» 1/4 cup cocoa powder
» 1 large egg
» 1/4 cup butter
» 1/2 teaspoon vanilla extract
» 1 cup milk

INSTRUCTIONS

Place everything in the bread machine's pan. Choose quick bread or a similar option. The bread is done when the bake cycle is finished. When the pan is finished, please remove it from the machine and lay it aside for 10 minutes. Before serving, remove the bread from the pan and allow it to cool.

272. CRANBERRY WALNUT BREAD

READY IN ABOUT: 2 HOURS
YIELDS: 1,5 LB LOAF

INGREDIENTS

» 1/4 cup water
» 1/4 cup rolled oats
» 1 egg
» 1 cup buttermilk
» 1-1/2 tablespoons margarine
» 3 tablespoons honey
» 1 teaspoon salt
» 3 cups bread flour
» 1/2 teaspoon ground cinnamon
» 1/4 teaspoon baking soda
» 3/4 cup dried cranberries
» 2 teaspoons active dry yeast
» 1/2 cup chopped walnuts

INSTRUCTIONS

Except for the walnuts and cranberries, put everything in the bread machine pan. Select the light crust and sweet cycle options on the machine. To begin, press the start button. At the beep signal, add the walnuts and cranberries. When the bake cycle ends, the bread is ready. Remove the pan and lay it aside for 10 minutes. Then take out the bread and let it cool before serving.

273. BROWN AND WHITE SUGAR BREAD

READY IN ABOUT: 3 HOURS
YIELDS: 1 1/2 LB LOAF

INGREDIENTS

» 1 cup milk
» 1/4 cup butter (softened)
» 1 egg
» 1/4 cup light brown sugar
» 1/4 cup granulated white sugar
» 2 tablespoons ground cinnamon
» 1/4 teaspoon salt
» 3 cups bread flour
» 2 teaspoons bread machine yeast

INSTRUCTIONS

Place all ingredients in the bread machine's baking pan in the manufacturer's recommended order. Close the cover on the bread maker and place the baking pan inside. Select the Sweet Bread option, followed by Medium Crust. To begin, press the start button. When the bake cycle ends, the bread is ready. Remove the baking pan carefully from the machine, and invert the bread loaf onto a wire rack to cool entirely before slicing. Cut the bread loaf into desired-sized slices with a sharp knife and serve.

274. HONEY SOY BREAD

READY IN ABOUT: 3 HOURS
YIELDS: 2 LB LOAF

INGREDIENTS

» 1 1/2 cups water
» 3 tablespoons canola oil
» 3 tablespoons honey
» 3 tablespoons dark brown sugar
» 1 large egg
» 2 cups whole wheat flour
» 1 1/2 cups bread flour
» 1/2 cup full-fat soy flour
» 2 tablespoons wheat germ
» 1/3 cup nonfat dry milk
» 2 tablespoons gluten
» 2 teaspoons salt
» 1 tablespoon + 1/2 teaspoon bread machine yeast

INSTRUCTIONS

In the pan, layer the ingredients in the sequence specified in the manufacturer's directions. Set the crust too dark and begin the Whole Wheat cycle by pressing the Start button. Take the bread from the pan and lay it on a rack when the baking cycle is finished. Before slicing, allow it cool to room temperature.

275. TEFF HONEY BREAD

READY IN ABOUT: 3 HOURS
YIELDS: 2 LB LOAF

INGREDIENTS

» 1 1/2 cups water
» 3 tablespoons vegetable oil
» 3 tablespoons honey
» 3 1/4 cups bread flour
» 3/4 cup ivory or dark teff flour
» 1 tablespoon+ 2 teaspoons gluten
» 2 teaspoons salt
» 1 tablespoon + 1/2 teaspoon bread machine yeast

INSTRUCTIONS

In the pan, layer the ingredients in the sequence specified in the manufacturer's directions. Set the crust too dark and begin the Whole Wheat cycle by pressing the Start button. Take the bread from the pan and lay it on a rack when the baking cycle is finished. Before slicing, allow it cool to room temperature.

276. WHITE CHOCOLATE BREAD

READY IN ABOUT: 3 HOURS
YIELDS: 1 1/2 LB LOAF

INGREDIENTS

» 1 cup warm milk
» 1/4 cup warm water
» 1/4 cup butter (softened)
» 1 egg
» 2 tablespoons white sugar
» 2 tablespoons brown sugar
» 3 cups bread flour
» 1 teaspoon salt
» 1 teaspoon ground cinnamon
» 1 (.25 ounce) package active dry yeast
» 1 cup white chocolate chips

INSTRUCTIONS

Place all of the ingredients in the pan (excluding white chocolate chips) in the order indicated by the manufacturer. Choose a cycle and press the Start button. Add the white chocolate chips when the machine beeps, which should be roughly 5 minutes before the kneading cycle ends. Take out the bread from the pan and place it on a rack when the baking cycle is finished. Before slicing, allow it cool to room temperature.

277. PORTUGUESE SWEET BREAD

READY IN ABOUT: 3 HOURS
YIELDS: 1 1/2 LB LOAF

INGREDIENTS

» 1 egg (beaten)
» 1 cup milk
» 1/3 cup sugar
» 2 tablespoons margarine
» 3 cups bread flour
» 3/4 teaspoon salt
» 2 1/2 teaspoons active dry yeast

INSTRUCTIONS

Place all of the ingredients (mentioned above) in your bread machine. Choose the sweet bread option. To begin, press the start button. Set bake cycle standard. When the bake cycle ends, the bread is ready. Take it out from the pan of the bread machine and let it cool before serving.

278. PISTACHIO HORSERADISH APPLE BREAD

READY IN ABOUT: 3 HOURS
YIELDS: 2 LB LOAF

INGREDIENTS

» 3 cups wheat flour
» 2 whole eggs (beaten)
» 3 tablespoons horseradish (grated)
» 1/2 cup apple puree
» 1 tablespoon sugar
» 4 tablespoons olive oil
» 1/2 cup pistachios (peeled and chopped)
» 1 teaspoon instant yeast
» 1 cup + 1 tablespoon water
» 1 teaspoon salt

INSTRUCTIONS

In a mixing bowl, beat the eggs. To the bread maker bucket, add 1 cup plus 1 tablespoon water. Pour in the olive oil. Fill the bucket with flour, applesauce, pistachios, horseradish, and eggs. Mix thoroughly and create a small groove in the center. Toss in the yeast. From different sides, add salt and sugar to the bucket. Set your bread machine's program to Basic/White Bread and the crust type to Medium. Start by pressing the START button. Wait till the cycle is finished. When the loaf is done, take it from the bucket and set it aside to cool for 5 minutes. To remove the bread, gently shake the bucket. Let it cool before slicing and serving.

Chapter 11

QUICK BREAD
(NO YEAST)

279. MATCHA GREEN TEA QUICK BREAD

READY IN ABOUT: 2 1/2 HOURS
YIELDS: 1 1/2 LB LOAF

INGREDIENTS

» 2 cups Light Flour Blend/Whole-Grain Flour Blend
» 1 cup granulated cane sugar
» 1/2 cup tiger nut flour
» 1/2 cup millet flour
» 1/4 cup green matcha tea powder
» 1 tablespoon baking powder
» 2 teaspoons psyllium husk flakes or powder
» 1 teaspoon kosher salt
» 1/2 cup unsweetened soy/coconut milk
» 1/3 cup vegetable oil
» 3 large eggs (beaten)
» 1 teaspoon pure vanilla extract

INSTRUCTIONS

Mix the dry ingredients (mentioned above) in a mixing bowl. Whisk together the wet ingredients in a 4-cup glass measuring cup and pour into the bread pan. Spread the dry ingredients over the wet components with a spatula. Insert the bread pan into the machine, center it, and lock it in place. Close the lid and choose from the following options: Quick bread/cake cycle; Loaf size: 1 1/2 pound; Medium crust; Press Start

Remove the paddle and reshape the loaf when you hear the signal for the machine changing from the knead to the bake cycle if your machine has one. If the dough feels sticky, moisten your hands with a little water to aid in reshaping and flattening the top of the loaf. Allow the bread to finish baking while the cover is closed.

When the baking is finished, take the bread pan from the machine and place it on a wire cooling rack on its side. Allow for a few minutes in the pan before turning it upside down and sliding the loaf onto the wire rack. Allow the bread to cool before slicing it.

280. MORNING GLORY QUICK BREAD

READY IN ABOUT: 2 1/2 HOURS
YIELDS: 1 1/2 LB LOAF

INGREDIENTS

» 1/2 cup raisins
» 2 1/4 cups Light Flour Blend/Whole-Grain Flour Blend
» 3/4 cup dark brown sugar
» 1 teaspoon ground cinnamon
» 2 teaspoons xanthan gum
» 1/2 teaspoon ground ginger
» 8 ounces (227 g) canned crushed pineapple
» 3/4 cup grated peeled carrots
» 1/2 cup grated sweetened coconut
» 2 teaspoons baking powder
» 1/2 cup chopped walnuts
» 1/4 cup vegetable oil
» 2 large eggs (beaten)
» 3/4 teaspoon salt
» 1 teaspoon pure vanilla extract
» 1/4 cup water (at 27°C)

INSTRUCTIONS

Place the raisins, cover with water in a bowl, and microwave for 30 seconds. Set aside for 5 minutes to rehydrate before draining. Combine the flour blend, cinnamon, brown sugar, baking powder, salt, xanthan gum, and ginger in a mixing bowl. Combine the pineapple, carrots, coconut, almonds, and drained raisins in a large mixing bowl. Toss and stir to thoroughly coat everything with the dry ingredients. Whisk the wet ingredients in a 4-cup glass measuring cup and pour into the bread pan. Spread the dry ingredients over the wet components with a spatula. Insert the bread pan into the machine, center it, and lock it in place. Close the lid and choose from the following options: Quick bread/cake cycle; Loaf size: 1 1/2 pound; Light crust; Press Start.

When the baking is finished, take the bread pan from the machine and place it on a wire cooling rack on its side. Allow for a few minutes in the pan before turning it upside down and sliding the loaf onto the wire rack. Allow the bread to cool before slicing it.

281. PUMPKIN QUICK BREAD

READY IN ABOUT: 2 1/2 HOURS
YIELDS: 1 1/2 LB LOAF

INGREDIENTS

» 2 1/2 cups Light Flour Blend
» 1 1/2 cups granulated cane sugar
» 1/2 cup millet flour
» 1 tablespoon baking powder
» 2 teaspoons psyllium husk flakes or powder
» 2 teaspoons ground nutmeg
» 2 teaspoons ground cinnamon
» 1 teaspoon kosher salt
» 1 teaspoon ground allspice
» 1/2 teaspoon ground cloves
» 15 ounces canned pure pumpkin puree
» 1/2 cup vegetable or canola oil
» 3 large eggs (beaten)
» 1/4 cup water

INSTRUCTIONS

Blend the above-mentioned dry recipe items in a separate bowl, whisk the wet ingredients, and scrape them into the bread pan. Spread the dry ingredients over the wet components with a spatula. Insert the bread pan into the machine, center it, and lock it in place. Close the lid and choose from the following options: Quick bread/cake cycle; Loaf size: 1 1/2 pound; Medium crust; Press Start
When the baking is finished, take the bread pan from the machine and place it on a wire cooling rack on its side. Allow for a few minutes in the pan before turning it upside down and sliding the loaf onto the wire rack. Allow the bread to cool before slicing it.

282. SALTED CARAMEL QUICK BREAD

READY IN ABOUT: 2 1/2 HOURS
YIELDS: 1 1/2 LB LOAF

INGREDIENTS

» 2 cups Light Flour Blend/Whole-Grain Flour Blend
» 1 cup millet flour
» 1 cup granulated cane sugar
» 2 teaspoons baking powder
» 1 teaspoon salt
» 1 teaspoon xanthan gum
» 1/4 cup vegetable oil
» 3 large eggs (beaten)
» 1/2 cup unsweetened soy/coconut milk
» 1 teaspoon pure vanilla extract
» 1 cup gluten-free caramel bits/quartered standard caramel squares

For Serving:
» 1/4 cup gluten-free caramel sauce
» Coarse sea salt

INSTRUCTIONS

Mix the dry ingredients in a bowl. Whisk the wet ingredients in a 4-cup glass measuring cup and pour into the bread pan. Spread the dry ingredients over the wet components with a spatula. Insert the bread pan into the machine, center it, and lock it in place. Close the lid and choose from the following options: Quick bread/cake cycle; Loaf size: 1 1/2 pound; Light crust; Press Start.
Place the caramel chunks on top. Pay heed to the indicators signaling the transition from the knead to the bake cycle if your machine has one. Remove the paddle, reshape the loaf, and smooth the top when you hear it. Moisten your hands with water if it becomes dough sticky. Close the lid and leave the bread alone to finish baking.
When the baking is finished, take the bread pan from the machine and place it on a wire cooling rack on its side. Allow for a few minutes in the pan before turning it upside down and sliding the loaf onto the wire rack. Allow the bread to cool before slicing it upside down. Before slicing and serving, drizzle the loaf with caramel sauce and sprinkle with coarse sea salt.

283. TROPICAL QUICK BREAD

READY IN ABOUT: 2 1/2 HOURS
YIELDS: 1 1/2 LB LOAF

INGREDIENTS

» 2 cups Light Flour Blend/Whole-Grain Flour Blend
» 1 cup millet flour
» 2 teaspoons baking powder
» 3/4 cup granulated cane sugar
» 1 tablespoon psyllium husk flakes or powder
» 3/4 teaspoon salt
» 1/2 cup grated unsweetened coconut
» 1/2 cup unsweetened coconut milk
» 1/4 cup vegetable oil
» 3 large eggs (beaten)
» 1 teaspoon pure vanilla extract
» 8 ounces (227 g) canned crushed pineapple (drained)
» 1/3 cup coarsely chopped macadamia nuts

INSTRUCTIONS

Blend the dry ingredients (except the coconut) in a large mixing basin. Stir in the coconut and toss until all of the dry ingredients are nicely coated. Whisk the wet ingredients (excluding the pineapple) in a 4-cup glass measuring cup. Pour the mixture into the bread pan after stirring in the pineapple. Spread the dry ingredients over the wet components with a spatula. Insert the bread pan into the machine, center it, and lock it in place. Close the lid and choose from the following options: Quick bread/cake cycle; Loaf size: 1 1/2 pound; Medium crust; Press Start.
Add the macadamia nuts to the mix. Remove the kneading paddle and reshape the bread when you hear the indication for the machine switching from the knead to the bake cycle if your machine has one. If the dough feels sticky, moisten your hands with a little water to aid in reshaping and flattening the top of the loaf. Close the lid and leave the bread alone to finish baking.
When the baking is finished, take the bread pan from the machine and place it on a wire cooling rack on its side. Allow for a few minutes in the pan before turning it upside down and sliding the loaf onto the wire rack. Allow the bread to cool before slicing it.

284. WHITE CHOCOLATE PISTACHIO QUICK BREAD

READY IN ABOUT: 2 1/2 HOURS
YIELDS: 1 1/2 LB LOAF

INGREDIENTS

»   3 cups Light Flour Blend
»   1 cup granulated cane sugar
»   1 tablespoon baking powder
»   2 teaspoons psyllium husk flakes or powder
»   1 teaspoon kosher or fine sea salt
»   1 teaspoon ground cardamom
»   3/4 cup unsweetened coconut milk
»   1/4 cup water
»   2 tablespoons vegetable oil/unsalted butter
»   3 large eggs (beaten)
»   2 teaspoons pure vanilla extract
»   1 1/3 cups white chocolate chips
»   1/2 cup chopped pistachios

INSTRUCTIONS

Mix the dry ingredients (above mentioned) in a bowl and the wet ingredients in a separate 4-cup glass measuring cup, and pour into the bread pan. Spread the dry ingredients over the wet components with a spatula. Insert the bread pan into the machine, center it, and lock it in place. Close the lid and choose from the following options: Quick bread/cake cycle; Loaf size: 1 1/2 pound; Medium crust; Press Start.
Combine the white chocolate chips and pistachios in a mixing bowl, and after the first knead cycle, add it to the bread pan. When the baking is finished, take the bread pan from the machine and place it on a wire cooling rack on its side. Allow for a few minutes in the pan before turning it upside down and sliding the loaf onto the wire rack. Allow the bread to cool before slicing it.

285. DRIED CRANBERRY TEA QUICK BREAD

READY IN ABOUT: 2 1/2 HOURS
YIELDS: 1,5 LB LOAF

INGREDIENTS

»   1 1/2 cups dried cranberries
»   Boiling water as required
»   2 large eggs
»   2 teaspoons almond extract
»   1 teaspoon vanilla extract
»   1/4 cup canola/vegetable oil
»   3/4 cup frozen unsweetened apple juice concentrate (thawed)
»   1 cup sugar
»   1/2 teaspoon salt
»   1 1/4 cups unbleached all-purpose flour
»   1 cup whole wheat pastry flour
»   1/2 teaspoon baking soda
»   1 teaspoon ground cinnamon
»   1/2 teaspoon fresh-ground nutmeg
»   1 tablespoon baking powder

INSTRUCTIONS

Cover the cranberries over boiling water in a small bowl and set them aside for 20 minutes to soften. Using paper towels, absorb any excess liquid. Remove from the equation. Place the ingredients in the pan in the sequence listed in the manufacturer's instructions, starting with the dry ingredients and ending with the cranberries. Set the crust too dark if your machine has that option, and set up the machine for the Quick Bread/Cake cycle; push Start. It will be a thick batter. Check the loaf for doneness when the machine beeps at the end of the cycle.
When the bread shrinks slightly from the pan's sides, the sides are dark brown, and the top is firm to a mild pressure when touched with your finger, it's done. Allow 10 minutes for the bread to cool in the pan before turning it out right side up to cool entirely on a rack before slicing. Refrigerate after wrapping securely in plastic wrap.

286. FIG BREAD

READY IN ABOUT: 3 1/2 HOURS
YIELDS: A 2-POUND LOAF

INGREDIENTS

»   1 cup apple juice
»   4 tablespoons unsalted butter
»   1 cup dried figs (stemmed and cut into quarters)
»   grated zest (of 1 orange)
»   2 large eggs
»   1 teaspoon vanilla extract
»   2 1/2 teaspoons baking powder
»   1/3 cup sugar
»   2 cups unbleached all-purpose flour
»   1/2 teaspoon salt
»   1/2 teaspoon baking soda

INSTRUCTIONS

Heat the apple juice and butter in a small saucepan over medium-low heat on the stovetop or in a microwave-safe bowl until the butter is melted. Take the pan off the heat and stir in the figs and orange zest. Allow 1 hour for cooling to room temperature. Place the ingredients in the pan in the sequence specified by the manufacturer, beginning with the apple-fig mixture and ending with the liquid ingredients.

Set the crust too dark if your machine has that option, and set up the machine for the Quick Bread/Cake cycle; push Start. When the bread shrinks slightly from the pan's sides, the sides are dark brown, and the top is firm to a mild pressure when touched with your finger, it's done. Allow 10 minutes for the bread to cool in the pan before flipping it out, right side up, to cool entirely on a rack. Wrap firmly in plastic wrap and chill until ready to serve, up to 3 days.

287. BANANA AND WALNUT QUICK BREAD

READY IN ABOUT: 2 1/2 HOURS
YIELDS: 2 LB LOAF

INGREDIENTS

- » 1 1/2 cups mashed overripe bananas (2 large)
- » 1/4 cup sour cream
- » 1/2 cup vegetable oil
- » 2 large eggs
- » 1 teaspoon vanilla extract
- » 1/2 cup sugar
- » 1/2 teaspoon salt
- » 1/3 cup dark brown sugar
- » 1 teaspoon baking soda
- » 2 cups unbleached all-purpose flour
- » 1/2 teaspoon baking powder
- » 1/2 cup coarsely chopped walnuts

INSTRUCTIONS

In a small mixing bowl, mash the sour cream and bananas together with a fork. The combination can be used right away or refrigerated for up to 24 hours. In the bread pan, layer the banana mixture and the remaining ingredients in the sequence specified in the manufacturer's instructions. Set the crust too dark if your machine has that option, and set up the machine for the Quick Bread/Cake cycle; push Start. The batter will be rich and silky in texture. Check the bread for doneness when the machine beeps at the end of the cycle. When the bread shrinks slightly from the pan's sides, the sides are dark brown, and the top is firm to a mild pressure when touched with your finger, it's done. Allow 10 minutes for the bread to cool in the pan before flipping it out, right side up, to cool entirely on a rack. Refrigerate after wrapping securely in plastic wrap.

288. DARK AND WHITE CHOCOLATE QUICK BREAD

READY IN ABOUT: 2 1/2 HOURS
YIELDS: 2 LB LOAF

INGREDIENTS

- » 2 large eggs
- » 1 cup plain yogurt
- » 1/4 cup buttermilk
- » 1/4 cup vegetable oil
- » 2 teaspoons vanilla extract
- » 2/3 cup light brown sugar
- » 2 1/2 cups unbleached all-purpose flour
- » 1/3 cup unsweetened Dutch-process cocoa powder
- » 1 1/2 teaspoons baking soda
- » 1/2 teaspoon instant espresso powder
- » 1/4 teaspoon salt
- » 1/2 teaspoon baking powder
- » 1 cup white chocolate chips/ chunks broken off a bar of white chocolate

INSTRUCTIONS

In the pan, layer the ingredients in the sequence specified in the manufacturer's directions. Set the crust too dark if your machine has that option, and set up the machine for the Quick Bread/Cake cycle; push Start. When the cake starts to shrink slightly from the sides of the pan, the sides are dark brown, and the top is hard when gently pressed with your finger, it's done. Take the pan from the machine as soon as the bread is done. Allow 10 minutes for the bread to cool in the pan before turning it out right side up to cool entirely on a rack before slicing. Wrap securely with plastic wrap and keep refrigerated.

289. BOURBON NUT QUICK BREAD

READY IN ABOUT: 2 1/2 HOURS
YIELDS: 2 LB LOAF

INGREDIENTS

- » 2 large eggs
- » 2 1/4 cups unbleached all-purpose flour
- » 1/4 cup nut oil/vegetable oil
- » 1 1/2 teaspoons almond extract
- » 1 1/2 cups sour cream
- » 1/2 cup bourbon
- » 1/2 teaspoon salt
- » 1/2 teaspoon baking soda
- » 1 cup light brown sugar
- » 2 1/2 teaspoons baking powder
- » 1 1/2 teaspoons ground nutmeg
- » 1 teaspoon instant espresso powder
- » 1 1/4 cups coarsely chopped pecans/walnuts

INSTRUCTIONS

In the pan, layer the ingredients in the sequence specified in the manufacturer's directions. Set the crust too dark if your machine has that option, and set up the machine for the Quick

Bread/Cake cycle; push Start. When the bread shrinks slightly from the pan's sides, the sides are dark brown, and the top is firm to a mild pressure when touched with your finger, it's done. Allow 10 minutes for the bread to cool in the pan before flipping it out, right side up, to cool entirely on a rack. Before serving, wrap firmly in plastic wrap and chill for at least 3 days.

290. BEST CARDAMOM BREAD

READY IN ABOUT: 2 1/2 HOURS
YIELDS: 2 LB LOAF

INGREDIENTS

» 1/3 cup vegetable oil
» 3 large eggs
» 1/4 cup buttermilk
» 1 tablespoon vanilla extract
» 1 cup sour cream
» 2 teaspoons baking powder
» 3/4 cup sugar
» 1 teaspoon baking soda
» 1/2 teaspoon salt
» 2 1/4 cups unbleached all-purpose flour
» 2 1/2 teaspoons ground cardamom

INSTRUCTIONS

In the pan, layer the ingredients in the sequence specified in the manufacturer's directions. Set the crust too dark if your machine has that option, and set up the machine for the Quick Bread/Cake cycle; push Start. When the bread shrinks slightly from the pan's sides, the sides are dark brown, and the top is firm to a mild pressure when touched with your finger, it's done. Allow 10 minutes for the bread to cool in the pan before turning it out right side up to cool entirely on a rack before slicing. Wrap securely with plastic wrap and keep refrigerated.

291. GRANOLA FRUIT QUICK BREAD

READY IN ABOUT: 2 1/2 HOURS
YIELDS: 2 LB LOAF

INGREDIENTS

» 3/4 cup milk
» 1/4 cup plain yogurt
» 1/2 cup vegetable/nut oil
» 2 large eggs
» Grated zest of 1 lemon
» 1 teaspoon vanilla extract
» 3/4 cup sugar
» 1/2 teaspoon salt
» 1 tablespoon baking powder
» 1 cup whole wheat pastry flour
» 1 cup unbleached all-purpose flour
» 3/4 cup granola
» 1/2 cup chopped dried pineapple/golden raisins
» 1/2 teaspoon ground cinnamon/apple pie spice

INSTRUCTIONS

In the pan, layer the ingredients in the sequence specified in the manufacturer's directions. Set the crust too dark if your machine has that option, and set up the machine for the Quick Bread/Cake cycle; push Start. It will be a thick, lumpy batter. Check the loaf for doneness when the machine beeps at the end of the cycle. When the bread shrinks slightly from the pan's sides, the sides are dark brown, and the top is firm to a mild pressure when touched with your finger, it's done. Allow 10 minutes for the bread to cool in the pan before flipping it out, right side up, to cool entirely on a rack. If desired, brush the top with melted butter. Wrap firmly with plastic wrap and keep refrigerated or at room temperature.

292. WELSH BARA BRITH

READY IN ABOUT: 2 1/2 HOURS
YIELDS: 2 LB LOAF

INGREDIENTS

» 1 1/4 cups boiling water
» 2 Earl Grey tea bags (can be decaffeinated)
» 1 (8-ounce / 227-g) bag mixed dried fruit (chopped)
» 1 large egg
» 1/2 cup milk
» 1 tablespoon unsalted butter
» 3 tablespoons orange marmalade, ginger marmalade/apricot preserves
» 1 cup light brown sugar
» 3/4 teaspoon salt
» 2 3/4 cups unbleached all-purpose flour
» 1 cup dark or golden raisins
» 1/4 cup chopped candied orange peel/currants
» 2 3/4 teaspoons baking powder
» 2 teaspoons apple pie spice

INSTRUCTIONS

Fill a 4-cup glass measuring cup halfway with boiling water. Allow the tea bags to steep for 10 minutes before removing them and squeezing them dry. Stir in the dry fruit thoroughly. Allow 1 to 4 hours at room temperature to plump the fruit and bring it to room temperature. Place the ingredients in the pan in the order specified by the manufacturer's directions, including the fruit and all of the soaking liquid. Set the crust too dark if your machine has that option, and set up the machine for the Quick Bread/Cake cycle; push Start. The batter will be thick, silky, and packed with fruit that is equally distributed. When the machine beeps at the end of the cycle, hit Stop/Reset and set the machine to the Bake cycle for another 20 minutes to finish baking. When the bara brith shrinks slightly from the pan's sides, the sides are dark brown, and the top is firm to a little pressure when touched with your finger, it's done. Allow 10 minutes for the bread to cool in the pan before turning it out right side up to cool entirely on a rack before slicing. Refrigerate after wrapping securely in plastic wrap.

293. EASY PUMPKIN QUICK BREAD

READY IN ABOUT: 1 1/2 HOUR
YIELDS: 1,5 LB LOAF

INGREDIENTS

» 3 cups All-Purpose Flour
» 3 Eggs
» Cooking spray/ Baking spray
» 1/3 cup Vegetable Oil
» 1 1/2 cups Pumpkin Puree (canned or homemade)
» 1 cup Granulated Sugar
» 1 1/2 teaspoons Baking Powder
» 1/2 teaspoon Baking Soda
» 1/4 teaspoon Kosher Salt
» 3/4 teaspoon Ground Cinnamon
» 1/4 Teaspoon Ground Nutmeg
» 1/4 teaspoon Ground Ginger
» 1/2 cup chopped walnuts (optional)

INSTRUCTIONS

Collect the necessary components. Mix the vegetable oil, eggs, pumpkin puree, and sugar in a mixing bowl until well combined. Add baking powder and other ingredients with flour until combined. Set the bread machine to the cake or quick bread cycle after pouring the batter into the prepared pan. Add chopped nuts once the machine beeps. Remove the loaf from the pan and paddles and place it on a cooling rack.

294. APRICOT WALNUT QUICK BREAD

READY IN ABOUT: 2 1/2 HOURS
YIELDS: 1 1/2 LB LOAF

INGREDIENTS

» 2 1/4 cups Light Flour Blend
» 1 cup granulated cane sugar
» 3/4 cup millet flour
» 1 tablespoon baking powder
» 2 teaspoons psyllium husk flakes or powder
» 1 teaspoon ground ginger
» 1/2 teaspoon sea salt
» 1/4 cup vegetable oil / non-dairy butter
» 1/2 cup apricot nectar
» 3 large eggs (beaten)
» 1 cup chopped dried apricots
» 1/2 cup chopped walnuts (toasted)

INSTRUCTIONS

Blend the ingredients in a large mixing bowl. In a large mixing basin, combine the oil, apricot nectar, and eggs. Combine the chopped apricots and walnuts in a mixing bowl. Scrape the mixture into the bread pan. Spread the dry ingredients over the wet components with a spatula. Insert the bread pan into the machine, center it, and lock it in place. Close the lid and choose from the following options: quick or cake cycle; 1 1/2 pound; light crust loaf; Press Start.
When the baking is finished, take the bread pan from the machine and place it on a wire cooling rack on its side. Allow

for a few minutes in the pan before turning it upside down and sliding the loaf onto the wire rack. Allow the bread to cool before slicing it.

295. BANANA CHOCOLATE CHIP QUICK BREAD

READY IN ABOUT: 2 1/2 HOURS
YIELDS: 1 1/2 LB LOAF

INGREDIENTS

» 2 cups Light Flour Blend
» 1 cup granulated cane sugar
» 1/2 cup teff flour
» 1/2 cup buckwheat flour
» 1 tablespoon baking powder
» 1 tablespoon psyllium husk flakes or powder
» 1 teaspoon kosher or fine sea salt
» 3 large ripe bananas
» 1/3 cup vegetable oil
» 3 large eggs (beaten)
» 1 1/2 cups gluten-free, dairy-free semisweet chocolate chips

INSTRUCTIONS

Blend the ingredients in a large mixing bowl. Using a fork or a potato masher, mash the bananas into a pulp in a large mixing bowl. Whisk together the oil and eggs until smooth. Scrape the mixture into the bread pan. Spread the dry ingredients over the wet components with a spatula. Insert the bread pan into the machine, center it, and lock it in place. Close the lid and choose from the following options: quick or cake cycle; 1 1/2 pound; light crust loaf; Press Start.

Scrape the pan with the spatula after the first knead cycle to integrate all dry ingredients. Place the chocolate chips on top. When the baking is finished, take the bread pan from the machine and place it on a wire cooling rack on its side. Allow for a few minutes in the pan before turning it upside down and sliding the loaf onto the wire rack. Allow the bread to cool before slicing it.

296. BLUEBERRY QUICK BREAD WITH BROWN SUGAR CRUMBLE TOPPING

READY IN ABOUT: 2 1/2 HOURS
YIELDS: 1 1/2 LB LOAF

INGREDIENTS

» 1 1/2 cups Light Flour Blend or Whole-Grain Flour Blend
» 1 cup millet flour
» 1 cup granulated cane sugar
» 1 tablespoon baking powder
» 2 teaspoons psyllium husk flakes or powder
» 1 teaspoon kosher or fine sea salt

Wet Ingredients

» 1/2 cup unsweetened coconut milk (warmed to about 27°C)
» 1/3 cup vegetable oil

- » 3 large eggs (beaten)
- » 1 teaspoon pure vanilla extract
- » 1 1/4 cups fresh blueberries

Topping
- » 1/3 cup brown sugar
- » 2 tablespoons Light Flour Blend or Whole-Grain Flour Blend
- » 1/8 teaspoon ground cinnamon, nutmeg, mace, or cardamom

INSTRUCTIONS

Blend the ingredients in a large mixing bowl. Whisk the wet ingredients in a 4-cup glass measuring cup and pour into the bread pan. Spread the dry ingredients over the wet components with a spatula. Insert the bread pan into the machine, center it, and lock it in place. Close the lid and choose from the following options: quick or cake cycle; 1 1/2 pound; light crust loaf; Press Start.

Scrape the sides of the pan with the spatula after the first knead cycle to ensure all the dry ingredients are integrated. Add the blueberries and stir to combine. Close the lid and keep kneading. Meanwhile, in a separate dish, combine the topping ingredients with a fork.

Remove the kneading paddle and reshape the loaf when you hear the indication as the machine moves from the knead to the bake cycle. To reshape the loaf, moisten your hands with a little water if the dough feels sticky. Evenly distribute the topping over the dough. Allow the bread to finish baking while the cover is closed.

When the baking is finished, take the bread pan from the machine and place it on a wire cooling rack on its side. Allow for a few minutes in the pan before turning it upside down and sliding the loaf onto the wire rack. Allow the bread to cool before slicing it.

297. CARAMEL APPLE QUICK BREAD

READY IN ABOUT: 2 1/2 HOURS
YIELDS: 1 1/2 LB LOAF

INGREDIENTS

- » 2 1/2 cups light Flour Blend
- » 1 cup granulated cane sugar
- » 1/2 cup teff flour
- » 1/2 cup milk soy powder
- » 1 tablespoon baking powder
- » 1 tablespoon psyllium husk flakes or powder
- » 1 teaspoon kosher or fine sea salt
- » 3 large eggs (beaten)
- » 1/2 cup applesauce
- » 1/3 cup vegetable oil
- » 2 cups grated peeled apples
- » 1 1/2 cups gluten-free caramel bits

INSTRUCTIONS

Blend the ingredients in a large mixing bowl. Whisk together the eggs, applesauce, and oil in a separate large mixing basin. Scrape into the bread pan after stirring in the apples and caramel chunks. Using a spatula, spread the dry ingredients evenly over the wet components, totally covering them. Insert the bread pan into the machine, center it, and lock it in place. Close the lid and choose from the following options: quick or

cake cycle; 1 1/2 pound; medium crust loaf; Press Start. When the baking is finished, take the bread pan from the machine and place it on a wire cooling rack on its side. Allow for a few minutes in the pan before turning it upside down and sliding the loaf onto the wire rack. Allow the bread to cool before slicing it.

298. WALNUT QUICK BREAD WITH CHAI GLAZE

READY IN ABOUT: 2 1/2 HOURS
YIELDS: 1 1/2 LB LOAF

INGREDIENTS

- » 2 cups Light Flour Blend/Whole-Grain Flour Blend
- » 1 cup millet flour
- » 1 cup granulated cane sugar
- » 1/4 cup dairy-free chai powder
- » 1/4 cup Dari Free
- » 1 tablespoon baking powder
- » 1 tablespoon psyllium husk flakes or powder
- » 2 teaspoons instant espresso powder
- » 1 teaspoon kosher or fine sea salt
- » 3 large eggs (beaten)
- » 1/2 cup unsweetened soy or coconut milk
- » 1/3 cup vegetable oil
- » 1 teaspoon pure vanilla extract

Add-Ins
- » 1 cup chopped dates
- » 1 cup coarsely chopped walnuts

Chai Glaze
- » 3/4 cup confectioners' sugar
- » 2 tablespoons hot chai tea

INSTRUCTIONS

Blend the ingredients in a large mixing bowl. Whisk the wet ingredients in a 4-cup glass measuring cup and pour into the bread pan. Spread the dry ingredients over the wet components with a spatula. Insert the bread pan into the machine, center it, and lock it in place. Close the lid and choose from the following options: quick or cake cycle; 1 1/2 pound; medium crust loaf; Press Start.

Scrape the pan with the spatula after the first kneading cycle to integrate all dry ingredients. Combine the dates and nuts in a bowl. Remove the kneading paddle and reshape the bread when you hear the indication for the machine switching from the knead to the bake cycle if your machine has one. If the dough looks sticky, reshape the loaf with a lightly oiled spatula. Allow the bread to finish baking while the cover is closed.

When the baking is finished, take the bread pan from the machine and place it on a wire cooling rack on its side. Allow for a few minutes in the pan before turning it upside down and sliding the loaf onto the wire rack. Allow the bread to cool before slicing it.

If required, add more chai or hot water to the glaze ingredients to make a drizzle-like consistency. Pour the glaze over the bread after it has cooled and hardened. Cut into slices and serve.

299. DOUBLE CRANBERRY APPLESAUCE QUINOA QUICK BREAD

READY IN ABOUT: 2 1/2 HOURS
YIELDS: 1 1/2 LB LOAF

INGREDIENTS

» 2 cups Light Flour Blend
» 1 cup quinoa flakes
» 1 cup granulated cane sugar
» 1/2 cup milk soy powder
» 1 tablespoon baking powder
» 1 tablespoon psyllium husk flakes or powder
» 1 teaspoon kosher salt

Wet Ingredients
» 3 large eggs (beaten)
» 1/2 cup unsweetened applesauce, plain or cinnamon
» 1/3 cup vegetable oil
» 1 cup fresh cranberries (or frozen/ no need to thaw if frozen)
» 1/2 cup dried cranberries

INSTRUCTIONS

Blend the ingredients in a large mixing bowl. Whisk together the wet ingredients (excluding the cranberries) in a 4-cup glass measuring cup. Scrape the cranberries into the bread pan after stirring them in. Spread the dry ingredients evenly over the wet components using a spatula, totally covering them. Insert the bread pan into the machine, center it, and lock it in place. Close the lid and choose from the following options: quick or cake cycle; 1 1/2 pound; medium crust loaf; Press Start.

When the baking is finished, take the bread pan from the machine and place it on a wire cooling rack on its side. Allow for a few minutes in the pan before turning it upside down and sliding the loaf onto the wire rack. Allow the bread to cool before slicing it.

300. CURRANT WALNUT QUICK BREAD

READY IN ABOUT: 2 1/2 HOURS
YIELDS: 1 1/2 LB LOAF

INGREDIENTS

» 2 1/2 cups Light Flour Blend or Whole-Grain Flour Blend
» 1/2 cup buckwheat flour
» 1 cup granulated cane sugar
» 1 tablespoon psyllium husk flakes or powder
» 2 teaspoons baking powder
» 1/2 teaspoon sea salt
» 1/2 cup applesauce
» 1/3 cup vegetable oil
» 3 large eggs (beaten)
» 1 teaspoon pure vanilla extract

Add-Ins
» 1 cup coarsely chopped walnuts
» 3/4 cup dried currants or dark raisins

INSTRUCTIONS

Blend the ingredients in a large mixing bowl. Whisk the wet ingredients in a 4-cup glass measuring cup and pour into the bread pan. Spread the dry ingredients over the wet components with a spatula. Insert the bread pan into the machine, center it, and lock it in place. Close the lid and choose from the following options: quick or cake cycle; 1 1/2 pound; Light crust loaf; Press Start.
Scrape the pan with the spatula after the first kneading cycle to integrate all dry ingredients. Combine the walnuts and currants in a bowl and add them to the pan. Remove the kneading paddle and reshape the bread when you hear the indication for the machine switching from the knead to the bake cycle if your machine has one. If your dough becomes sticky, wet your hands with a little water to aid in reshaping and flattening the top of the loaf. Allow the bread to finish baking while the cover is closed.
When the baking is finished, take the bread pan from the machine and place it on a wire cooling rack on its side. Allow for a few minutes in the pan before turning it upside down and sliding the loaf onto the wire rack. Allow the bread to cool before slicing it.
Note: Currants are small raisins that are tarter. In your grocery shop, you might come across Zante currants, which are small grapes that are sweeter than true currants. In this recipe, any version will work, but if you can't get them, black raisins will suffice.

301. LEMON QUICK BREAD

READY IN ABOUT: 2 1/2 HOURS
YIELDS: 1 1/2 LB LOAF

INGREDIENTS

» 2 1/2 cups Light Flour Blend
» 1/2 cup almond flour/meal
» 1/2 cup Better Than Milk soy powder or coconut milk powder (40 g)
» 1 1/4 cups granulated cane sugar
» 1 tablespoon baking powder
» 1 tablespoon psyllium husk flakes or powder
» 1 teaspoon kosher or fine sea salt
» 3 large eggs (beaten)
» 1 lemon
» 1/2 cup squeezed lemon juice
» 1/3 cup vegetable or canola oil

INSTRUCTIONS

Whisk together the ingredients in a large mixing bowl. Whisk the wet ingredients in a 4-cup glass measuring cup and pour into the bread pan. Spread the dry ingredients evenly over the wet components using a spatula, totally covering them. Insert the bread pan into the machine, center it, and lock it in place. Close the lid and choose from the following options: quick or cake cycle; 1 1/2 pound; medium crust loaf; Press Start.
When the baking is finished, take the bread pan from the machine and place it on a wire cooling rack on its side. Allow for a few minutes in the pan before turning it upside down

and sliding the loaf onto the wire rack. Allow the bread to cool before slicing it.

302. ORANGE GLAZED QUICK BREAD

READY IN ABOUT: 2 1/2 HOURS
YIELDS: 1 1/2 LB LOAF

INGREDIENTS

- » 2 1/2 cups Light Flour Blend or Whole-Grain Flour Blend
- » 1 cup granulated cane sugar
- » 1/2 cup millet flour
- » 1/4 cup coconut milk powder
- » 1 tablespoon baking powder
- » 1 tablespoon psyllium husk flakes or powder
- » 1 teaspoon kosher or fine sea salt
- » 1/3 cup vegetable oil
- » 3 large eggs (beaten)
- » 1/2 cup fresh orange juice or water (at 27°C)
- » 1 teaspoon orange extract
- » 1/4 cup chopped candied orange peel

For glaze
- » 3/4 cup confectioners' sugar
- » 2 tablespoons freshly squeezed orange juice
- » 1 to 2 tablespoons) hot water

INSTRUCTIONS

Blend with the dry ingredients in a large mixing bowl. Whisk the wet ingredients (excluding the candied orange peel) in a 4-cup glass measuring cup. Pour the mixture into the bread pan after adding the orange peel. Spread the dry ingredients over the wet components with a spatula. Insert the bread pan into the machine, center it, and lock it in place. Close the lid and choose from the following options: quick or cake cycle; 1 1/2 pound; medium crust loaf; Press Start.
When the baking is finished, take the bread pan from the machine and place it on a wire cooling rack on its side. Allow for a few minutes in the pan before turning it upside down and sliding the loaf onto the wire rack. Allow for at least 2 hours of cooling time before glazing and slicing the bread. For the glaze: combine the confectioners' sugar and orange juice to make the glaze. Add the water little by little at a time until the required consistency is reached. Drizzle the glaze over the bread and set aside for 15 minutes before slicing.

303. ALMOND QUICK BREAD WITH CARDAMOM

READY IN ABOUT: 2 1/2 HOURS
YIELDS: 1 1/2 LB LOAF

INGREDIENTS

- » 2 1/2 cups Light Flour Blend
- » 1/2 cup almond flour
- » 1/4 cup coconut milk powder
- » 1 cup granulated cane sugar
- » 1 tablespoon baking powder
- » 1 tablespoon psyllium husk flakes or powder
- » 2 teaspoons ground cardamom
- » 1 teaspoon salt

- » 1 cup slivered almonds (toasted)
- » 3 large eggs (beaten)
- » 3/4 cup water
- » 1/4 cup vegetable/canola oil

INSTRUCTIONS

Blend the dry ingredients (except the slivered almonds) in a large mixing basin. Set aside after adding the almonds. Blend the wet ingredients in a 4-cup glass measuring cup and pour into the bread pan. Spread the dry ingredients evenly over the wet components using a spatula, totally covering them. Insert the bread pan into the machine, center it, and lock it in place. Close the lid and choose from the following options: quick or cake cycle; 1 1/2 pound; medium crust loaf; Press Start.

When the baking is finished, take the bread pan from the machine and place it on a wire cooling rack on its side. Allow for a few minutes in the pan before turning it upside down and sliding the loaf onto the wire rack. Allow the bread to cool before slicing it.

304. BUTTERNUT SQUASH QUICK BREAD

READY IN ABOUT: 2 1/2 HOURS
YIELDS: 1 1/2 LB LOAF

INGREDIENTS

- » 2 1/2 cups Light Flour Blend /Whole-Grain Flour Blend
- » 1/2 cup butternut squash flour
- » 1 cup granulated cane sugar
- » 1 tablespoon baking powder
- » 1 tablespoon psyllium husk flakes or powder
- » 1 teaspoon kosher or fine sea salt
- » 3/4 teaspoon ground nutmeg
- » 3 large eggs (beaten)
- » 1/2 cup unsweetened coconut milk
- » 1/4 cup vegetable oil
- » 2 teaspoons pure vanilla extract
- » 1 cup grated peeled butternut squash

INSTRUCTIONS

Place the bread pan on the counter with the beater paddle inside. Unless your machine's manufacturer specifies otherwise, put the liquids first, followed by the dry ingredients. Blend the dry ingredients in a large mixing bowl. Blend the wet ingredients (except the grated squash) in a 4-cup (1 liter) glass measuring cup. Add the squash and pour the mixture into the bread pan. Spread the dry ingredients evenly over the wet components using a spatula, totally covering them. Place the bread pan in the center of the machine and lock it in place. Shut the lid and choose quick or cake cycle; 1 1/2 pound; Light crust loaf; Press Start.
When the baking is finished, take the bread pan from the machine and place it on a wire cooling rack on its side. Allow for a few minutes in the pan before turning it upside down and sliding the loaf onto the wire rack. Allow the bread to cool before slicing it.

305. SUGAR-FREE BANANA BREAD

READY IN ABOUT: 2 HOURS
YIELDS: 1 1/2 LB LOAF

INGREDIENTS

» 1/4 cup 1% low-fat milk
» 1/4 cup canola oil
» 1/2 cup whole wheat flour
» 1/2 cup all-purpose flour
» 1/2 cup cake flour
» 1/4 cup low-fat sour cream
» 2 eggs
» 1 cup mashed banana
» 1 teaspoon vanilla extract
» 1 1/4 cups Fiber One Honey cereal (crushed)
» 2/3 cup Splenda sugar substitute
» 1/2 teaspoon baking soda
» 1 teaspoon baking powder
» 1/2 teaspoon salt
» 1/2 cup pecans (chopped)

INSTRUCTIONS

Collect the necessary components. Combine the dry ingredients in the mixing basin (flour through salt). Combine all of the ingredients in a mixing bowl and pour into the bread pan. Use the quick bread setting with light crust color. Remove the pan from the machine once it has finished baking. Allow the bread to rest for about 10 minutes before removing it from the pan and putting it on a wire rack to cool completely.

306. CITRUS CRANBERRY BREAD

READY IN ABOUT: 1 1/2 HOUR
YIELDS: 1,5 LB LOAF

INGREDIENTS

» 3/4 cup milk
» 3/4 cup sugar
» 2/3 cup melted butter
» 2 eggs
» 1/4 teaspoon ground nutmeg
» 1/4 cup freshly squeezed orange juice
» 1 tablespoon orange zest
» 1 1/2 teaspoons baking powder
» 1 teaspoon pure vanilla extract
» 1/2 teaspoon salt
» 2 1/4 cups all-purpose flour
» 1 cup sweetened dried cranberries
» 1/2 teaspoon baking soda

INSTRUCTIONS

Combine the ingredients (milk, sugar, butter, eggs, orange juice, zest, and vanilla) in your bread machine. Press Start after programming the machine for quick or rapid bread. In a medium mixing basin, combine the flour, cranberries, baking powder, baking soda, salt, and nutmeg while the

wet ingredients are mixed. When the machine indicates that the initial quick mixing is complete, add the dry ingredients. Remove the bucket from the machine after the loaf is done. Allow 5 minutes for the bread to cool. Remove the loaf from the bucket with a little shake and place it on a cooling rack.

307. COCONUT GINGER BREAD

READY IN ABOUT: 1 1/2 HOUR
YIELDS: 2 LB LOAF

INGREDIENTS

» 1 cup + 2 tablespoon Half & Half
» 1 1/4 cup toasted shredded coconut
» 2 large eggs
» 1/4 cup oil
» 1 teaspoon coconut extract
» 1 teaspoon lemon extract
» 3/4 cup sugar
» 1 tablespoon grated lemon peel
» 2 cups all-purpose flour
» 2 tablespoon finely chopped candied ginger
» 1 tablespoon baking powder
» 1/2 teaspoon salt

INSTRUCTIONS

In your bread machine pan, combine all of the ingredients. Choose the fast bread option. To begin, press the start button. Select the bake cycle, and the bread will be ready when it finishes. Remove the pan from the machine and set it aside to cool. Remove the bread from the pan and set it aside. Allow your bread to cool down on a wire rack for at least 20 minutes before serving.

308. RASPBERRY BREAD WITH STREUSEL TOPPING

READY IN ABOUT: 2 HOURS AND 15 MINUTES
YIELDS: 1 1/2 LB LOAF

INGREDIENTS

» 2 cups Light Flour Blend/Whole-Grain Flour Blend
» 1 cup millet flour
» 1 cup granulated cane sugar
» 1 tablespoon baking powder
» 1 tablespoon psyllium husk flakes or powder
» 1 teaspoon kosher or fine sea salt
» 1/2 cup unsweetened coconut milk (warmed)
» 1/4 cup vegetable oil / unsalted butter (melted and cooled)
» 2 large eggs (beaten)
» 2 teaspoons pure vanilla extract

Add-ins

» 1 1/3 cups fresh raspberries

Streusel Topping

» 3/4 cup light brown sugar
» 1/4 cup Light Flour Blend/Whole-Grain Flour Blend

- » 1/8 teaspoon salt
- » 2 tablespoons unsalted butter

INSTRUCTIONS

Place the bread pan on the counter with the beater paddle inside. Add the water first in the pan, then the dry ingredients. Insert the bread pan into the machine, center it, and lock it in place. Close the lid and choose from the following option: Quick bread/cake cycle with 1 1/2 pound; Loaf size: pick Light crust and then hit Start.

Scrape the pan with a spatula after the first kneading cycle to ensure all the dry ingredients are combined. Place the raspberries on top. Allow the machine to finish mixing and kneading before closing the cover. In a small mixing bowl, combine the streusel ingredients with a fork. It should be like the appearance of damp sand.

Remove the kneading paddle and reshape the bread when you hear the indication for the machine switching from the knead to the bake cycle if your machine has one. Evenly sprinkle the streusel on top. Close the lid and leave the bread alone to finish baking.

When the baking is finished, take the bread pan from the machine and place it on a wire cooling rack on its side. Allow for a few minutes in the pan before turning it upside down and sliding the loaf onto the wire rack. Allow the bread to cool before slicing it upside down.

309. QUICK ZUCCHINI BREAD

READY IN ABOUT: 2 1/2 HOURS
YIELDS: 1 1/2 LB LOAF

INGREDIENTS

- » 2 cups Light Flour Blend
- » 1 cup millet flour
- » 1 cup brown sugar
- » 1 tablespoon baking powder
- » 2 teaspoons psyllium husk flakes or powder
- » 1 1/2 teaspoons ground cinnamon
- » 1/2 teaspoon kosher salt
- » 1/3 cup vegetable oil
- » 1 teaspoon pure vanilla extract
- » 3 large eggs (beaten)
- » 1 cup grated zucchini
- » 1/2 cup raisins or currants (optional)

INSTRUCTIONS

Blend the dry ingredients mentioned above in a mixing bowl. In a large mixing basin, whisk together the wet ingredients (excluding the zucchini). Add the zucchini and mix well. Into the bread pan, scrape the wet ingredients. Spread the dry ingredients over the wet components with a spatula. Insert the bread pan into the machine, center it, and lock it in place. Close the lid and choose from the following options: Express bake or quick bread/cake cycle; Loaf size: 1 1/2 pound; Medium crust; Press Start

When the baking is finished, take the bread pan from the machine and place it on a wire cooling rack on its side. Allow for a few minutes in the pan before turning it upside down and sliding the loaf onto the wire rack. Allow the bread to cool before slicing it upside down.

310. GOLDEN CORN BREAD

READY IN ABOUT: 2 HOURS
YIELDS: 1 LB LOAF

INGREDIENTS

- » 1 1/3 cups all-purpose flour
- » 1 cup buttermilk
- » 1 tablespoon baking powder
- » 2 eggs
- » 1 cup cornmeal
- » 1/4 cup sugar
- » 1 teaspoon salt
- » 1/4 cup melted butter

INSTRUCTIONS

Follow the manufacturer's recommendations for adding buttermilk, butter, and eggs to your bread machine. Press START after programming the machine for Quick/Rapid Bread mode. While the wet ingredients are being combined in the machine, combine flour, cornmeal, sugar, baking powder, and salt in a small bowl. When the machine indicates that the first rapid mix is complete, add the dry ingredients. Wait until the entire cycle is finished. Remove the bucket from the oven after the loaf is done and set it aside to cool for 5 minutes. Remove the loaf from the basket with a little shake and place it on a cooling rack.

311. QUICK BANANA BREAD

READY IN ABOUT: 2 HOURS
YIELDS: 2 LB LOAF

INGREDIENTS

- » 2 Eggs, lightly beaten
- » 3 Bananas, ripe & MEDIUM-sized bananas
- » 1 Teaspoon Vanilla Extract
- » 8 Tablespoons Unsalted Butter
- » 2 Cups all-purpose Flour
- » 1 Cup Light Brown Sugar
- » 1/2 Teaspoon salt
- » 1 Teaspoon baking Soda
- » 1 Teaspoon baking Powder
- » 1/2 Cup chopped Walnuts or Mini Chocolate Chips (optional)

INSTRUCTIONS

Collect the necessary components. Set aside the eggs, butter, milk, and bananas in the bread pan. Combine the dry ingredients in the mixing basin (flour through salt). Combine all of the ingredients in a mixing bowl and pour into the bread pan. Use the quick bread setting with light crust color. Add the walnuts or chocolate chips when the machine beeps. Remove the pan from the machine once it has finished baking. Allow the bread to rest for about 10 minutes before removing it from the pan and putting it on a wire rack to cool completely.

Chapter 12
FOCACCIA AND PIZZA RECIPES

312. PIZZA DOUGH

READY IN ABOUT: 2 HOURS
SERVINGS: 2 PIZZA DOUGH
YIELDS: 2 LB LOAF

INGREDIENTS

» 1 1/2 cups Water

» 1 1/2 tablespoons Vegetable Oil

» 3 3/4 cups Bread Flour

» 1 tablespoon + 1 teaspoon Granulated Sugar

» 1 1/2 teaspoons salt

» 1 1/2 teaspoons Active Dry Yeast

INSTRUCTIONS

Collect the necessary components. In the sequence advised by the manufacturer, add the ingredients to your bread maker. Select the dough-making cycle. When the bread machine has finished, drop the dough onto a lightly floured surface. Place something on top of the dough and set it aside for 10 minutes. Separate the dough into two halves. Keep one half covered and set away. Set aside 2 big pizza pans that have been lightly brushed with olive oil and sprinkled with cornmeal. Roll out half dough on a gently floured board to fit the prepared pan. Toppings such as sauce, cheese, and veggies can be added as desired. Preheat your oven to 425 degrees Farhenhieght and bake for 20 minutes, or until the sides are golden and the cheese is bubbling. Continue with the remaining dough.

313. BEST PIZZA DOUGH

READY IN ABOUT: 2 HOURS
SERVINGS: 2 PIZZA DOUGHS
YIELDS: 2 LB LOAF

INGREDIENTS

» 1 1/2 cups beer/ water

» 1 tablespoon honey/ sugar

» 2 tablespoons extra virgin olive oil

» 1 1/2 teaspoon salt

» 4 1/4 cups bread flour

» 2 teaspoon bread machine yeast

INSTRUCTIONS

In the order specified, pour the ingredients into the bread pan. Securely place the bread pan in the baking chamber and close the cover. Connect the unit to a wall outlet. Select DOUGH from the drop-down menu. START/STOP by pressing the START/STOP button. When the dough is ready, the complete signal will sound. Remove the bread pan from the baking chamber with potholders and place dough on a gently floured surface. Place something on top of the dough and set it aside for 10 minutes. Separate the dough into two halves. Keep one half covered and set away. Set aside 2 big pizza pans that have been lightly brushed with olive oil and sprinkled with cornmeal. Roll out half dough on a gently floured board to fit the prepared pan. Toppings such as sauce, cheese, and veggies can be added as desired. Preheat your oven to 425 degrees Farhenhieght and bake for 20 minutes, or until the sides are golden and the cheese is bubbling. Continue with the remaining dough.

314. WHOLE WHEAT PIZZA DOUGH

PREP TIME: 1 HOUR
COOK TIME: 20 MINUTES
SERVINGS: 2 PIZZA
YIELDS: 2 LB LOAF

INGREDIENTS

- » 1 1/3 cups water (80°F – 90°F)
- » 1/4 cup olive oil
- » 1 1/2 teaspoon salt
- » 2 1/2 cups bread flour
- » 1 cup whole wheat flour
- » 2 teaspoon bread machine yeast

INSTRUCTIONS

In the order specified, pour the ingredients into the bread pan. Close the cover and secure the bread pan in the baking chamber. Connect the unit to a wall outlet. DOUGH is the option to choose. START/STOP by pressing the START/STOP button. When the dough is ready, the complete signal will sound. Remove the bread pan from the baking chamber with potholders and set the dough on a lightly floured board. Allow the dough to rest for 10 minutes after inverting a large mixing bowl over it. The dough should be divided in half. Keep one half covered and set away. Set aside 2 big pizza pans that have been lightly brushed with olive oil and sprinkled with cornmeal. Roll out half piece of the dough on a gently floured board to fit the prepared pan. Toppings such as sauce, cheese, and veggies can be added as desired. Preheat your oven before to about 425 degrees F and bake for 20 minutes, or until the sides are golden and the cheese is bubbling. Repeat with the rest of the dough.

315. GLUTEN-FREE PIZZA DOUGH

READY IN ABOUT: 2 HOURS
SERVINGS: 3 12-INCH PIZZA DOUGHS
YIELDS: 2 LB LOAF

INGREDIENTS

- » 1 cup buttermilk
- » 1/4 cup water
- » 2 large eggs
- » 1 egg white
- » 3 tablespoon olive oil
- » 1 1/2 cups tapioca flour
- » 1 cup white rice flour
- » 1 cup brown rice flour
- » 1/2 cup potato starch
- » 1 teaspoon salt
- » 1 tablespoon Sugar
- » 1 tablespoon xanthan gum
- » 2 tablespoon bread machine yeast

INSTRUCTIONS

In the order specified, pour the ingredients into the bread pan. Securely place the bread pan in the baking chamber and close the cover. Connect the unit to a wall outlet. Select DOUGH from the drop-down menu. START/STOP by pressing the START/STOP button. When the dough is ready, the complete signal will sound. Remove the bread pan from the baking chamber with potholders and place dough on a gently floured surface. Divide the dough into three equal parts. 2 pieces should be set aside and covered. Set aside 3 12-inch pizza pans that have been lightly brushed with olive oil and sprinkled with cornmeal. Place 1/3rd of the dough on the prepared pizza pan and gently press it to evenly cover the bottom. Preheat your oven before then baking (to 425 degrees Fahrenheit)for 15 minutes. Add desired toppings such as sauce, cheese, and vegetables to the top. Put it in the oven again for 12 minutes, or until the edges are brown and the cheese has melted. Repeat with the rest of the dough.

316. PANCETTA, PEPPER & OLIVE PIZZAS

READY IN ABOUT: 2 HOURS AND 20 MINUTES
SERVINGS: 2 PIZZA DOUGHS
YIELDS: 2 LB LOAF

INGREDIENTS

- » 1 cup + 2 tablespoon water
- » 2 tablespoon olive oil
- » 3 1/4 cups strong white flour
- » 1 teaspoon salt
- » 2 teaspoon caster/superfine sugar
- » 1 1/2 teaspoon instant dry yeast

Topping

- » 2 tablespoon olive oil
- » 2 garlic cloves
- » 1 cup diced smoked pancetta
- » 2 large red peppers, halved lengthways, deseeded and sliced
- » 400g/14oz can chopped tomatoes with herbs (drained)
- » 2 tablespoon tomato purée/paste
- » 1 heaping cup pitted black olives, drained
- » 3/4 cup freshly grated Parmesan cheese
- » Sea salt
- » Freshly ground black pepper
- » Basil leaves to garnish (optional)

INSTRUCTIONS

To begin, make the dough. Fill the bread pan halfway with water, then halfway with oil. Sprinkle the flour over the liquid, completely covering it. Separate the salt and sugar in the pan's corners. Make a small well in between flour and sprinkle the yeast on top. Close the lid, select "Basic Dough" or "Pizza Dough" on the machine's menu, and push Start. Set aside two 12-inch pizza pans that have been greased or floured in the meantime. Toss the topping together. In a frying pan, heat the oil, then add the garlic and cook for 30 seconds. Stir in the pancetta and cook over high heat until it releases its fat and is faintly browned. Put aside the pan from the heat. Sauté the peppers in the pan until they are slightly softened. Remove the skillet from the heat and combine the peppers with the pancetta. Remove the dough from the machine when it's done, knock it back on a lightly floured surface, and split it in half. To make a 30cm (12in) circular, roll out each piece of dough thinly. Using a spatula, transfer each round to a baking sheet.

Preheat the oven to 425 degrees F. Combine the tomatoes, tomato purée/paste, and salt and pepper in a mixing bowl. To within 1cm of the edge, spread this mixture evenly over the pizza bases. Distribute the pepper and pancetta mixture equally over the tomatoes, then top with olives. Sprinkle parmesan cheese on top. Bake until the topping becomes brown and the bases are crisp. Serve hot, garnished with basil leaves if desired.

317. BASIC PIZZA DOUGH

READY IN ABOUT: 1 HOUR
YIELDS: 2 LB LOAF

INGREDIENTS

- » 1 1/3 cups water
- » 1/4 cup extra virgin olive oil
- » 3 1/2 cups unbleached all-purpose flour
- » 1 tablespoon sugar
- » 1 1/2 teaspoons salt
- » 2 1/2 teaspoons bread machine yeast

INSTRUCTIONS

Put all ingredients in the pan and layer all ingredients in the sequence specified in the manufacturer's directions. Select the dough/pizza dough cycle and hit the Start button. It will be a soft dough ball. Press Stop and unplug the machine when it beeps at the end of the cycle (about 15 minutes). Take out the pan from the machine as soon as possible and turn the machine off. On a lightly floured work area, roll out the dough and let it rest for about 15 minutes covered. Divide the mixture into the number of servings you want. By kneading each portion a few times and folding the sides into the middle, flatten each section into a disc. Cover with a moist towel and set aside. Rest the dough on the work surface for 30 minutes or until it has doubled in size.

Alternatively, you may put the Refrigerate dough for up to 24 hours in plastic food storage containers. Before rolling out, let the dough rest for 20 minutes at room temperature. The Dough balls can be frozen for up to three months; let them defrost before using.

318. SEMOLINA PIZZA DOUGH

READY IN ABOUT: 1 HOUR
YIELDS: 2 LB LOAF

INGREDIENTS

- » 3 tablespoons olive oil
- » 1 1/2 cup warm water
- » 3 1/3 cups unbleached all-purpose flour
- » 2/3 cup semolina pasta flour (durum flour)
- » 1 tablespoon sugar
- » 2 teaspoons salt
- » 2 1/2 teaspoons bread machine yeast

INSTRUCTIONS

Put all ingredients in the pan and layer all ingredients in the sequence specified in the manufacturer's directions. Select the dough/pizza dough cycle and hit the Start button. It will be a soft dough ball. Press Stop and unplug the machine

when it beeps at the end of the cycle (about 15 minutes). Take out the pan from the machine as soon as possible and turn the machine off. On a lightly floured work area, roll out the dough and let it rest for about 15 minutes covered. Divide the mixture into the number of servings you want. By kneading each portion a few times and folding the sides into the middle, flatten each section into a disc. Cover with a moist towel and set aside. Rest the dough on the work surface for 30 minutes or until it has doubled in size.

Alternatively, you may put the Refrigerate dough for up to 24 hours in plastic food storage containers. Before rolling out, let the dough rest for 20 minutes at room temperature. The Dough balls can be frozen for up to three months; let them defrost before using.

319. CORNMEAL PIZZA DOUGH

READY IN ABOUT: 1 HOUR
YIELDS: 2 LB LOAF

INGREDIENTS

- » 1 1/2 cups water
- » 1/4 cup olive oil
- » 3 2/3 cups unbleached all-purpose flour
- » 1/3 cup medium-grind yellow cornmeal
- » 1 teaspoon salt
- » 2 1/2 teaspoons bread machine yeast

INSTRUCTIONS

Put all ingredients in the pan and layer all ingredients in the sequence specified in the manufacturer's directions. Select the dough/pizza dough cycle and hit the Start button. It will be a soft dough ball. Press Stop and unplug the machine when it beeps at the end of the cycle (about 15 minutes). Take out the pan from the machine as soon as possible and turn the machine off. On a lightly floured work area, roll out the dough and let it rest for about 15 minutes covered. Divide the mixture into the number of servings you want. By kneading each portion a few times and folding the sides into the middle, flatten each section into a disc. Cover with a moist towel and set aside. Rest the dough on the work surface for 30 minutes or until it has doubled in size.

Alternatively, you may put the Refrigerate dough for up to 24 hours in plastic food storage containers. Before rolling out, let the dough rest for 20 minutes at room temperature. The Dough balls can be frozen for up to three months; let them defrost before using.

320. THIN CRUST PIZZA DOUGH

READY IN ABOUT: 1 1/2 HOUR
SERVINGS: 1 PIZZA DOUGH
YIELDS: 1 LB LOAF

INGREDIENTS

- » 3/4 cup warm water
- » 2 cups all-purpose flour
- » 1/2 teaspoon salt
- » 1/4 teaspoon white sugar
- » 1 teaspoon active dry yeast
- » 2 teaspoons olive oil

INSTRUCTIONS

Pour the heated water into the bread machine's pan, and then sprinkle the flour on top. Season with salt and sugar, and then add the yeast. Push the start button on the machine and select the dough setting. Transfer the dough to a well-floured surface when the machine says it's done. Preheat the oven to 425 degrees Fahrenheit. Roll or stretch the dough into a 14-inch-wide thin crust. Keep the dough thick around the edges and brush it with olive oil. Bake for 5 minutes in a preheated oven before removing to top with selected seasonings and finishing baking for about 15 minutes more.

321. NO SUGAR-ADDED PIZZA DOUGH

READY IN ABOUT: 1 HOUR
SERVINGS: 2 PIZZA DOUGHS
YIELDS: 1 1/2 LB LOAF

INGREDIENTS

» 1 cup warm water
» 2 tablespoon oil
» 1 teaspoon salt
» 3 cups unbleached all-purpose flour
» 1 tablespoon Active dry yeast

INSTRUCTIONS

Put all ingredients in the pan and layer all ingredients in the sequence specified in the manufacturer's directions. Select the dough/pizza dough cycle and hit the Start button. It will be a soft dough ball. Press Stop and unplug the machine when it beeps at the end of the cycle (about 15 minutes). Take out the pan from the machine as soon as possible and turn the machine off. On a lightly floured work area, roll out the dough and let it rest for about 15 minutes covered. Knead the dough and split it in half. Make two balls and wrap them in a clean towel. By kneading each portion a few times and folding the sides into the middle, flatten each section into a disc. Cover with a moist towel and set aside. Rest the dough on the work surface for 30 minutes or until it has doubled in size.

Alternatively, you may put the Refrigerate dough for up to 24 hours in plastic food storage containers. Before rolling out, let the dough rest for 20 minutes at room temperature. The Dough balls can be frozen for up to three months; let them defrost before using.

322. GARLIC FOCACCIA

READY IN ABOUT: 2 HOURS
SERVINGS: 2 12-INCH DOUGHS
YIELDS: 2 LB POUND

INGREDIENTS

» 1 1/8 cups water
» 2 tablespoons extra virgin olive oil
» 3 1/4 cups bread flour
» 1 1/2 teaspoons salt
» 1 teaspoon garlic powder
» 1/4 teaspoon dried oregano
» 2 1/2 teaspoons bread machine yeast
» Cornmeal or coarse semolina (for sprinkling)

For the topping:

» 1/4 cup extra virgin olive oil
» 6 large cloves garlic (minced)

INSTRUCTIONS

In the pan, layer the dough ingredients in the sequence specified in the manufacturer's instructions. Start the Dough cycle by pressing the Start button. Drizzle olive oil over a 17-by-11-inch baking sheet and liberally sprinkle with cornmeal or semolina. When the machine beeps at the end of the cycle, press Stop and disconnect it. Remove the dough from the bread pan as soon as possible and place it on a lightly floured work surface. Divide the dough into two equal parts. Press and flatten a piece of dough with the palm of your hand until it is 14 inches thick. Place it in the pan. Repeat it with the other half of the dough. With a few inches between them, the two parts will fit on the baking sheet. Brush olive oil on the tops. Allow rising at room temperature for about 25 minutes, covered lightly with plastic wrap. Preheat the oven to 450°F and set a baking stone on the bottom rack 20 minutes before baking. Gently poke deep indentations all over the dough surface with your fingertips. Brush the dough with olive oil again and sprinkle the garlic on top. If you have any extra olive oil, drizzle it over the top. Low the temperature of your oven to 400 degrees Fahrenheit. Bake for 15 minutes, or until the focaccias are well browned, in the pan on the hot stone. Serve warm from the oven or slide onto a cooling rack.

323. WINE FOCACCIA

READY IN ABOUT: 2 HOURS
SERVINGS: 1 FOCACCIA
YIELDS: 2 LB LOAF

INGREDIENTS

For the dough:
» 1 1/8 cups water
» 1/2 cup dry white wine
» 3 tablespoons extra virgin olive oil
» 4 cups bread flour
» 2 teaspoons salt
» 2 1/2 teaspoons bread machine yeast
» Cornmeal/coarse semolina (for sprinkling)

For the topping:
» 1/4 cup extra virgin olive oil
» 3 tablespoons dried basil

INSTRUCTIONS

Place the dough ingredients in the pan in the sequence specified in the manufacturer's instructions to produce the dough. Start the Dough cycle by pressing the Start button. Brush an olive oil-coated 14-inch circular pizza pan or a 13-by-9-inch metal baking pan with cornmeal or semolina. When the machine beeps at the end of the cycle, press Stop and disconnect it. Remove the dough from the bread pan as soon as possible and place it on a lightly floured work surface. Press and flatten it with the palm of your hand. To stretch the dough to fit the pan, lift it onto the pan and gently pull and press it, then cover with oiled plastic wrap and allow it to rise at room temperature until it becomes doubled in size. In a separate bowl, combine the oil and basil to make the topping.

Allow sitting at room temperature for 20 minutes. In the meantime, preheat your oven to 450°F and set a baking stone on the bottom rack. If not baking stone, preheat to 400 degrees F. Gently poke deep indentations all over the dough surface with your fingertips. Pour the herb oil over the dough and allow it to pool in the indentations. Bake for about 25 minutes. Let it cool, then serve hot out of the oven.

324. CLASSICAL PIZZA

READY IN ABOUT: 2 HOURS
SERVINGS: 2 9-INCH PIZZA
YIELDS: 1 1/2 LB LOAF

INGREDIENTS

» 2 tablespoons active dry yeast
» 2 1/2 cups Light Flour Blend/Whole-Grain Flour Blend
» 1/2 cup cornstarch (potato starch)
» 1 tablespoon dried oregano
» 2 1/2 teaspoons psyllium husk flakes or powder
» 2 teaspoons salt
» 1 1/2 teaspoons granulated cane sugar
» 1/8 teaspoon ascorbic acid, optional
» Finely ground cornmeal for the bottom of the dough (substitute coarsely ground oats or finely ground nuts if you cannot have corn)
» 1 cup water
» 3 large egg whites
» 2 teaspoons apple cider vinegar

INSTRUCTIONS

In a large mixing basin, combine the dry ingredients (excluding the cornmeal). Remove from the equation. Combine the wet ingredients in a 2-cup glass measuring cup and pour into the bread pan. Spread the dry ingredients over the wet components with a spatula. Pour the yeast into a shallow well in the center of the flour mixture. Insert the bread pan into the machine, center it, and lock it in place. Close the lid and choose from the following options: Cycle of dough; Size of loaf: 1 1/2 pound.
When the dough is smooth and lump-free, push stop to end the cycle and turn the machine off. Take the pan out of the machine. Form the dough into a ball.
Lightly oil two baking sheets, line them with parchment paper and sprinkle cornmeal on top. Divide the dough into two halves with an oiled bench scraper or knife. Place one piece on each of the prepared baking sheets. Working from the center out, press the dough into a 9-inch circle. Place a nonstick or oiled pizza pan upside down over the dough, then invert the dough onto the pan using one hand beneath the parchment and the other on top of the pan. Remove the parchment off the dough with care.
Push the dough outward around the edge with one hand on the outside and the other on the inside about 1 inch from the edge to create a lip to help contain the toppings—your outer hand will keep it from expanding too much. Repeat with the remaining dough piece. Poke holes all over the center of the

crust (not the thicker edge) with the tines of a fork or a docker to help prevent bubbles. Allow to rise for about 20 minutes, uncovered.
Let your dough rest, preheat the oven to 350 degrees F and arrange a rack in the upper third of the oven.
Poke the dough in the center many times more. Bake until the top is golden brown. When tapped on the edge, the crust should sound hollow. Take the crust out from the oven when it's done. Apply a light coating of pizza sauce to the dough's center, spreading it out to the rising edge. Finish with shredded cheese and any other toppings you choose. Because the pizza will only be in the oven for a few minutes, make sure all of your toppings are ready to go. Bake again until the crust is deep golden brown and hollow when tapped. Put the pizza under the broiler for a few minutes if the cheese isn't completely melted. Keep checking it to make sure it doesn't burn. Cool the pizza for 10 minutes on a wire rack (this allows the steam to escape, keeping the crust crispy). Before serving, place it on a cutting board and cut it into wedges.

325. CHEESY HERBED PIZZA

READY IN ABOUT: 2 HOURS
SERVINGS: 2 12-INCH PIZZAS
YIELDS: 2 LB LOAF

INGREDIENTS

» 1 tablespoon active dry yeast
» 3 cups Light Flour Blend/Whole-Grain Flour Blend
» 1/2 cup cornstarch, potato starch (not potato flour)
» 1/4 cup milk powder
» 1/4 cup cheddar cheese powder
» 1/4 cup) lightly packed finely grated Parmesan cheese
» 1 tablespoon psyllium husk flakes or powder
» 2 teaspoons granulated cane sugar
» 2 teaspoons baking powder
» 1 1/2 teaspoons salt
» 1/2 teaspoon dried oregano
» 1/2 teaspoon onion powder
» 1/2 teaspoon garlic powder
» 1/8 teaspoon ascorbic acid, optional
» 1 1/2 cups water
» 1 teaspoon apple cider vinegar

Topping
» Pizza Sauce pesto,
» shredded cheese
» chopped vegetables
» fresh herbs
» thinly sliced meats
» Chopped fresh basil

INSTRUCTIONS

Lightly grease two baking pans lined with parchment paper. Preheat the oven to 400°C and place oven racks in the upper and lower thirds. In a separate bowl, measure out the yeast and leave it aside. Mix the remaining dry ingredients in a mixing bowl. Combine the wet ingredients in a 2-cup glass measuring cup and pour into the bread pan. Spread the dry ingredients over the wet components with a spatula. Pour the yeast into a shallow well in the Centre. Place the pan in the machine and lock it in place in the Centre. Close the lid and choose from the following options: Cycle of dough; Size of loaf: 1 1/2 pound. Allow 15 minutes for the machine to mix the dough until it is smooth and free of lumps. Press the stop button, switch off the machine, and remove the bread pan to cancel the cycle.

Scoop the dough out of the bread pan and onto one of the baking sheets with a spatula. Divide it into two equal pieces by pressing it into a flattened disc. Transfer half of the dough to the second baking sheet. Lightly grease your hands and roll each piece of dough into a 10- to a 12-inch rectangle (the thinner you make it, the crispier the crust). To help hold the toppings on the baked pizza and make the edge a little thicker than the middle, push a shallow "moat" about 1/2 inch (1 cm) from the edge with your fingertips. Poke holes all over the Centre of the crust with the tines of a fork. Allow the dough to rest for 30 to 45 minutes, uncovered until they have slightly risen. They will puff out rather than rise dramatically. Bake (15 to 20 minutes) until the center of each crust is fully baked, moving the pans and switching racks halfway through, and tapping the center to pop any bubbles that have developed and flatten the dough.

Reduce the heat to 350°Farhenheight, remove the pans from the oven and add whatever toppings you want. Again put the pizzas in the oven and bake for 15 to 20 minutes (until the dough is golden brown on top and bottom), the toppings are hot and bubbly, and any additional cheese is melted. Transfer the pizzas to wire cooling racks using the parchment, then remove the parchment to allow the steam to escape. If preferred, sprinkle with a sprinkling of chopped fresh basil. Allow at least 5 minutes for the pizzas to rest before cutting and serving.

326. PRETZELS PIZZA

READY IN ABOUT: 2 HOURS
SERVINGS: 3 8-INCH PIZZAS
YIELDS: 1 1/2 LB LOAF

INGREDIENTS:

» 1 tablespoon active dry yeast
» 3 cups Light Flour Blend/Whole-Grain Flour Blend
» 1/2 cup cornstarch, potato starch (not potato flour)
» 2 teaspoons psyllium husk flakes or powder
» 2 teaspoons kosher or fine sea salt
» 1/2 teaspoon baking powder
» 1/8 teaspoon ascorbic acid (optional)
» 1 1/3 - 1 1/2 cups water
» 2 teaspoons apple cider vinegar
» 1 teaspoon honey

For baking Soda Wash

» 1/4 cup water
» 1/4 teaspoon baking soda

Topping

» Melted butter or olive oil for brushing
» Pretzels salt
» Cheese
» Chopped vegetables

» herbs
» cold meats

INSTRUCTIONS

In a bowl, measure out the yeast and leave it aside. Mix the remaining dry ingredients in a mixing bowl. Whisk the wet ingredients (start with 1 1/3 cup water) in a 2-cup glass measuring cup and pour into the bread pan. Spread the dry ingredients on top with a spatula. Pour the yeast into a shallow well in the Centre. Insert the bread pan into the machine, center it, and lock it in place. Close the lid and choose from the following options: Cycle of dough; Size of loaf: 1 1/2 pound

Allow 15 minutes for the machine to mix the dough until it is smooth and free of lumps, putting the dough onto the beater blade as it tends to go to the pan's edges. It will be a very soft and slightly sticky dough. Press the stop button, switch off the machine, and remove the bread pan to cancel the cycle. Take the dough out from the pan and onto the baking sheet with a spatula. More oil should be brushed on top and pressed into a flattened disc. Preheat your oven already to about 400 degrees Fahrenheit (200 degrees Celsius). Divide the dough into thirds for individual pizzas. Put one of the dough balls in the center of a baking sheet. Oil your hands and then press the dough into an 8-inch (20-cm) circle with your palms. To help hold the toppings on the baked pizza and make the edge a little thicker than the middle, push a shallow "moat" about 1/2 inch (1 cm) from the edge with your fingertips. As much as possible, smooth the middle. If your hands are stuck, add a bit more oil. Rep with the rest of the dough.

Poke holes all over the Centre of the crust with the tines of a fork or a docker (not the thicker edge). Allow it to rise for 45 minutes, uncovered. In a small basin, whisk together the baking soda and water until completely dissolved. Brush the tops and edges of each pizza lightly. Bake for 10 minutes. If necessary, remove from the oven and tap the center to pop any bubbles that have developed and flatten the dough. Coat the rims with melted butter, and liberally sprinkle with pretzel salt. Add toppings to the middle.

Reduce the heat to 350°Farhenheight bake for at least 15 minutes or until the crust is browned on top and bottom, the toppings are hot and bubbly, and any additional cheese has melted. Transfer to a wire rack to cool for about 10 minutes before slicing and serving, slipping the parchment out from under the pizza.

327. CHEWY FOCACCIA

READY IN ABOUT: 2 HOURS
SERVINGS: 1 12-INCH FOCACCIA
YIELDS: 1 1/2 LB LOAF

INGREDIENTS:

» 2 teaspoons active dry yeast
» 2 cups Light Flour Blend/Whole-Grain Flour Blend
» 1/4 cup milk powder
» 1 tablespoon granulated cane sugar
» 2 teaspoons psyllium husk flakes or powder
» 1 teaspoon baking powder
» 1 teaspoon kosher or fine sea salt
» 1/8 teaspoon ascorbic acid, optional
» 2 large eggs (beaten)

- » 1/2 cup water
- » 2 tablespoons vegetable/olive oil
- » 2 teaspoons apple cider vinegar

Topping
- » Olive oil, for brushing Coarse Sea salt

INSTRUCTIONS

In a bowl, measure out the yeast and leave it aside. Mix the remaining dry ingredients in a mixing bowl. Combine the wet ingredients in a 2-cup glass measuring cup and pour into the bread pan. Spread the dry ingredients over the wet components with a spatula. Pour the yeast into a shallow well in the Centre. Put the pan into the machine and secure it. Close the lid and choose from the following options: Cycle of dough; Size of loaf: 1 1/2 pound.

Allow 15 minutes for the machine to mix the dough until it is smooth and free of lumps. Press the stop button, switch off the machine, and remove the pan to cancel the cycle. Scoop the dough onto the baking sheet from the bread pan. Brush the top with olive oil and flatten the dough into an 8-by-12-inch rectangle with your hands. Make dimples all over the dough's surface using your fingertips. Season it well with coarse salt. Put the pan aside and let the dough rise for 30 minutes, uncovered. Cover the pan with greased plastic wrap and let it rise for up to an hour if you want a taller loaf. Preheat your oven before to about 350 degrees Fahrenheit while the dough is rising. Bake for 20 to 24 minutes, flipping the pan halfway through until puffed and golden brown. Remove the baking sheet from inside the oven and put the focaccia onto a wire cooling rack using parchment paper as a guide. Remove the parchment and maintain the crispiness of the crust. Let for at least 30 minutes of cooling time. To serve, cut into squares or narrow rectangles. Refrigerate any leftovers tightly wrapped in plastic wrap for up to two days.

328. PIZZA FOCACCIA

READY IN ABOUT: 2 HOURS
SERVINGS: 1 8X12-INCH PIZZA
YIELDS: 1 LB LOAF

INGREDIENTS

- » 2 teaspoons active dry yeast
- » 2 cups Light Flour Blend/ Whole-Grain Flour Blend
- » 1/4 cup milk powder
- » 4 teaspoons cheddar cheese powder
- » 1 tablespoon granulated cane sugar
- » 2 teaspoons psyllium husk flakes or powder
- » 2 teaspoons baking powder
- » 2 teaspoons dried oregano
- » 2 teaspoons onion powder
- » 1 1/2 teaspoons tomato powder
- » 1 teaspoon salt
- » 1/8 teaspoon ascorbic acid (optional)
- » 1/3 cup water
- » 2 large eggs
- » 2 tablespoons vegetable/olive oil
- » 2 teaspoons apple cider vinegar

Topping
- » Olive oil, for brushing
- » 1/4 cup Pizza Sauce
- » 2 tablespoons minced fresh basil

INSTRUCTIONS

In a bowl, measure out the yeast and leave it aside. Mix the remaining dry ingredients in a mixing bowl. Combine the wet ingredients in a 2-cup glass measuring cup and pour into the bread pan. Spread the dry ingredients over the wet components with a spatula. Pour the yeast into a shallow well in the Centre. Place the pan in the machine and lock it in place in the Centre. Close the lid and choose from the following options: Cycle of dough; Size of loaf: 1 1/2 pound. Allow 15 minutes for the machine to mix the dough until it is smooth and free of lumps. Press the stop button, switch off the machine, and remove the pan to cancel the cycle. Scoop the dough onto the baking sheet from the bread pan. Brush the top with olive oil and flatten the dough into an 8x12-inch rectangle with your hands. Make dimples all over the dough's surface with your fingertips or knuckles. Spread a thin layer of sauce on top of the dough and sprinkle basil on top. Set the pan aside, let the dough rise for about 30 minutes, uncovered. It will not become double, but it will puff up. Preheat the oven to 350°F while the dough is rising. Bake for 25 minutes, or until puffed and golden brown. Take out the pizza from the oven and place it on a wire cooling rack using parchment paper. Allow it cool for 20 minutes before serving in squares or skinny rectangles. Refrigerate any leftovers tightly wrapped in plastic wrap for up to two days.

329. ITALIAN HERBED FOCACCIA

READY IN ABOUT: 2 HOURS
SERVINGS: 1 8X12-INCH PIZZA
YIELDS: 1 LB LOAF

INGREDIENTS:

- » 2 teaspoons active dry yeast
- » 2 cups Light Flour Blend/Whole-Grain Flour Blend
- » 1/4 cup milk powder
- » 1 tablespoon granulated cane sugar
- » 1 tablespoon dried oregano
- » 2 to 3 teaspoons dried basil
- » 2 teaspoons psyllium husk flakes or powder
- » 1 teaspoon baking powder
- » 1 teaspoon kosher or fine sea salt
- » 1/8 teaspoon ascorbic acid (optional)
- » 2 large eggs
- » 1/2 cup water
- » 2 tablespoons vegetable/olive oil
- » 2 teaspoons apple cider vinegar
- » 1/2 teaspoon minced garlic

Topping
- » Olive oil (for brushing)
- » Coarse sea salt (optional)
- » 2 teaspoons chopped fresh rosemary
- » 2 to 3 teaspoons grated Parmesan cheese (optional)

INSTRUCTIONS

In a bowl, measure out the yeast and leave it aside. Mix the flour, baking powder and salt in a separate bowl, then mix the remaining dry ingredients in it. Combine the wet ingredients in a 2-cup glass measuring cup. Spread the dry ingredients over the wet components with a spatula. Pour the yeast into a shallow well in the center. Put the pan in the machine and lock it in place in the Centre. After closing the lid, select: Cycle of dough; Size of loaf: 1 1/2 pound.

Allow 15 minutes for the machine to mix the dough until it is smooth and free of lumps. Press the stop button, switch off the machine, and remove the pan to cancel the cycle. Scoop the dough onto the baking sheet from the bread pan. Brush the top. Using your hands, press the dough into an 8x12-inch rectangle. Make dimples all over with your fingers or knuckles.

Combine the coarse salt and rosemary in a bowl. Set the timer. Put the pan aside and let the dough rise for 30 minutes, uncovered. It is not going to double, but it will puff up a little. Preheat your oven before to about 350 degrees Fahrenheit while the dough is rising. Bake until puffed and golden brown. Take out the focaccia, then transfer it to a wire rack, then sprinkle with salt and rosemary. If preferred, sprinkle with Parmesan and leave aside to cool for at least 20 minutes before serving.

330. ROSEMARY FOCACCIA

READY IN ABOUT: 2 HOURS
SERVINGS: 1 8X12-INCH PIZZA
YIELDS: 1 LB LOAF

INGREDIENTS:

- » 2 teaspoons active dry yeast
- » 2 cups Light Flour Blend/Whole-Grain Flour Blend
- » 1/4 cup milk powder
- » 1 tablespoon granulated cane sugar
- » 2 teaspoons psyllium husk flakes/powder
- » 1 teaspoon baking powder
- » 1 teaspoon salt
- » 1/8 teaspoon ascorbic acid (optional)
- » 2 large eggs
- » 1/2 cup water
- » 2 tablespoons (finely minced) fresh rosemary
- » 2 tablespoons vegetable/ olive oil
- » 2 teaspoons apple cider vinegar

Topping
- » Olive oil, for brushing
- » Fresh rosemary sprigs
- » Coarse Sea salt

INSTRUCTIONS

In a bowl, measure out the yeast and leave it aside. Mix the remaining dry ingredients in a separate mixing bowl. Combine the wet ingredients in a 2-cup glass measuring cup and pour into the bread pan. Spread the dry ingredients over the wet components with a spatula. Pour the yeast into a shallow well in the Centre. Place the pan in the machine and lock it in place in the Centre. Close the lid and choose from the following options: Cycle of dough; Size of loaf: 1 1/2 pound.

Allow 15 minutes for the machine to mix the dough until it is smooth and free of lumps. Press the stop button, switch off the machine, and remove the pan to cancel the cycle.

Scoop the dough onto the baking sheet from the bread pan. Brush the top with a little extra oil and push the dough into an 8x12-inch rectangle with your hands. Make dimples all over the dough's surface with your fingertips or knuckles. Fresh rosemary sprigs are strewn across the top, and coarse salt is sprinkled on top. Let the dough rise for 30 to 35 minutes, uncovered, while the pan rests. It will not become double in size, but it will puff up. Preheat the oven to 350° Fahrenheit while the dough is rising.

Bake the focaccia for 20 minutes, or until puffy and golden brown. Take out the focaccia from the oven and place it on a wire cooling rack. Allow at least 20 minutes to cool before cutting into squares or skinny rectangles to serve. If desired, add fresh rosemary sprigs to the basket or tray. Refrigerate any leftovers tightly wrapped in plastic wrap for up to two days.

331. OLIVE FOCACCIA

READY IN ABOUT: 2 HOURS
SERVINGS: 1 8X12-INCH PIZZA
YIELDS: 1 LB LOAF

INGREDIENTS

- » 2 teaspoons active dry yeast
- » 2 cups Light Flour Blend/Whole-Grain Flour Blend
- » 1/4 cup milk powder
- » 1 tablespoon granulated cane sugar
- » 2 teaspoons psyllium husk flakes or powder
- » 1 teaspoon baking powder
- » 1 teaspoon kosher or fine sea salt
- » 1/8 teaspoon ascorbic acid (optional)
- » 2 large eggs (beaten)
- » 1/2 cup water
- » 2 tablespoons vegetable/olive oil
- » 2 teaspoons apple cider vinegar

Topping
- » Olive oil, for brushing
- » 1/2 cup pitted black olives (drained well and coarsely chopped)
- » Coarse Sea salt (optional)

INSTRUCTIONS

In a bowl, measure out the yeast and leave it aside. Mix the remaining dry ingredients in a separate mixing bowl. Combine the wet ingredients in a 2-cup glass measuring cup and pour into the bread pan. Spread the dry ingredients over the wet components with a spatula. Pour the yeast into a shallow well in the Centre. Place the pan in the machine and lock it in place in the Centre. Close the lid and choose from the following options: Cycle of dough; Size of loaf: 1 1/2 pound.

Allow 15 minutes for the machine to mix the dough until it is smooth and free of lumps. Press the stop button, switch off the machine, and remove the pan to cancel the cycle. Scoop the dough onto the baking sheet from the bread pan. Brush the top with olive oil and flatten the dough into an 8x12-inch rectangle with your hands. Make dimples all over the dough's surface with your fingertips or knuckles. Arrange the olives on top in a uniform layer, gently pushing them into the dough. If desired, lightly season with coarse salt. Let the dough rise for about half-hour, uncovered, in the pan. It will not double in size, but it will puff up. Preheat your oven 350°F while the dough rises, then bake the focaccia for 20 minutes, or until puffy and golden brown. Take out the focaccia from the oven and place it on a wire cooling rack. Allow at least 20 minutes to cool before cutting into squares or skinny rectangles to serve. Refrigerate any leftovers tightly wrapped in plastic wrap for up to two days.

332. TRIPLE GARLIC FOCACCIA

READY IN ABOUT: 2 HOURS
SERVINGS: 1 8X12-INCH PIZZA
YIELDS: 1 LB LOAF

INGREDIENTS

» 2 teaspoons active dry yeast

» 2 cups Light Flour Blend/Whole-Grain Flour Blend

» 1/4 cup milk powder

» 1 tablespoon granulated cane sugar

» 2 teaspoons psyllium husk flakes or powder

» 1 teaspoon baking powder

» 1 teaspoon salt

» 1 teaspoon garlic powder

» 1/8 teaspoon ascorbic acid (optional)

» 2 large eggs (beaten)

» 1/2 cup water

» 2 tablespoons vegetable/olive oil

» 2 teaspoons apple cider vinegar

TOPPING

» Olive oil (for brushing)

» Garlic cloves (peeled and quartered lengthwise)

» 1 teaspoon minced garlic or Roasted Garlic

» 2–3 tablespoons unsalted butter/non-dairy butter/olive oil

» Coarse Sea salt

INSTRUCTIONS

In a bowl, measure out the yeast and leave it aside. Mix the remaining dry ingredients in a separate mixing bowl. Combine the wet ingredients in a 2-cup glass measuring cup and pour into the bread pan. Spread the dry ingredients over the wet components with a spatula. Pour the yeast into a shallow well in the Centre. Place the pan in the machine and lock it in place in the Centre. Close the lid and choose from the following options: Cycle of dough; Size of loaf: 1 1/2 pound.

Allow 15 minutes for the machine to mix the dough until it is smooth and free of lumps. Press the stop button, switch off the machine, and remove the pan to cancel the cycle. Scoop the dough onto the baking sheet from the bread pan. Brush the top with olive oil and flatten the dough into an 8x12-inch rectangle with your hands. Make dimples all over the dough's surface with your fingertips or knuckles. Insert as

many pieces of garlic as you and your family choose into the dimples. Put the pan aside and let the dough rise for about 30 minutes, uncovered. It will not double in size, but it will puff up. Preheat your oven (350°F while the dough is rising. In a small bowl, combine the minced garlic and melted butter. Bake for 20, or until puffed and golden brown. Brush the top with garlic butter, season with coarse salt, then transfer the focaccia to a wire cooling rack. Allow at least 20 minutes to cool before cutting into squares or skinny rectangles to serve. Refrigerate any leftovers tightly wrapped in plastic wrap for up to two days.

333. ARTISAN FOCACCIA DOUGH

READY IN ABOUT: 2 HOURS
SERVINGS: 2 10X10 FOCACCIA
YIELDS: 2 LOVES

INGREDIENTS

» 2 teaspoon bread machine yeast

» 1 1/2 cups water

» 3 1/2 cups bread flour

» 2 teaspoon honey

» 2 1/2 teaspoon sea salt

» 1/2 cup whole wheat flour

INSTRUCTIONS

In the order specified, pour the ingredients into the bread machine pan. Close the cover and secure the bread pan in the baking chamber. Connect the unit to a wall outlet. Select ARTISAN from the drop-down menu. START/STOP by pressing the START/STOP button. When the dough is ready, the complete signal will sound. Turn the dough out onto a floured surface. (If the kneading paddle is still in the dough, remove it.) To eliminate air from the dough, punch it down and knead it. Set aside for 10 minutes and cover it to allow flavors to meld.
Divide the dough into two equal parts. Place a piece of dough on a large baking sheet that has been coated with olive oil and cornmeal. Use the heel of your hand, flatten the dough into a 10 x 10-inch square. Brush olive oil over the top. At 1-inch intervals, press flour-coated fingertips into the dough. Repeat with the remaining dough half. Let it rise for 45 minutes also cover it during this time, or until it becomes doubled in size. Lightly press your fingertips into the focaccia once more. Garlic pepper, dried parsley, and Rosemary garlic blend are sprinkled on top. Bake for 20 to 23 minutes at 425 degrees Fahrenheit, or until golden and loaves test done. Cool the focaccia on a wire rack. Serve immediately.

334. SAUSAGE AND PEPPER CALZONE

READY IN ABOUT: 3 HOURS
SERVINGS: 3 9-INCH DOUGH
YIELDS: 1 1/2 LB LOAF

INGREDIENTS

For the Dough:

» 1 1/8 cups water

- » 3 tablespoons olive oil
- » 2 1/2 cups unbleached all-purpose flour
- » 1/2 cup semolina pasta flour (durum flour)/whole wheat flour
- » 1 1/2 teaspoons salt
- » 2 3/4 teaspoons bread machine yeast

For the filling:
- » 3/4 pound sweet/hot Italian sausage
- » 3 to 4 tablespoons olive oil
- » 2 to 3 red bell peppers (cut in half and sliced)
- » 1 medium yellow onion (thinly sliced)
- » Salt
- » Freshly -ground black pepper
- » 1/3 cup grated Parmesan/Asiago cheese

INSTRUCTIONS

To prepare the dough, layer all dough components in the pan in the sequence specified by the manufacturer. Select the Dough cycle and then push the Start button. Then prepare the filling while the dough cycle is running. Place the sausages in a medium skillet after pricking them with a fork. Add 12 inches of water, cover, and cook for 15 minutes, or until the water has evaporated. Uncover the sausages and continue to cook and brown them on all sides. Remove them from the heat and set them aside to cool. In a separate skillet, combine the oil, peppers, and onions. Cook until soft and lightly browned over medium-high heat. Remove from the fire, season to taste with salt and pepper, and set aside to cool. Preheat the oven to 425°F 20 to 30 minutes before baking. A large baking sheet should be oiled or lined with parchment paper.

Press Stop and unplug the machine when the machine beeps at the end of the cycle. Take the pan from the machine as soon as possible and transfer the dough to a lightly floured work surface. Make three equal parts of the dough. Flatten each part with your hand before flattening it out into a 9-inch round with a rolling pin. To avoid sticking, lightly dust the work surface with flour as needed. Cover half of one round of dough with a third of the filling and sausage slices, leaving a 1-inch border.

Brush the dough's edge with water and fold it in half to make a half-moon-shaped turnover. To form a braided edge, press the edges together to secure them, and then fold over the entire border in 1-inch sections. Put the calzone on the prepared baking sheet. Make a few slits in the top to let the steam out. Repeat with the remaining two dough pieces. Bake in the preheated oven for 25–30 minutes, or until golden brown and crisp. Remove the calzones from the baking pan and place them on a cooling rack. Allow 10 minutes to cool before slicing or eating by hand.

Chapter 13

BREAD BAKED IN OVEN

335. HOMEMADE SLIDER BUNS

READY IN ABOUT: 3 1/2 HOURS
SERVINGS: 18 BUNS
YIELDS: 2 LB LOAF

INGREDIENTS

- » 1 1/4 cup Milk
- » 1 Egg
- » 1/4 cup White Sugar
- » 2 tablespoons Butter
- » 3/4 teaspoon Salt
- » 3 3/4 cups All-Purpose Flour
- » 1 package Active Dry Yeast
- » Flour (for surface)

INSTRUCTIONS

Add all ingredients to the pan of your bread maker. Select the dough cycle in the bread machine. After the dough cycle is finished, lay out the dough to about a 1-inch thickness on a floured surface. A biscuit cutter or a tiny glass cut out 18 buns and set them on a prepared baking sheet. Allow one hour for the buns to rise or until they have doubled in size. Bake for 10 minutes at 350°F (180°C). Brush the melted butter on the tops of the baked buns before serving.

336. EASY MINI BURGER BUNS

READY IN ABOUT: 3 1/2 HOURS
SERVINGS: 18 BUNS
YIELDS: 1 1/2 LB LOAF

INGREDIENTS

- » 1/2 cup warm Water
- » 2 1/4 teaspoons Bread Machine Yeast
- » 2/3 cup Whole Milk
- » 1 Egg
- » 3 tablespoons melted butter
- » 2 1/2 tablespoons Sugar
- » 1 1/4 teaspoons salt
- » 3 cups All-Purpose Flour
- » Butter or oil for greasing the bowl

Optional Toppings:

- » 1 Egg white
- » 1 tablespoon Water
- » 1/4 cup Sesame seeds/Poppy seeds/as needed
- » Melted Butter

INSTRUCTIONS

Collect the necessary components. Whisk together the water, milk, melted butter, and egg in a small bowl. In the bread machine, combine the milk mixture, flour, sugar, salt, and instant or bread machine yeast in the sequence recommended by the manufacturer. Toggle the dough cycle on. Place the finished dough on a floured work surface. Flatten the dough into a rectangle, split it into pieces, and roll it into balls. Cover with a kitchen towel and let rise for 30 minutes on 2 parchment-lined baking pans. Brush with egg wash and seeds, if using, and bake for 15 to 18 minutes at 375°F. If the egg wash and seeds were not used, brush with melted butter if desired. Allow the buns to cool, split them in half, and fill them with your favorite sandwich fixings.

337. HONEY BUTTER MILK BREAD

READY IN ABOUT: 2 1/2 HOURS
YIELDS: 1 1/2 LOAF

INGREDIENTS

» 1/2 cup Water
» 3 cups Bread Flour
» 2 teaspoons Active Dry Yeast
» 1 1/2 teaspoons salt
» 3/4 cup Buttermilk
» 1 tablespoon unsalted butter
» 3 tablespoons Honey
» Sesame seeds/Poppy seeds/Caraway seeds (for garnish)
» 1 Egg White (with 2 teaspoons Water)

INSTRUCTIONS

Collect the necessary components. In the bread machine pan, mix all ingredients such as yeast, flour, salt, buttermilk, butter, honey, and water—in the sequence recommended by the bread machine manufacturer. Choose between basic or white bread with a light or medium crust. Then shape the bread into a loaf using the dough cycle. Brush the loaf with an egg wash made with 1 big egg white and 2 teaspoons of water on a greased baking sheet or in a loaf pan. Sprinkle sesame seeds on top of the loaf if desired. Bake for at least 30 minutes at 375 degrees F, or until the bread sounds hollow when softly tapped on the bottom. Serve and have fun.

338. AUTHENTIC FRENCH BREAD

READY IN ABOUT: 3 HOURS
YIELDS: 2 LB LOAF

INGREDIENTS

» 1 1/4 cup water
» 2 teaspoons salt
» 4 cups bread flour
» 2 1/2 teaspoons active dry yeast
» Cornmeal as needed

INSTRUCTIONS

In a bread pan, combine all ingredients except cornmeal, select dough, and click Start. The machine will sound when the dough has risen sufficiently. Take the pan from the bread machine and put dough out onto a lightly floured worktop or cutting board.

Apply a light dusting of flour on the top(s) and rub it in. Place the loaves on a cornmeal-dusted cookie sheet. Cover and rise for 30 to 45 minutes in a warm oven until doubled in size (Hint: To slightly warm the oven, put it to Warm for 1 minute, turn it off and place the wrapped dough in the oven to rise.) Before preheating, remove the pan from the oven. Place one pan of hot water on the oven's bottom rack. (This will produce steam, which is required for a crisp, genuine crust.) Preheat the oven to 450°F, and when ready, slash the tops of the rolls or baguettes straight down the middle, about 12 inches deep, using an extremely sharp knife or razor blade. Make three diagonal slits on the oblong loaf. Make an X or a # on the top of the round loaf. Bake for 20 minutes for round or oblong

loaves, 15 minutes for baguettes, and 10 to 12 minutes for rolls.
Grab it from the oven and cool on a cooling rack. It's preferable to eat this as soon as possible once it's been baked. To keep the crisp crust, don't wrap it in plastic wrap or store it in bags.

339. ARTISAN APRICOT PECAN BOULE

READY IN ABOUT: 3 HOURS
YIELDS: 1 1/2 LB LOAF

INGREDIENTS

» 1/3 cup water
» 1 cup apricot nectar
» 2 tablespoon vegetable oil
» 1 tablespoon maple syrup
» 2 teaspoon salt
» 1 3/4 cups whole wheat flour
» 1 3/4 cups bread flour
» 2 1/4 teaspoon bread machine yeast
» 2/3 cup dried cranberries
» 2/3 cup chopped pecans

INSTRUCTIONS

In the order specified, pour the ingredients into the bread pan. Close the cover and secure the bread pan in the baking chamber. Connect the unit to a wall outlet. ARTISAN is the option to choose. To begin, press the START button. Add the cranberries and pecans when the "add ingredient" beep sounds. When the dough is done, the entire signal will sound. Take it out. (If the kneading paddle is still in the dough, remove it.) To eliminate air from the dough, punch it down and knead it. Set it aside and cover for 10 minutes. Make a dough ball, lay it on a lightly greased baking sheet, and seam side down. Cover with something and let rise for 45 minutes, or until doubled in size. Remove the cover and lightly flour the loaves. Cut a cross into the top loaf with a sharp knife or razor blade about 3 inches long and 14 inches deep. Preheat oven at 425°F and bake for 25 minutes, or until golden brown and loaves test done. Cool the bread on a wire rack. Let it cool before serving.

340. ARTISAN SEMOLINA BOULES

READY IN ABOUT: 3 HOURS
SERVINGS: 4 LOAVES
YIELDS: 2 LB LOAF

INGREDIENTS

» 2 cups water
» 3 tablespoon olive oil
» 4 teaspoon sugar
» 1 tablespoon finely chopped garlic
» 1 1/2 teaspoon crushed dried rosemary
» 1 1/2 teaspoon sea salt
» 2 cups semolina flour
» 2 3/4 cups bread flour
» 4 teaspoon vital wheat gluten

» 2 teaspoon bread machine yeast

INSTRUCTIONS

In the order specified, pour the ingredients into the bread pan. Close the cover and secure the bread pan in the baking chamber. Connect the unit to a wall outlet. ARTISAN is the option to choose. START/STOP by pressing the START/STOP button. When the dough is ready, the complete signal will sound. (If the kneading paddle is still in the dough, remove it.) To eliminate air from the dough, punch it down and knead it. Allow flavors to meld by letting it rest. Divide the dough into four equal halves. Make each into a ball and place on a lightly greased baking sheet, seam side down. Cover with and let rise for 45 minutes, or until doubled in size. Remove the cover and lightly flour the loaves. Cut a cross about 3 inches long and 14 inches deep into each loaf with a sharp knife or razor blade. Preheat oven at 425°F and bake for 25 minutes, or until golden brown and loaves test done. Cool the bread on a wire rack. Allow bread to cool before serving.

341. CANDY CANE CHERRY BRAID

READY IN ABOUT: 3 HOURS
YIELDS: 2 LB LOAF

INGREDIENTS

» 2 large eggs
» Warm Water
» 3 tablespoon unsalted butter/margarine (cut in pieces)
» 1/4 cup dry skim milk powder
» 1/4 cup sugar
» 1/2 cup candied cherries
» 1/4 cup candied lemon peel
» 2 teaspoon grated lemon peel
» 1 teaspoon salt
» 1/2 teaspoon almond extract
» 3 3/4 cups bread flour
» 2 teaspoons active dry or bread machine yeast
» 1/2 cup toasted almonds (chopped)

INSTRUCTIONS

Add enough water to the eggs in a measuring cup to equal 1 1/4 cups. Pour the batter into a bread pan. In the order listed, pour the remaining ingredients into the bread pan, excluding the nuts. Close the cover and secure the bread pan in the baking chamber. Close the dispenser lid after adding the almonds. Connect the unit to a wall outlet. DOUGH is the option to choose. START/STOP by pressing the START/STOP button. When the dough is ready, the complete signal will sound.

Remove the pan from the baking chamber with potholders and set the dough on a lightly floured board. Divide the dough into three equal halves. Roll each piece into an 18-inch rope. Braid all three strands together and tuck the ends under to seal. Place it on a baking sheet that has been buttered. Curve one end to make it look like a candy cane. Allow rising until twice in size (about 45 minutes). Preheat your oven at 375°Farhenheit and bake for 30 minutes, or until golden brown and hollow when tapped on the bottom. Allow cooling on a wire rack.

342. APRICOT BRAID

READY IN ABOUT: 3 HOURS
SERVINGS: 3 LOAVES
YIELDS: 2 LB LOAF

INGREDIENTS

» 3/4 cup warm water
» 1/4 cup apricot nectar
» 2 large eggs
» 2 tablespoon sugar
» 2 tablespoon unsalted butter/margarine (cut in pieces)
» 2 teaspoon salt
» 4 cups bread flour
» 2 teaspoon bread machine yeast
» 1 cup dried apricots, chopped
» 1/2 cup toasted, skinned hazelnuts, chopped
» 1/2 teaspoon ground cinnamon
» 1 tablespoon honey

INSTRUCTIONS

In a bread pan, layer the first eight ingredients in the order stated. Close the cover and secure the bread pan in the baking chamber. Connect the unit to a wall outlet. Choose DOUGH. START/STOP by pressing the START/STOP button. When the dough is ready, the complete signal will sound. Meanwhile, combine the apricots, hazelnuts, cinnamon, and honey in a mixing bowl. Set aside, covered. Take the pan from the baking chamber using potholders and place dough on a gently floured counter. Place a mixing bowl over the top of the dough and set aside for 10 minutes. Divide the dough into three equal halves. Roll out each piece in a 6 x 14-inch rectangle on a lightly floured board. 1/3 of the apricot mixture spread down one long edge of the rectangle. Roll up jellyroll style and press the edges together to seal. Repeat with the remaining two dough pieces. Place these ropes on a baking sheet that has been lightly oiled. Braid the ropes loosely. To seal the braid, tuck the ends under it. Put it aside in a warm area and cover it to rise for about 40 minutes. Preheat the oven and bake at 375°F for about 25 minutes, or until brown.

343. APPLE FILLED BAKED DOUGHNUTS

READY IN ABOUT: 2 1/2 HOURS
SERVINGS: 22 DOUGHNUTS
YIELDS: 1 LB LOAF

INGREDIENTS

» 1/4 cup milk
» 1/4 cup + 2 tablespoon water
» 1 large egg
» 1/4 cup sugar
» 2 tablespoon unsalted butter
» 1/2 teaspoon salt
» 2 1/2 cups bread flour
» 2 1/4 teaspoon bread machine yeast

INSTRUCTIONS

Apple Filling:

In a bowl, mix 1 cup finely chopped apples, 1/4 cup raisins, 1 1/2 tbsp. Sugar, 1/2 teaspoon ground cinnamon and 1 tsp. Fresh lemon juice.

In the order specified, pour the ingredients into the bread pan. Close the cover and secure the bread pan in the baking chamber. Connect the unit to a wall outlet. DOUGH is the option to choose. START/STOP by pressing the START/STOP button. When the dough is ready, the complete signal will sound. Prepare the filling in the meantime. Cover and store in the refrigerator. Take the pan from the baking chamber with potholders and set the dough on a lightly floured board. Let the dough be there for 10 minutes after inverting a large mixing bowl over it. Remove the filling from the fridge and drain thoroughly. Cut the dough into 22 pieces.

Roll each piece into a 2-inch circular. Put 1 teaspoon apple filling in the center. Bring the edges up to cover the filling and press the edges together to seal them. Place each dough ball on a greased baking sheet, seam side down, about 2-inches apart. Allow rising until twice in size (about 45 minutes). Preheat oven at 375°F and bake for 14 minutes, or until gently browned and fully done. In a deep bowl, combine 3 tablespoons of confectioners' sugar and 2 tablespoons of water. In a second shallow bowl, put 1/3 cup granulated sugar. To completely cover doughnuts, roll each one in the confectioners' mixture and then in granulated sugar. Allow cooling on a wire rack.

344. GRISSINI

READY IN ABOUT: 2 1/2 HOURS
SERVINGS: ABOUT 60 GRISSINI
YIELDS: 1 1/2 LB LOAF

INGREDIENTS

» 1 cup water
» 1/3 cup olive oil
» 2 teaspoon sugar
» 1 1/2 teaspoon salt
» 3 cups bread flour
» 2 teaspoon bread machine yeast

INSTRUCTIONS

In the order specified, pour the ingredients into the bread pan. Close the cover and secure the bread pan in the baking chamber. Connect the unit to a wall outlet. DOUGH is the option to choose. START/STOP by pressing the START/STOP button. When the dough is ready, the complete signal will sound. Remove the bread pan from the baking chamber with potholders and set the dough on a lightly floured board. Let the dough be there for 10 minutes after inverting a large mixing bowl over it. The dough should be divided in half. Roll 1/2 of the dough into a 13 × 15 inch rectangle on a gently floured board. If preferred, 1 tbsp of extra virgin olive oil is brushed all over the Dough. Cut the dough lengthwise into 30 thin strips with a pastry cutter. Place the strips on a baking sheet that has been gently oiled. Preheat oven at 425°F and bake for 14 minutes, or until golden and completely done. Set breadsticks on a wire rack to cool. Repeat with the remaining dough half. Note: Grissini is Italian-style pencil-thin breadsticks.

345. THE ITALIAN BREAD

READY IN ABOUT: 3 1/2 HOURS
SERVINGS: 2 LOAVES
YIELDS: 2 LB LOAF

INGREDIENTS

» 1 1/3 cups warm water (110°F)
» 4 cups unbleached all-purpose flour
» 1 1/2 teaspoons salt
» 1 tablespoon light brown sugar
» 1 1/2 teaspoon olive oil
» 1 package active dry yeast (.25 ounce)
» 1 egg
» 1 tablespoon water
» 2 tablespoons cornmeal

INSTRUCTIONS

In your bread machine's pan, combine everything except the last 3 ingredients. Choose the dough cycle and press the Start button.

Place the dough on a floured surface to deflate it. Make two loaves out of the dough and place them seam side down on a cutting board that has been liberally dusted with cornmeal. Cover the loaves with a moist cloth and let rise for about 40 minutes, or until doubled in volume. Preheat the oven to 375°F in the meantime.

Combine the egg and 1 tablespoon water in a small mixing basin. Brush the egg mixture on the risen bread. With a sharp knife, make a single long, fast cut along the center of the loaves. Shake the cutting board gently to ensure that the loaves do not cling together. If they stick, loosen them with a spatula or pastry knife. With one swift yet careful motion, slide the loaves onto a baking sheet.

Bake for 30/35 minutes in a preheated oven or until loaves sound hollow when tapped on the bottom.

346. SWEDISH CARDAMOM BREAD

READY IN ABOUT: 3 HOURS
YIELDS: 1 1/2 LB LOAF

INGREDIENTS

» 1/4 cup of sugar
» 3/4 cup of warm milk
» 3/4 teaspoon cardamom
» 1/2 teaspoon salt
» 1/4 cup of softened butter
» 1 egg
» 2 1/4 teaspoons bread machine yeast
» 3 cups all-purpose flour
» 5 tablespoons milk for brushing
» 2 tablespoons sugar for sprinkling

INSTRUCTIONS

In your bread machine's pan, combine everything except the milk for brushing and the sugar for sprinkling. Choose a dough cycle. To begin, press the start button. When the cycle is through, you should have an elastic and smooth dough. It should be twice as big. Place the dough on a floured surface.

Divide the mixture into three balls. Allow 10 minutes to pass. Roll the balls into 14-inch long strands. Braid the shapes together. Keep the ends firm by pinching them under and placing them on a baking sheet. Brush the milk over the braid. Lightly dust with sugar. Bake for 25 min at 375 degrees F in your oven. Cover with foil for the last 10 minutes of cooking. It helps to avoid over-browning. Place on a cooling rack to cool.

347. NUT SWIRLS

READY IN ABOUT: 3 HOURS
SERVINGS: 12 SWIRLS
YIELDS: 1 1/2 LB LOAF

INGREDIENTS

For Dough:
» 1 cup milk
» 1/4 cup butter
» 1 egg
» 1/3 cup sugar
» 3 1/2 cups all-purpose flour
» 1 1/2 teaspoon active dry yeast
» 1/2 teaspoon salt

For nut crumb:
» 2/3 cup butter
» 1/2 cup sugar
» 3/4 cup all-purpose flour
» 1 cup ground hazelnuts
» 2 cups candied hazelnuts

For glaze:
» 1 egg yolk
» 2 tablespoons milk
» 1 1/2 cup butter

INSTRUCTIONS

In a bread machine, knead the dough. Allow 45 minutes for it to rest and rise. Roll out the dough into a 15x10-inch rectangle layer. Grease the dough evenly with the melted butter. To make the crumble topping, combine the butter and sugar in a mixing bowl, add the flour and nuts and rub the mixture together until it crumbles. Sprinkle it evenly over the dough. Form a cylinder out of the dough. Cut it into 1-inch (2-3 cm) thick round slices using a sharp knife. Place these slices over a baking sheet lined with greased parchment paper, stretch them out slightly to form a prolate shape, and brush with a milk-based egg wash. Allow 30 minutes for resting. Preheat oven at 400°F and bake 15 minutes in a preheated oven until golden brown, then remove from oven. Serve.

348. MUFFINS GOLDEN HIVE

READY IN ABOUT: 3 HOURS
SERVINGS: 12 MUFFINS
YIELDS: 1 LB LOAF

INGREDIENTS

For Dough:
» 2/5 cup milk
» 1/4 cup butter
» 1 egg
» 1/3 cup sugar
» 2 1/2 cups all-purpose flour
» 1 teaspoon active dry yeast
» 1/2 teaspoon salt

For glaze:
» 3 tablespoons butter
» 1/4 cup sugar
» 1 tablespoon honey
» 3/4 cup ground almonds
» 2 tablespoons cream

For filling:
» 1/2 cup butter
» 1 tablespoon powdered sugar
» 1 tablespoon vanilla sugar
» 2/3 cup vanilla pudding (prepared)

INSTRUCTIONS

In a bread machine, knead the dough. Allow 45 minutes for it to rest and rise. Place 12 equal pieces of dough in buttered cupcake cups. Allow 30 minutes for resting. Preheat oven to 400°F. In a saucepan, combine all of the glaze ingredients and bring to a low boil. Drizzle the glaze on the tops of the cupcakes. Cook for 20 minutes in a preheated oven. To create the filling, combine butter, powdered sugar, and vanilla sugar in a mixing bowl. Using a mixer, create a foam and gradually add vanilla pudding to the mixture, tablespoon by the spoonful. Cut the baked muffins in half horizontally. Using vanilla cream, cover one side of the cake. Place the remaining parts on top of each other. Serve

349. ROMAN BREAD

READY IN ABOUT: 3 HOURS
YIELDS: 1 1/2 LB LOAF

INGREDIENTS

For the Dough:
» 1 cup water
» 3 cups bread flour
» 1 tablespoon sugar
» 1/3 cup chopped yellow onion
» 1 1/2 teaspoons salt
» 2 1/2 teaspoons bread machine yeast

For the topping:

» 3 tablespoons olive oil
» 1 1/2 tablespoons dried rosemary
» Coarse Sea salt (for sprinkling)

INSTRUCTIONS

To produce the dough, layer the ingredients in the pan in the sequence specified by the manufacturer. Start the Dough cycle by pressing the Start button. Drizzle olive oil over a big rectangle baking sheet. Press Stop and unplug the machine when the machine beeps at the end of the cycle. Take the pan and flip the dough out onto the baking sheet. Press and flatten this dough into a 1-inch-thick oval with oily fingers or a rolling pin. Cover it around with plastic wrap and allow it to rise at room temperature for about 40 minutes or until doubled in size. Preheat your oven at 425°F and set a baking stone on the bottom rack 20 minutes before baking. Preheat the oven at 400°F if you aren't using a baking stone. Cut a large tic-tac-toe grid into the top of the dough using a small, sharp knife, no more than 12 inches deep. Spray the olive oil over the top and sprinkle the rosemary on top. Cook for 20 to 25 minutes, or until golden brown. Sprinkle coarse salt on the bread when it comes out of the oven. Serve warm or at room temperature the same day it's made, sliced into squares.

350. ITALIAN WHOLE WHEAT FLATBREAD

READY IN ABOUT: 3 HOURS
YIELDS: 2 LB LOAF

INGREDIENTS

» 2/3 cup water
» 1 cup milk
» 3 tablespoons extra virgin olive oil
» 3 cups unbleached all-purpose flour
» 1 cup whole wheat flour
» 2 1/4 teaspoons SAF yeast/2 3/4 teaspoons bread machine yeast
» 3 to 4 tablespoons extra virgin olive oil for drizzling
» 2 teaspoons coarse sea salt (for sprinkling)

INSTRUCTIONS

In the pan, layer the dough ingredients in the sequence specified in the manufacturer's instructions. Start the Dough cycle by pressing the Start button. Although the dough will be soft, it will still be able to form a dough ball. Lightly grease a 15-by-10-by-1-inch metal jelly roll pan. Press Stop and unplug the machine when the machine beeps at the end of the cycle. Remove the bread pan immediately and turn the dough out onto the prepared pan. To fit the pan, press and flatten the dough with the heel of your hand. Cover around with plastic wrap and let rise at room temperature for 1 hour, or until doubled in mass. Preheat the oven at 450°F and set a baking stone on the center rack 20 minutes before baking. Gently dimple the dough with your fingertips or knuckles all over the surface. Pour the olive oil over the dough and allow it to pool in the indentations. Bake for 25–30 minutes, or until golden brown. Season the bread with salt and pepper.

351. CHALLAH

READY IN ABOUT: 3 HOURS
YIELDS: 2 LB LOAF

INGREDIENTS

» 4 cups bread flour
» 1/2 cup white sugar
» 1 tablespoon honey
» 1/2 cup vegetable oil
» 2 1/2 teaspoons salt
» 1 cup warm water
» 1 tablespoon water
» 2 1/4 teaspoons bread machine yeast
» 2 large eggs, room temperature
» 1 egg, beaten

INSTRUCTIONS

Fill the bread machine pan with warm water, sugar, honey, vegetable oil, salt, 2 eggs, flour, and yeast in the sequence indicated by the manufacturer. Select the Dough cycle and push the Start button.
Take the pan from the baking chamber using potholders and place dough on a gently floured counter, punch it down, and set it aside for 5 minutes.
Make a half-dozen cuts in the dough. Then divide into three equal halves, roll into 12- to 14-inch ropes, and braid into a loaf. Carry out the same procedure with the remaining half. Environment the loaves on a greased cookie sheet, spritz with water, cover with plastic wrap and let rise in a warm place (draft-free) for about 1 to 1 1/2 hours, or until doubled in size. Preheat the oven to 350°Fahrenheit. 1 egg and 1 tablespoon water, beaten together in a small bowl. Brush the egg mixture on the risen bread. Cook for 20 to 25 minutes in a preheated oven. Cover with foil if it starts to brown too quickly.

352. WHOLE WHEAT ROLLS

READY IN ABOUT: 1 1/2 HOUR
YIELDS: 2 LB LOAF

INGREDIENTS

» 1 1/4 cups water
» 4 cups whole wheat flour
» 1 1/2 teaspoons salt
» 2 tablespoons oil
» 2 tablespoons molasses
» 2 tablespoons maple syrup
» 1 tablespoon active dry yeast

INSTRUCTIONS

In a bread pan, layer the first eight ingredients in the order stated. Close the cover and secure the bread pan in the baking chamber. Connect the unit to a wall outlet. Choose DOUGH. START/STOP by pressing the START/STOP button. To hand shape the roll, take the dough from the mixer and place it on a lightly floured cutting board. Form the dough into 12 balls by dividing it into 12 equal portions. Brush the rolls lightly with melted butter or butter substitute and place them in greased muffin tins. Allow rising for 15-20 minutes in a warm place, covered with wax paper and a clean cloth.

Preheat the oven to 375°F and bake the rolls for 15-20 minutes. Keep leftovers refrigerated.

353. FRENCH BAGUETTES

READY IN ABOUT: 2 HOURS
SERVINGS: 2 BAGUETTES
YIELDS: 1 1/2 LB LOAF

INGREDIENTS

» 1 cup water
» 2 1/2 cups bread flour
» 1 1/2 teaspoon bread machine yeast
» 1 teaspoon salt
» 1 tablespoon white sugar
» 1 tablespoon water
» 1 egg yolk

INSTRUCTIONS

Place all of the ingredients in the pan (except water and egg yolk) in the order recommended by the manufacturer. Select Dough cycle, and press Start.

When the cycle is through, transfer the dough to an oiled bowl and turn to coat both sides. Allow rising for 30 min. in a warm area, or until doubled in bulk. If the indentation stays when the dough is touched, it is ready.

Knead the dough. Roll out the dough into a 16x12-inch rectangle on a lightly floured surface. Divide the dough in half to make two 8x12-inch rectangles. Starting at the 12-inch side, roll up each half of dough tightly, hammering out any air bubbles as you go. To get to the tapered end, gently roll back and forth. Place on a greased cookie sheet 3 inches apart. Make deep diagonal slits every 2 inches across the loaves, or one longitudinal slash each loaf. Allow 30 to 40 minutes for the dough to rise in a warm area or until it has doubled in bulk.

Preheat the oven to 375°F. Brush the tops of the bread with an egg yolk and 1 tablespoon water mixture. Bake for 20 to 25 minutes, or until golden brown.

354. SOFT WHOLE WHEAT DINNER ROLLS

READY IN ABOUT: 2 HOURS
YIELDS: 2 LB LOAF

INGREDIENTS

» 2/3 cup milk
» 1/2 cup sour cream
» 1/4 cup honey
» 2 large eggs
» 4 tablespoons butter/margarine (cut into pieces)
» 3 cups unbleached All-Purpose flour
» 1 cup whole wheat flour
» 1/2 cup toasted wheat germ
» 1 1/2 teaspoons salt
» 1/2 teaspoons bread machine yeast

INSTRUCTIONS

Place all of the ingredients in the pan in the sequence specified by the maker. Start the Dough cycle by pressing the Start button.

Place a large baking sheet with parchment paper or grease it. Press Stop and unplug the machine when the machine beeps at the end of the cycle. On a lightly floured surface, on a board, roll the dough. Cut half the dough and roll each half into a 2- to 3-inch cylinder. Cut the cylinder into 8 equal sections using a metal dough scraper or a chef's knife. Make a total of 16 equal sections by repeating the process with the second cylinder. Pat, each section into an oval, then roll up from a short side to form a little compact cylinder approximately 4 inches long. Place the rolls in two rows of eight long sides facing each other. Brush the tops of the buns with melted butter. Cover it loosely with plastic wrap around it, let the bread rise at room temperature for 45 minutes or double in size.

Preheat the oven to 375°F 20 minutes before baking. Bake for 25 minutes, or until golden brown, with the baking sheet in the center of the oven. Remove the rolls from the pans and place them on a cooling rack to cool. Serve warm or cool at room temperature before reheating.

355. WHOLE WHEAT HAMBURGER & HOT DOG BUNS

READY IN ABOUT: 2 1/2 HOURS

Serving: 10 Pieces of Hamburger, 12 Hotdog buns

YIELDS: 1 1/2 LOAF

INGREDIENTS

» 3 Teaspoon Active Dry Yeast
» 1 Cup of Water
» 1 Egg
» 1 teaspoon of Salt
» 1/4 Cup Butter
» 1/4 Cup Sugar
» 2 cup All-Purpose Flour
» 1 cup Whole Wheat Flour

INSTRUCTIONS

In a bread pan, combine the dough ingredients, select the Dough setting and press Start.

The machine will beep when the dough has risen sufficiently. Remove the bread pan from the machine and transfer the dough onto a lightly floured worktop or cutting board. Using cooking spray, grease a baking pan or sheet. For hamburger buns, roll dough into balls and flatten, or shape into six-inch rolls for hot dog buns. Place these on a baking sheet that has been prepared. Cover and rise for 30 to 45 minutes in a warm oven (90-95°F) until doubled in size. (Hint: To slightly warm the oven, put it to Warm for 1 minute, then turn it off and place the wrapped dough in the oven to rise. Before preheating, remove the pan from the oven.) Preheat the oven to 400 degrees Fahrenheit and bake for 12 to 15 minutes, or until golden brown. Take out the pan(s) from the oven and place them on racks to cool. When you're ready to use the buns, cut them in half horizontally. These will last 3 to 4 weeks in the freezer if stored in a plastic bag.

356. SOUTHERN SPICY CORNBREAD

READY IN ABOUT: 3 1/2 HOURS
YIELDS: 1,5 LB LOAF

INGREDIENTS

» 1 1/4 cup water
» 1/4 cup nonfat dry milk powder
» 1 egg
» 1 teaspoon salt
» 1/3 cup cornmeal
» 1 1/2 teaspoon red pepper flakes
» 2 tablespoon white sugar
» 1 teaspoon bread machine yeast
» 2 tablespoon shortening
» 3 cup bread flour /all-purpose flour
» 2/3 cup frozen corn kernels

INSTRUCTIONS

Add all of the ingredients in the bread machine pan in the order specified by the manufacturer. Close the cover of the machine and place the pan inside. Select the Dough cycle and begin the process. Put the dough on a floured surface and press out all the air when the cycle is finished. Pinch the seam and roll the dough into a tight loaf. Place the loaf in a 9x5-inch loaf pan and set aside for about 40 minutes. Preheat the oven to 375 degrees Fahrenheit. Bake for 30-35 minutes in the oven.

357. CREAM CHEESE BREAD

READY IN ABOUT: 1 1/2 HOUR
YIELDS: 1 LB LOAF

INGREDIENTS

» 1/2 cup water
» 1/2 cup cream cheese
» 1 tablespoon butter
» 1 egg
» 1 tablespoon Sugar
» 1 teaspoon salt
» 2 cups bread flour
» 1 1/2teaspoons Active dry yeast

INSTRUCTIONS

Place the ingredients in the pan in the sequence recommended by the manufacturer of your bread maker. Use a dough cycle. Take the dough from the machine and shape it into a loaf in a prepared 9x5 loaf pan. Allow rising until twice in size. Preheat oven to 350°F and bake for 35 minutes.

358. ROASTED GARLICKY DRY JACK BREAD

READY IN ABOUT: 2 1/2 HOURS
YIELDS: 2 LB LOAF

INGREDIENTS

» 3 to 4 ounces (85- to 113-g) garlic
» 2/3 cup grated dry jack cheese
» 1 1/2 cups water
» 1 tablespoon gluten
» 4 cups bread flour
» 2 1/4 teaspoons salt
» 1 and 1/2 teaspoon bread machine yeast

INSTRUCTIONS

Preheat the oven to 350 degrees Fahrenheit. Add the garlic to a small baking dish and bake for 40 to 45 minutes, or until tender when touched with a finger. Allow cooling to room temperature after removing from the oven. Slice the roasted garlic head in half horizontally. Add all of the ingredients in the pan in the sequence specified by the maker. Select Dough Cycle and press Start. When the dough cycle is finished, turn it out onto a floured surface and knead it a few times before dividing it in two.
Form each half into a round or oval loaf, place on an oiled baking sheet, and allow the bread to rise until doubled in size. Bake for 25-30 min at 350°F, or until golden brown and hollow when tapped. Cool for at least 15 minutes on wire racks before slicing.

359. FLUFFY PEASANT BREAD

READY IN ABOUT: 3 HOURS
YIELDS: 1 LB LOAF

INGREDIENTS

» 3/4 cup water
» 2 cups flour
» 2 tablespoons olive oil
» 1 1/2 tablespoons sugar
» 1 tablespoon salt
» 1 tablespoon yeast
» 1 1/2 tablespoons rosemary
» rosemary to garnish

INSTRUCTIONS

In the bread machine's pan, combine all the ingredients according to the manufacturer's instructions. Set the machine on dough cycle.
When the cycle is finished, remove the dough from the machine and set them on a lightly greased baking sheet. Form the dough into a rectangular mound by hand, spreading it thinly, about an inch or two thick. Allow rising for about 1 hour in a warm area or until doubled in size. Brush with olive oil and season with salt and rosemary, if preferred.
Preheat oven to 375°F and bake for 20-25 minutes, or until crust is golden and crunchy. The loaf is supposed to have a flatter shape than a high-rise bread.
Tear the bread into pieces using your hands and serve with olive oil scented with fresh ground pepper.

360. DOUGHNUTS GLAZED WITH CHOCOLATE

READY IN ABOUT: 10 HOURS
SERVINGS: 24 DOUGHNUTS
YIELDS: 1,5 LB LOAF

INGREDIENTS

For the Doughnuts:
- » 1/2 cup Milk
- » 1/2 cup Water
- » 2 tablespoons Butter
- » 1 Egg
- » 1/3 cup Granulated Sugar
- » 3 cups All-Purpose Flour
- » 1 teaspoon salt
- » 2 teaspoons Active Dry Yeast
- » Oil, for deep-frying of Doughnuts

For the Chocolate Glaze:
- » 2 tablespoons Butter
- » 2 tablespoons Cocoa Powder
- » 3 tablespoons Hot Water
- » 1 1/2 cups Confectioners' Sugar
- » 1/2 teaspoon Vanilla Extract

INSTRUCTIONS

In the bread machine, combine all of the ingredients. At the end of the kneading cycle, wrap the pan with plastic wrap and place it in the refrigerator. Roll out the dough and make its thickness of about 1/2 inch on a lightly floured board. (Alternatively, place the mixture in a lightly greased mixing bowl.) Make knots or cruller shapes out of the strips, or cut doughnut shapes out of them. Cover it and then leave to rise for 1 hour. Fry till bright and browned in oil at 360°F. Use the chocolate icing recipe below or your preferred icing.

Glaze: Chocolate or Vanilla

Melt the butter in mentioned quantity over low heat in a small saucepan; add the Chocolate and water. Stir regularly until the mixture reaches a thick consistency. Off from heat and gradually whisk in powdered sugar and vanilla until creamy. Add more hot water, 1/2 teaspoon at a time, until the consistency is drizzling. If you want vanilla icing, leave off the Chocolate and add 1 1/2 teaspoons vanilla instead.

361. SWEET POTATO ROLLS

READY IN ABOUT: 1 1/2 HOUR
SERVINGS: 24 ROLLS
YIELDS: 2 LB LOAF

INGREDIENTS

- » 1 cup Mashed Sweet Potatoes
- » 3/4 cup Milk
- » 3 tablespoons Melted Butter
- » 1 Egg
- » 4 cups All-Purpose Flour
- » 4 tablespoons Sugar
- » 1 teaspoon salt
- » 2 1/4 teaspoons Active Dry Yeast

INSTRUCTIONS

Collect the necessary components. 2 medium sweet potatoes are peeled and cut into cubes. Over high heat, bring a saucepan of salted water to a boil. Reduce the heat to low and add the sweet potato cubes to the boiling water. Cook, and cover it for about 20 minutes, or until the vegetables are soft. Drain and mash thoroughly. Allow it cool completely before measuring out 1 cup for the recipe. In the bread machine, combine all ingredients in the sequence recommended by the manufacturer. Use the basic dough cycle to make the dough. When the cycle is through, break portions of dough into balls and lay them in a prepared 9-inch square baking pan so they're barely touching but not too close together—about 1.75 ounces in weight per roll for a total of 24 rolls. Allow the rolls to rise for about 45 minutes in a warm, draft-free environment. Preheat the oven to 375° F and bake for 20–23 minutes, or until nicely browned. While they're still hot, brush the tops with melted or softened butter.

362. PRETZELS

READY IN ABOUT: 1 1/2 HOUR
SERVINGS: 12-14 PRETZELS
YIELDS: 2 LB LOAF

INGREDIENTS

- » 1 1/2 cups Water
- » 1 tablespoon Light Brown Sugar
- » 3 1/2 cups All-Purpose Flour
- » 2 teaspoons Active Dry Yeast
- » 2 quarts Water
- » Salt (according to taste)
- » 1/3 cup Baking Soda

INSTRUCTIONS

In your bread machine, add the first five ingredients in the sequence recommended by the manufacturer. After the cycle is finished, turn the dough onto a lightly floured surface and set it aside to rest. Prepare two baking sheets and a third baking sheet with a rack. The dough should be divided into 12 to 14 equal pieces. Each component should be rolled into a 15-inch rope.
With each rope, make a U and then cross the ends. Pick up the ends, twist them together, and fold them in half to form a pretzel shape. To seal, pinch the edges together. Put the pretzels on a baking sheet that has been salted.
In a large saucepan, combine the 2 quarts of water. Bring the water to a boil. Reduce the heat and add the baking soda. Place 2 to 3 pretzels in the baking soda bath at a time. Allow for a 2-minute simmer. Remove the pretzels using a slotted spoon. Place on a cooling rack to cool. Transfer the pretzels to the salted baking pans once they have all come out of the baking soda bath. Preheat the oven for about 350°F and bake for 8 to 12 minutes, or until golden brown.

363. HOT CROSS BUNS

READY IN ABOUT: 3 HOURS
YIELDS: 1,5 LB LOAF

INGREDIENTS

» 3/4 cup lukewarm Milk
» 2 teaspoons Pure Vanilla Extract
» 1 Egg
» 3 cups All-Purpose Flour
» 1/3 cup Granulated Sugar
» 1 scant teaspoon salt
» 3 teaspoons Active Dry Yeast
» 1/4 cup unsalted Butter
» 1 1/2 teaspoons Ground Cinnamon
» 3/4 to 1 cup Currants
» 1 Egg Yolk
» 2 tablespoons Water

FOR THE ICING:

» 1 1/2 cups Confectioners' Sugar
» 2 tablespoons Milk
» 1/2 teaspoon Pure Vanilla Extract

INSTRUCTIONS

Collect the necessary components. Combine the 3/4 cup milk, 2 teaspoons vanilla extract, and the egg in a mixing bowl. In the bread machine, add the milk mixture, flour, granulated sugar, salt, yeast, and butter to the bread machine manufacturer. Set your bread machine on the dough cycle and, when the beep sounds, add cinnamon and currants or chopped dried fruit. If the mixture becomes to be too dry, add a small amount of water.
Remove the dough to a gently floured board once it has doubled in volume. Leave it for a few minutes after punching it down and kneading it 6 to 8 times. Greased a 9-inch square baking pan. Small pieces of dough (approximately 2 to 2 1/4 ounces apiece) should be torn out and shaped into balls. Put the dough balls in the baking pan that has been prepared. Allow the dough to rise in a warm location for 40 minutes after covering it with a cloth. Preheat the oven to 350 degrees Fahrenheit. Mix the egg yolk and 2 tablespoons of water in a mixing bowl. Brush the egg yolk mixture lightly over the tops of the buns. Bake them until they become golden brown on top. Place the pan on a cooling rack to finish cooling. Combine the confectioners' sugar, 2 tablespoons milk, and 1/2 teaspoon vanilla extract in a mixing bowl and whisk until smooth. For a dripping consistency, add small amounts of hot water or additional confectioners' sugar as needed. Use a spoon or a decorating bag; drizzle crosses on the tops of the buns.

364. BASIC SWEET BUN

READY IN ABOUT: 3 HOURS
SERVINGS: 10 BUNS
YIELDS: 2 LB LOAF

INGREDIENTS

» 1 cup water
» 1 egg
» 1/4 cup butter
» 1/3 cup sugar
» 3 1/2 cups all-purpose flour
» 1/2 teaspoon lemon zest
» 1 1/2 teaspoon active dry yeast
» 1/2 teaspoon salt

After beeping:

» Chocolate drops/raisins/spices

INSTRUCTIONS

In a bread machine, knead the dough. Allow 45 minutes for resting. Remove the dough from the bread machine. Divide it into 10 equal halves and place it on a floured surface, from the ready-to-use dough, form buns. Put them over a baking sheet with parchment paper that has been greased. Using a towel, cover the dish. Allow the buns to rise and rest for 30 minutes in a warm location. Brush the buns with a mixture of egg, cream, and sweet milk (2/3 cup (160 ml) warm milk and 1/3 cup (65 g, 2.4 oz.) sugar. Preheat your oven to 400F (200 degrees C). Bake until they become golden brown, about 20 minutes.

365. BERRY CRUMB CAKE

READY IN ABOUT: 4 1/2 HOURS
YIELDS: 2 LB LOAF

INGREDIENTS

» 3/4 cup sour cream
» 1 large egg plus 2 egg yolks
» 1/4 cup water
» 4 cups unbleached all-purpose flour
» Grated zest of 1 large orange
» 1/4 cup sugar
» 1 1/2 teaspoons salt
» 1 tablespoon + 1 teaspoon bread machine yeast
» 3/4 cup unsalted butter

For the Streusel Topping:

» 2/3 cup sugar
» 1 1/3 cups unbleached all-purpose flour
» 1 tablespoon ground cinnamon/apple pie spice
» 1 1/2 teaspoons vanilla extract or 2 1/2 teaspoons vanilla powder
» 1/2 cup + 3 tablespoons unsalted butter (chilled and cut into pieces)
» 3 cups fresh blueberries (rinsed and picked over, or frozen unsweetened blueberries, unthawed)
» 1/2 cup confectioners sugar (for dusting)

INSTRUCTIONS

In the sequence specified in the manufacturer's directions, place all dough ingredients in the pan, except the butter. Start the Dough cycle by pressing the Start button. Set a timer for 10 minutes in the kitchen. It will be a firm yet springy dough.

Open the cover when the timer goes off. Add a slice or two of butter at a time while the machine is running, allowing the butter to mix before adding more fully. Adding all of the parts will take a minute or two. Put the lid back on. Set the timer for 30 minutes after the Knead 2 step is completed and let the dough rise in the machine. The machine should then be unplugged after pressing Stop. Transfer the dough to a greased 4-quart plastic bucket, wrap in plastic wrap, and chill overnight.

To prepare the topping, put the flour, sugar, and cinnamon in the work bowl of a food processor. Then dribble in the vanilla while the motor is going, then stop and add the butter chunks. Pulse until the mixture is crumbly and forms large clumps. Please do not overmix the ingredients. Place in a plastic jar with a lid.

Then, line an 18-by-12-by-1-inch jelly roll pan with parchment paper. Using butter-flavored cooking spray, coat the sides and bottom of the pan. The dough will be cold and stiff when you turn it out onto a lightly floured work surface. Flatten out the dough with a roller into a rectangle that will fit in the pan. Transfer to the pan, pressing down to ensure a tight fit. Cover it with wrap (plastic) and set it aside to rise for 3 hours or until it has doubled in size. Preheat the oven to 350°F.

Uncover the pan and sprinkle the blueberries on top, gently pressing them into the dough. Loosen the topping and sprinkle it over the entire pan, covering all dough and berries with a fork. Bake it for 30–35 minutes, or until golden brown around the edges and a cake tester inserted in the center comes out clean. Dust the pan with powdered confectioners' sugar and place it on a wire rack. Warm the dish before serving.

366. EASY DONUTS

READY IN ABOUT: 2 HOURS
SERVINGS: 8 DONUTS
YIELDS: 1,5 LB LOAF

INGREDIENTS

» 2/3 cups milk
» 1/4 cup water
» 1/2 cup of warm water
» 1/4 cup softened butter
» 1 egg slightly beaten
» 1/4 cup granulated sugar
» 1 teaspoon salt
» 3 cups bread machine flour
» 2 1/2 teaspoon bread machine yeast
» Oil for deep frying
» 1/4 cup confectioners' sugar

INSTRUCTIONS

In a bread machine pan, combine milk, water, butter, egg, sugar, salt, flour, and yeast. Select the dough setting and press the start button. To begin, press the start button. When the dough cycle ends, remove it from the pan and place it on a lightly floured surface. Roll out dough to a thickness of 12 inches with a lightly floured rolling pin. Use a lightly powdered donut cutter or a round cookie cutter to cut the dough. Transfer the made doughnuts to a baking sheet lined with wax paper. Cover with a clean tea towel after adding another layer of wax paper. Allow 30-40 minutes for the dough to rise. In a deep-fryer or large, heavy saucepan, heat vegetable oil to 375°F (190°C). Fry doughnuts in batches of two or three at a time until golden brown on both sides, about 3 minutes. Using a paper towel, absorb excess liquid. Sprinkle confectioners' sugar on top.

367. CINNAMON ROLLS

READY IN ABOUT: 4 HOURS
YIELDS: 2 LB LOAF

INGREDIENTS

» 1 cup milk
» 1/4 cup water
» 1 teaspoon vanilla
» 1/2 cup butter
» 2 eggs (beaten)
» 1/2 teaspoon salt
» 1/2 cup sugar
» 5 cup bread flour
» 3 teaspoon instant active yeast

For the Filling:
» 1/2 cup soft butter
» 1 cup brown sugar
» 5 tablespoon cinnamon
» 3/4 cups chopped nuts

Icing:
» 2-ounce cream cheese
» 1/4 cup butter
» 1 cup icing sugar
» 1/2 teaspoon vanilla
» 1/8 teaspoon lemon extract or oil

INSTRUCTIONS

Layer the ingredients in the sequence specified in the manufacturer's directions in the pan. Select the "DOUGH" option and press the start button. Spray a counter with cooking spray, turn out the dough, and shape it into an oval. Allow 10 minutes to rest after covering with plastic wrap. Meanwhile, grease and set aside a 9x13x2 glass pan. On the sprayed counter, stretch and roll the dough into a rectangle 15x24 inches after it has rested. Smear your butter all over the rectangle with a spatula, almost to the edges. Mix the cinnamon, sugar, and nuts together and sprinkle over the top. Starting with the long edge nearest to you, roll up the dough (not too tight, or centers will pop up when baking). Pinch the seam closed with your fingers once it's wrapped up. With a knife, mark 1.5-inch portions along with the roll. Now slide a foot-long strand of unflavored dental floss under the roll until it reaches one of your knife marks. Bring the floss ends up above the roll and crosses them over each other.

This will cut off a nice portion of meat. This ensures that your cuts are precise and clean and that the roll is not squished as it would be if you cut it with a knife. Continue slicing down the roll until it's all cut apart. Place it in a greased baking pan. (Leave some space between the rolls because they will expand and fill the pan as they bake.)

Allow 45-60 minutes to rise after covering with plastic wrap. Remove the plastic wrap and bake for 20-25 min at 350°F. To make the icing, add the butter and cream cheese in a medium mixing bowl and beat until creamy. Mix in the sugar, lemon, and vanilla until smooth.

Allow to cool slightly before icing.

368. CINNAMON BABKA

READY IN ABOUT: 3 HOURS AND 45 MINUTES
YIELDS: 1 1/2 LB LOAF

INGREDIENTS

For the Dough
» 3/4 cup milk, warm (85°F)
» 3 1/2 - 4 c unbleached all-purpose flour
» 4 Tablespoon unsalted butter
» 1 teaspoon salt
» 3 Tablespoon sugar
» 2 egg yolks
» 2 eggs, whole
» 1 teaspoon pure vanilla extract
» 2 1/4 teaspoon active dry yeast

For the Filling
» 1 Tablespoon cinnamon
» 1 cup brown sugar
» 1/4 teaspoon salt
» 1 egg white
» 2 Tablespoon unsalted butter (melted and cooled)

For the Egg Wash
» 1 egg white, lightly beaten

INSTRUCTIONS

Combine the warmed milk and yeast in a small basin. Set aside for 5-10 minutes, or until the yeast starts to foam. In a medium mixing bowl, beat the butter and sugar together with an electric hand mixer while the yeast is starting. One at a time, add the egg yolks, beating well after each addition. One at a time, add the vanilla and entire eggs, beating well after each addition. Set aside this mixture.

Stir the yeast mixture, then pour it into the bread machine's bowl (fitted with the dough paddles). Over the milk, pour the egg and butter mixture. Add the salt and 3 cups of flour. Set the Dough Cycle on your bread machine and press start. As the dough begins to knead, keep an eye on it. Once the ingredients appear to be thoroughly combined, add more flour, a quarter cup (or less) at a time, letting the machine knead between each addition until the dough comes together and pulls away from the bowl's sides.

When the cycle is finished, the bread should have roughly doubled in bulk. For the filling, whisk together all of the filling ingredients in a medium bowl until smooth. Remove from the equation.

Grease a 9x5 loaf pan and line it with parchment paper that has been buttered.

Remove the dough from the rising bowl and place it on a floured board. Roll out the dough into an 18x15-inch rectangle after punching it down. Fill dough equally with filling, leaving a 1-inch border on the long sides.

Begin rolling the dough from one of the long sides.

Cut the roll lengthwise in half, creating two strands.

Twist the two strands together as much as possible, striving to retain the cut (exposed filler) side on top

Finally, make a figure 8 with the twisted dough, keeping the cut sides up as much as possible. Place the twisted figure 8 in the loaf pan that has been greased and lined

Allow for a 30-minute rise by loosely covering the dough in the pan with plastic wrap, then preheat your oven to 350°F. Sprinkle the top of the bread with the egg wash when the dough has risen slightly and appears puffy. Bake for 45-55 minutes at 350°F, or until the top crust is brown and the loaf sounds hollow when tapped. (To collect any filling that may bubble out of the loaf, lay a piece of aluminum foil or an aluminum foil coated baking sheet on the rack under the bread.) When the loaf is done, leave it to cool in the pan for 10 minutes before gently removing it to cool for another 10-20 minutes before slicing.

369. HARPER'S LOAF

READY IN ABOUT: 2 HOURS
YIELDS: 1 1/2 LB LOAF

INGREDIENTS

» 1 1/8 cups water
» 2 large eggs
» 3 tablespoons peanut oil
» 3 tablespoons honey
» 3 tablespoons unsalted butter, cut into pieces
» 2 cups whole wheat flour
» 1 1/2 cups bread flour
» 1 1/2 teaspoons salt
» 1 tablespoon bread machine yeast
» 2 tablespoons rolled oats for sprinkling
» 2 tablespoons sunflower seeds for sprinkling

INSTRUCTIONS

Place all of the ingredients in the pan in the sequence specified by the maker. Start the Dough cycle by pressing the Start button. Brush two 8-by-4-inch loaf pans with peanut oil on the bottom and sides. Turn the dough out onto a clean work surface and allow it to deflate naturally.

Divide the dough into four equal halves using your metal bench scraper or knife without further working it. Roll into four fat oblong sausages, each about 10 inches long, using your palms. Place two of the pieces next to each other. Wrap one piece of dough around the other 2 to 3 times to produce a fat twist effect, holding both pieces of dough together at one end. To make the second loaf, repeat the process. Place the pans in the oven and tuck the ends under. Apply a little layer of peanut oil on the tops. Cover loosely it with plastic wrap, and let it rise at room temperature for 45 minutes to 1 hour (or until the dough becomes doubled in bulk and is approximately 1 inch beyond the rims of the pans). Set the oven tray in the center and preheat to 350°F (20 minutes before baking) (reduce the temperature by 25° if using glass pans).

Using more peanut oil, brush the tops of the loaves. Sprinkle the oats and sunflower seeds on the top. Bake them for 40 to 45 minutes, or until the loaves are golden brown and the sides of the pan have slightly contracted. Lift one end of a loaf out of the pan to check for even browning on the bottom, then tap the top and bottom surfaces with your finger; it should sound hollow, and an instant-read thermometer should read 200°F. Remove the loaves from the pans as soon as possible and lay them on a cooling rack. Before slicing, allow it cool to room temperature.

Chapter 14

SOURDOUGH BREAD

370. SOURDOUGH WALNUT BREAD

READY IN ABOUT: 2 1/2 HOURS
YIELDS: 1 1/2 POUND LOAF

INGREDIENTS:

- » 2 tablespoons active dry yeast
- » 2 cups Light Flour Blend
- » 1/2 cup buttermilk powder
- » 3 tablespoons granulated cane sugar
- » 1 tablespoon baking powder
- » 2 teaspoons salt
- » 1 teaspoon xanthan gum
- » 1 cup) finely chopped walnuts
- » 1 cup sourdough starter (at room temperature)
- » 4 tablespoons unsalted butter (melted)
- » 3 large eggs (beaten)
- » 1/4 cup warm water
- » 1 teaspoon apple cider vinegar

INSTRUCTIONS

In a bowl, measure out the yeast and leave it aside. Whisk together the remaining dry ingredients (excluding the walnuts) in a large mixing basin. Add the walnuts and mix well. Remove from the equation. Combine the wet ingredients in a 4-cup glass measuring cup and pour into the bread pan. Spread the dry ingredients evenly over the wet components using a spatula, totally covering them. Pour the yeast into a shallow well in the center. Put the pan in the machine and lock it in place in the center. Close the lid and choose from the following options: Cycle of Gluten-Free; 1 1/2 pound Loaf size; medium crust.

Remove the bread pan from the machine and place it on a wire cooling rack on its side. Allow for a few minutes in the pan before turning it upside down and sliding the loaf onto the wire rack. If the paddle is stuck in the bottom of the bread, remove it before slicing, cool the loaf upside down for at least 2 hours.

371. SOURDOUGH ENGLISH MUFFIN BREAD

READY IN ABOUT: 2 HOURS
YIELDS: 1 1/2 POUND LOAF

INGREDIENTS

- » 2 teaspoons active dry yeast
- » 1 1/2 cups Light Flour Blend/Whole-Grain Flour Blend
- » 1 1/2 cups potato starch (not potato flour)
- » 1 tablespoon salt
- » 2 teaspoons psyllium husk flakes or powder
- » 1 teaspoon honey
- » 3/4 to 1 cup warm water
- » 1 cup sourdough starter (at room temperature)
- » 2 large eggs (beaten)
- » 1/4 cup olive/vegetable oil
- » 1 teaspoon apple cider vinegar

Topping

- » 1 to 2 teaspoons unsalted butter or non-dairy butter substitute (melted)
- » Fine-ground cornmeal

INSTRUCTIONS

In a bowl, measure out the yeast and leave it aside. Combine the remaining dry ingredients in a large mixing bowl. Blend the honey and water in a 4-cup glass measuring cup to dissolve the honey. Return to the whisk and add the remaining wet ingredients. Pour the batter into the bread pan.

Spread the dry ingredients evenly over the wet components using a spatula, totally covering them. Pour the yeast into a shallow well in the center. Put the pan in the machine and lock it in place in the center. Close the lid and choose from the following options: Cycle of Gluten-Free; 1 1/2 pound Loaf size; medium crust.

After the mix/kneads cycle is complete, carefully brush the top of the dough with melted butter and a light dusting of cornmeal. During the rise and bake processes, close the lid and do not open. Pull the pan from the machine and place it on a wire cooling rack on its side. To get it out of the pan and onto the wire rack, you may need to beat it on the counter. If the paddle is stuck in the bottom of the bread, carefully remove it. Allow at least 2 hours for the bread to cool upside down before slicing.

372. SOURDOUGH CIABATTA

READY IN ABOUT: 2 HOURS
YIELDS: 2 LB LOAF

INGREDIENTS

» 4 teaspoons active dry yeast
» 3 cups Light Flour Blend/Whole-Grain Flour Blend
» 1/2 cup milk powder
» 3 tablespoons granulated cane sugar
» 2 teaspoons psyllium husk flakes/powder
» 2 teaspoons salt
» 1 cup sourdough starter (at room temperature)
» 3 large eggs (beaten)
» 1/4 cup+2 tablespoons warm water
» 3 tablespoons vegetable/olive oil

Topping

» Vegetable oil
» Coarse Sea salt (optional)

INSTRUCTIONS

Brush a long, thin baking pan with vegetable oil generously. Place the pan with parchment paper and leave it stretched over two sides to create "handles" that will make removing the bread from the pan much easier. Oil the parchment lightly. Place the bread pan on the counter with the beater paddle inside. In a bowl, measure out the yeast and leave it aside. Combine the remaining dry ingredients in a large mixing bowl. Combine the wet ingredients in a 4-cup glass measuring cup and pour into the bread pan. Spread the dry ingredients evenly over the wet components using a spatula, totally covering them. Pour the yeast into a shallow well in the center. Put the pan in the machine and lock it in place in the center. Close the lid and choose from the following options: Dough cycle; Loaf size: 1 1/2 pound.

When the dough is done, cancel the cycle using the stop button, turn off the machine, and remove the pan. Use a spatula to scoop the dough into the prepared baking pan. Smooth the dough with damp fingers and a teaspoon of vegetable oil on top. Let the dough rise for 30 minutes, uncovered, to the top of the pan or slightly over it. Preheat your oven to 350°F while the dough is rising. If desired, lightly season the top with coarse salt. Bake for 30 to 45 minutes, or until golden brown. Remove the bread from the oven and flip it out of the pan right away. Cool for 30 to 60 minutes, right

side up, on a wire rack before slicing.

373. SOURDOUGH FOCACCIA

READY IN ABOUT: 2 HOURS
YIELDS: 1 1/2 LB LOAF

INGREDIENTS

» 2 teaspoons active dry yeast
» 1 1/4 cups Light Flour Blend/Whole-Grain Flour Blend
» 1/4 cup milk powder
» 1 tablespoon granulated cane sugar
» 2 teaspoons psyllium husk flakes/powder
» 1 teaspoon salt
» 1/8 teaspoon ascorbic acid (optional)
» 3/4 cup sourdough starter
» 2 large eggs (beaten)
» 1/4 cup warm water
» 2 tablespoons vegetable/olive oil
» 2 teaspoons apple cider vinegar

Topping

» Olive oil Coarse Sea salt

INSTRUCTIONS

Brush a baking sheet generously with oil after lining it with parchment. In a bowl, measure out the yeast and leave it aside. Combine the remaining dry ingredients in a large mixing bowl. Combine the wet ingredients in a 2-cup glass measuring cup and pour into the bread pan. Spread the dry ingredients evenly over the wet components using a spatula, totally covering them. Pour the yeast into a shallow well in the center. Put the pan in the machine and lock it in place in the center. Close the lid and choose from the following options: Cycle of dough; Size of loaf: 1 1/2 pound.

When the dough is done, cancel the cycle using the stop button, turn off the machine, and remove the pan. Take out the dough from the pan and place it on an oiled baking sheet. Brush the top with a little extra oil and flatten the dough into a 12 x 8-inch (30 x 20-cm) rectangle with your hands. Make dimples all over the dough's surface with your fingertips or knuckles. Oil a piece of plastic wrap and place it over the dough, oiled side down. Let the dough rise for 1 hour while the pan is set aside to rest. It will not double, but it will puff up.

Preheat the oven to 350°F while the dough is rising. Remove the plastic wrap and thoroughly season the dough with coarse salt. Bake it for 20 to 25 minutes, or until the focaccia becomes puffy and golden brown. Let it cool for a few minutes on a wire rack. To serve, cut into squares or narrow rectangles. Wrap the uncut loaf or pieces tightly in plastic wrap and store them on the counter overnight or in the refrigerator for up to 3 days. Freeze leftovers for longer storage.

374. SOURDOUGH BUCKWHEAT BREAD

READY IN ABOUT: 2 HOURS
YIELDS: 1 1/2 POUND LOAF

INGREDIENTS

» 1 cup Light Flour Blend
» 1 cup+2 tablespoon buckwheat flour
» 1/4 cup milk powder
» 2 tablespoons firmly packed brown sugar
» 2 tablespoons active dry yeast
» 4 tablespoons flaxseed meal/ground flaxseed
» 3 teaspoons baking powder
» 2 teaspoons xanthan gum
» 2 teaspoons dried minced onions/shallots
» 1 teaspoon caraway powder
» 1 teaspoon kosher salt
» 1/2 teaspoon dried dill weed
» 3 tablespoons honey
» 1/2 cup+1 tablespoon warm water
» 1 cup sourdough starter
» 3 large eggs (beaten)
» 3 tablespoons olive oil
» 2 teaspoons apple cider vinegar

INSTRUCTIONS

In a bowl, measure out the yeast and leave it aside. Combine the remaining dry ingredients in a large mixing bowl. Blend the honey and water in a 4-cup (1-liter) glass measuring cup to dissolve the honey. Return to the whisk and add the remaining wet ingredients. Pour the batter into the bread pan. Spread the dry ingredients evenly over the wet components using a spatula, totally covering them. Pour the yeast into a shallow well in the center. Put the pan in the machine and lock it in place in the center. Close the lid and choose from the following options: Cycle of Gluten-Free; Loaf size: 1 1/2 pound; Medium crust.

Remove the pan from the machine and place it on a wire cooling rack on its side. Allow for a few minutes in the pan before turning it upside down and sliding the loaf onto the wire rack. If the paddle is stuck in the bottom of the bread, carefully remove it. Allow at least 2 hours for the bread to cool upside down before slicing.

375. SOUR PUMPERNICKEL BREAD

READY IN ABOUT: 2 1/2 HOURS
YIELDS: 1 1/2 POUND LOAF

INGREDIENTS

» 2 tablespoons active dry yeast
» 1 1/4 cups Light Flour Blend
» 3/4 cup buckwheat flour
» 2 tablespoons firmly packed brown sugar
» 3 tablespoons flaxseed meal/ground flaxseed
» 2 teaspoons unsweetened cocoa powder
» 2 teaspoons baking powder
» 2 teaspoons xanthan gum
» 1 teaspoon kosher or fine sea salt
» 1 teaspoon onion powder
» 1/2 teaspoon caraway powder
» 1/2 cup warm water
» 3 tablespoons molasses (not blackstrap)
» 1 cup sourdough starter
» 3 large eggs (beaten)
» 1/4 cup olive oil

INSTRUCTIONS

In a small bowl, measure out the yeast and leave it aside. Combine the remaining dry ingredients in a large mixing bowl. Blend the water and molasses in a 4-cup glass measuring cup to dissolve the molasses. Return to the whisk and add the remaining wet ingredients. Pour the batter into the bread pan. Spread the dry ingredients evenly over the wet components using a spatula, totally covering them. Pour the yeast into a shallow well in the center. Insert the bread pan into the machine, center it, and lock it in place. Close the lid and choose from the following options: Cycle of Gluten-Free; Loaf size: 1 1/2 pound; Medium crust.

Remove the pan from the machine and place it on a wire cooling rack on its side. Allow for a few minutes in the pan before turning it upside down and sliding the loaf onto the wire rack. If the paddle is stuck in the bottom of the bread, carefully remove it. Allow at least 2 hours for the bread to cool upside down before slicing.

376. SOURDOUGH FLATBREAD WITH FRESH TOMATOES AND ZA'ATAR

READY IN ABOUT: 3 HOURS
YIELDS: 1 LB LOAF

INGREDIENTS

» 1/2 teaspoon active dry yeast
» 1 cup Light Flour Blend/Whole-Grain Flour Blend
» 1 teaspoon granulated cane sugar
» 3/4 teaspoon salt
» 1/2 teaspoon xanthan gum
» 1/2 cup sourdough starter
» 1/2 cup warm water
» 1 large egg (beaten)
» 1 tablespoon olive/vegetable oil

Topping

» 1/2 cup olive oil
» 2 tablespoons za'atar
» 1/4 cup grated Parmesan cheese (optional)
» 2 cups cherry tomatoes (cut in half)
» 1/2 cup pine nuts
» salt

INSTRUCTIONS

In a small bowl, measure out the yeast and leave it aside. Combine the remaining dry ingredients in a large mixing bowl. Whisk the wet ingredient) in a 2-cup glass measuring cup. Pour the batter into the bread pan. Spread the dry ingredients evenly over the wet components using a spatula, totally covering them. Pour the yeast into a shallow well in the center. Place the bread pan in the machine, center it, and lock it in place. Close the lid and choose from the following options: Dough cycle; Loaf size: 1 pound.

Allow 5 minutes for the machine to mix the dough until it is smooth and free of lumps. Meanwhile, grease a large mixing bowl. Cancel the cycle, switch off the machine, and remove the bread pan when the dough is done. Transfer the dough to the oiled basin with a spatula. Apply a thin layer of oil to the top and sides. Wrap the bowl with a clean dish towel and leave aside for 1 to 1 1/2 hours to rest and rise. Although it will not double in size, it will puff up. Preheat the oven to 500°F while the dough is rising. Place 2 baking sheets with parchment paper and lightly oil them.

In a small bowl, combine the olive oil, za'atar, and Parmesan cheese, if used, for the topping. When the dough has finished rising, gently deflate it with a spoon. When portioning the dough, use 1/4 cup dough for each medium flatbread or 2 tablespoons for each flatbread. Place the dough on the baking pans with plenty of space between each one. Each medium flatbread should be pressed into a flat oval, and each flatbread should be pressed into a flat circle, 1/4 inch (6 mm) thick. It's easier to fit two on each baking sheet if the dough is formed into ovals.

Bake it for 10 minutes, or until golden brown and cooked through in the center. Take it out from the oven and let it cool for 15 to 20 minutes on wire racks. While the flatbreads are cooling, evenly distribute the tomatoes and pine nuts among them, spreading them out. If desired, top with a small amount of the za'atar mixture and a light dusting of salt. Serve while the bread is still warm, cut into quarters.

377. SOURDOUGH SANDWICH BREAD

READY IN ABOUT: 2 1/2 HOURS
YIELDS: 1 1/2 LB LOAF

INGREDIENTS

» 2 tablespoons active dry yeast
» 2 cups Light Flour Blend
» 1/2 cup milk powder
» 3 tablespoons granulated cane sugar
» 1 tablespoon baking powder
» 2 teaspoons salt
» 1 teaspoon xanthan gum
» 1 cup sourdough starter (at room temperature)
» 4 tablespoons unsalted butter (melted)
» 3 large eggs (beaten)
» 1/4 cup water

INSTRUCTIONS

In a small bowl, measure out the yeast and leave it aside. Combine the remaining dry ingredients in a large mixing bowl. Whisk the wet ingredients in a 4-cup glass measuring cup and pour into the bread pan. Spread the dry ingredients over the wet components with a spatula. Pour the yeast into a shallow well in the center. Insert the bread pan into the machine, center it, and lock it in place. Close the lid and choose from the following options: Cycle of Gluten-Free; Loaf size: 1 1/2 pound; Medium crust.

Remove the bread pan from the machine and place it on a wire cooling rack on its side. Allow for a few minutes in the pan before turning it upside down and sliding the loaf onto

the wire rack. If the paddle is stuck in the bottom of the bread, remove it before slicing, cool the loaf upside down for at least 2 hours.

378. WHITE SOURDOUGH BREAD

READY IN ABOUT: 3 HOURS
YIELDS: 1 1/2 LB LOAF

INGREDIENTS

» 3/4 cup sourdough starter (Next-Day White Sourdough Starter)
» 1/2 cup fat-free milk
» 2 tablespoons unsalted butter (melted)
» 1 1/2 tablespoons honey
» 3 cups bread flour
» 1 1/2 teaspoons salt
» 2 teaspoons bread machine yeast

INSTRUCTIONS

Place all of the ingredients in the pan in the sequence specified by the maker. Set the crust too dark and begin the Basic cycle by pressing the Start button. (The Delay Timer is not compatible with this recipe.) When the bake cycle ends, the bread is ready. Take out the bread from the pan and place it on a rack when the baking cycle is finished. Before slicing, allow it cool to room temperature.

379. SOURDOUGH CORNMEAL BREAD

READY IN ABOUT: 3 HOURS
YIELDS: 1 1/2 LB LOAF

INGREDIENTS

» 1 1/4 cups white flour sourdough starter (Next-Day White Sourdough Starter)
» 1/2 cup + 2 tablespoons fat-free milk
» 2 tablespoons olive oil
» 3 tablespoons honey/molasses
» 2 1/2 cups bread flour
» 2/3 cup yellow cornmeal
» 1 1/2 teaspoons salt
» 2 teaspoons bread machine yeast

INSTRUCTIONS

Place all of the ingredients in the pan in the sequence specified by the maker. Set the crust to medium and begin the Basic cycle by pressing the Start button. (The Delay Timer is not compatible with this recipe.) Remove the bread from the pan and place it on a rack when the baking cycle is finished. Before slicing, allow it cool to room temperature.

Chapter 15

OTHER RECIPES

380. BOHEMIAN BLACK BREAD

READY IN ABOUT: 2 1/2 HOURS
YIELDS: 1 1/2 LB LOAF

INGREDIENTS

- » 1 1/8 cups water
- » 3 tablespoons butter (melted)
- » 1 1/2 tablespoons molasses
- » 1 3/4 cups bread flour
- » 1 cup medium or dark rye flour
- » 1/4 cup wheat bran
- » 2 tablespoons unsweetened Dutch-process cocoa powder
- » 1 tablespoon gluten
- » 1 1/2 teaspoons instant espresso powder
- » 1 1/2 teaspoons caraway seeds
- » 1/2 teaspoon fennel seeds
- » 1 1/2 teaspoons salt
- » 2 teaspoons SAF yeast / 2 1/2 teaspoons bread machine yeast

INSTRUCTIONS

Place all of the ingredients in the pan in the sequence specified by the maker. Set the crust to medium and begin the Basic or Whole Wheat cycle by pressing the Start button. (The Delay Timer can be used to make this dish.) Take out the bread from the pan and place it on a rack when the baking cycle is finished. Before slicing, allow it cool to room temperature.

381. SUNFLOWER PUMPERNICKEL RYE

READY IN ABOUT: 2 1/2 HOURS
YIELDS: 1 1/2 LB LOAF

INGREDIENTS

- » 1 1/3 cups water
- » 3 1/2 tablespoons molasses
- » 2 tablespoons butter, melted
- » 1 1/2 cups bread flour
- » 1 cup medium or dark rye flour
- » 1/2 cup whole wheat flour
- » 1/4 cup cornmeal
- » 3 tablespoons unsweetened Dutch-process cocoa powder
- » 2 tablespoons brown sugar
- » 1 1/2 tablespoons nonfat dry milk
- » 1 1/2 tablespoons gluten
- » 1/2 teaspoon instant espresso powder
- » 2 teaspoons caraway seeds
- » 1 1/2 teaspoons salt
- » 2 1/2 teaspoons SAF yeast/ 1 tablespoon bread machine yeast
- » 1/3 cup raw sunflower seeds

INSTRUCTIONS

Place all of the ingredients in the pan, except the sunflower seeds, in the sequence specified by the manufacturer. Set the crust to medium and begin the Basic or Whole Wheat cycle by pressing the Start button. (The Delay Timer is not compatible with this recipe.) Add the sunflower seeds when the machine whistles, or between Knead 1 and Knead 2. Take out the bread from the pan and place it on a rack when the baking cycle is finished. Before slicing, allow it cool to room temperature.

382. DUTCH SUGAR LOAF

READY IN ABOUT: 2 1/2 HOURS
YIELDS: 1 1/2 LB LOAF

INGREDIENTS

- » 2/3 cup sugar cubes
- » 1 1/2 teaspoons ground cinnamon
- » Small pinch of ground cloves
- » 1 1/8 cups fat-free milk
- » 1 1/4 teaspoons salt
- » 1 tablespoon unsalted butter/ margarine
- » 3 cups bread flour
- » 1 tablespoon gluten
- » 2 1/2 teaspoons bread machine yeast

INSTRUCTIONS

Place the sugar cubes in a hefty transparent freezer bag and crack them with the smooth side of a meat hammer. Do not smash them; ideally, the chunks should be no smaller than quarter cubes. Toss the spices into the bag to coat. Remove from the equation.

Place the ingredients in the pan in the order listed in the manufacturer's directions, except for the spice-coated sugar cubes. Set the crust to medium and select the Sweet Bread cycle from the menu; push Start. (The Delay Timer is not compatible with this recipe.) Press Pause after five minutes of kneading and sprinkle in half of the sugar cube mixture. To restart the cycle, press Start. Press Pause after three minutes and add the remaining sugar cube mixture. To restart the cycle, press Start. Take out the bread from the pan and place it on a rack when the baking cycle is finished. If you slice it before it cools to normal temperature, the sugar syrup will seep out.

383. ORANGE CINNAMON BREAD

READY IN ABOUT: 3 HOURS
YIELDS: 1 1/2 LB LOAF

INGREDIENTS

- » 1/2 cup orange juice
- » 1/3 cup milk
- » 1 large egg
- » 3 tablespoons unsalted butter
- » 3 cups bread flour
- » 1/4 cup sugar
- » Grated zest of 1 orange
- » 1 tablespoon gluten
- » 2 teaspoons ground cinnamon
- » 1 1/4 teaspoons salt
- » 2 teaspoons SAF yeast/ 2 1/2 teaspoons bread machine yeast

For the vanilla-orange glaze:

- » 3/4 cup sifted confectioners' sugar
- » 1 1/2 to 2 tablespoons orange juice
- » 1 teaspoon vanilla extract

INSTRUCTIONS

To prepare the dough, layer all dough components in the pan in the sequence specified by the manufacturer. Set the crust to medium and begin the Basic cycle by pressing the Start button. (The Delay Timer is not compatible with this recipe.) Take out the bread from the pan and place it on a rack when the baking cycle is finished. Under the rack, place a plate or a piece of waxed paper. To make the glaze, mix the confectioners' sugar, orange juice, and vanilla extract in a small bowl until smooth. Drizzle the glaze over the bread with a large spoon, allowing it to trickle down the edges. Allow it cool to room temperature before slicing to solidify the glaze.

384. MEXICAN CHOCOLATE BREAD

READY IN ABOUT: 2 1/2 HOURS
YIELDS: 1 1/2 LB LOAF

INGREDIENTS

- » 1/2 cup milk
- » 1/2 cup orange juice
- » 1 large egg plus 1 egg yolk
- » 3 tablespoons unsalted butter
- » 2 1/2 cups bread flour
- » 1/4 cup light brown sugar
- » 3 tablespoons unsweetened Dutch-process cocoa powder
- » 1 tablespoon gluten
- » 1 1/4 teaspoons salt
- » 1 teaspoon instant espresso powder
- » 3/4 teaspoon ground cinnamon
- » 1/2 cup bittersweet chocolate chips
- » 2 teaspoons SAF yeast/ 2 1/2 teaspoons bread machine yeast

INSTRUCTIONS

Place all of the ingredients in the pan in the sequence specified by the maker. Set the crust to medium and select the Sweet Bread cycle from the menu; push Start. (The Delay Timer is not compatible with this recipe.)

Take out the bread from the pan and place it on a rack when the baking cycle is finished. Before slicing, allow it cool to room temperature.

385. PAIN AUX TROIS PARFUMS

READY IN ABOUT: 2 1/2 HOURS
YIELDS: 1 1/2 LB LOAF

INGREDIENTS

- » 1/2 cup milk
- » 1/2 cup water
- » 1 large egg plus 1 egg yolk
- » 3 tablespoons pistachio oil/ melted unsalted butter
- » 1 teaspoon mint extract
- » 2 2/3 cups bread flour
- » 1/4 cup sugar
- » 3 tablespoons unsweetened Dutch-process cocoa powder
- » 1 tablespoon + 1 teaspoon gluten
- » 1 teaspoon salt
- » 2 1/2 teaspoons bread machine yeast

- » 1/2 cup bittersweet chocolate chips
- » 1/3 cup chopped pistachios

INSTRUCTIONS

Place all of the ingredients in the pan, except the chocolate chips and pistachios, in the sequence specified by the maker. Set the crust to light and select the Sweet Bread cycle from the menu; press Start. (The Delay Timer is not compatible with this recipe.) Add the chocolate chips and pistachios when the machine whistles, or between Knead 1 and Knead 2. Take out the bread from the pan and place it on a rack when the baking cycle is finished. Before slicing, allow it cool to room temperature.

386. ITALIAN CHOCOLATE BREAD WITH AMARETTO ICING

READY IN ABOUT: 2 1/2 HOURS
YIELDS: 1 1/2 LB LOAF

INGREDIENTS

For the nuts:
- » 2 cups water
- » 3 tablespoons baking soda
- » 2 ounces whole hazelnuts (1/2 cup)

For the dough:
- » 2 cup milk
- » 1 large egg
- » 2 tablespoons amaretto liqueur
- » 3 tablespoons unsalted butter, cut into pieces
- » 2 7/8 cups bread flour
- » 1/3 cup sugar
- » 2 tablespoons unsweetened Dutch-process cocoa powder
- » 1 tablespoon gluten
- » 1 1/4 teaspoons salt
- » 1 teaspoon ground cinnamon
- » 2 1/2 teaspoons bread machine yeast

For the amaretto icing:
- » 1/2 cup sifted confectioners' sugar
- » 1 1/4 tablespoon amaretto liqueur
- » 1 to 2 teaspoons hot milk

INSTRUCTIONS

Boil the water in a saucepan to peel the nuts. Combine the baking soda and nuts in a mixing bowl. Boil for 3–5 minutes, or until the water turns black. Pour the nuts into a colander and run them under cold water to drain. Remove each skin with your fingertips and set the nuts on a clean dish towel. Place on a clean baking sheet after patting dry. Stir the nuts twice during the ten to fifteen minutes of toasting. Cool completely on the baking pan. Chop the nuts coarsely. To prepare the dough, layer all ingredients in the pan according to the manufacturer's directions, start adding the dry ingredients and end with the nuts. Set the crust to medium and select the Sweet Bread cycle from the menu; push Start. (The Delay Timer is not compatible with this recipe.)
Remove the bread from the pan after the baking cycle is finished and place it on a rack with a sheet of parchment paper or a large plate below. To prepare the icing, whisk together all of the ingredients in a small bowl until smooth. Add a few drops of milk to adjust the consistency. Drizzle or pour over the top of the loaf with a large spoon in a back and forth motion. The glaze will harden as it cools.

387. THANKSGIVING SANDWICH BREAD

READY IN ABOUT: 3 1/2 HOURS
YIELDS: 1 1/2 LB LOAF

INGREDIENTS

- » 2 cups Light Flour Blend
- » 1 cup sorghum flour
- » 1/2 cup milk powder
- » 2 tablespoons granulated cane sugar
- » 2 tablespoons flaxseed meal/ground flaxseed
- » 2 tablespoons gluten-free oats
- » 2 teaspoons baking powder
- » 2 tablespoons active dry yeast
- » 2 teaspoons xanthan gum
- » 1 1/2 teaspoons kosher or fine sea salt
- » 1 1/2 teaspoons dried poultry seasoning
- » 3/4 teaspoon onion powder
- » 2 large eggs (beaten)
- » 1 1/4 cups + 1 tablespoon warm water
- » 1/4 cup olive oil
- » 2 teaspoons apple cider vinegar

INSTRUCTIONS

Place the bread pan on the counter with the beater paddle inside. Add the water first in the pan, then the dry ingredients except for the yeast. In the center of these ingredients, make a well with a spoon and add the yeast. Insert the bread pan into the machine, center it, and lock it in place. Close the lid and choose from the following option: Cycle gluten-free with 1 12 pound/750 g Loaf size: pick Medium crust, and then hit Start. When the baking is finished, take the bread pan from the machine and place it on a wire cooling rack on its side. Allow for a few minutes in the pan before turning it upside down and sliding the loaf onto the wire rack. Allow the bread to cool before slicing it upside down.

388. WHITE AND DARK CHOCOLATE TEA CAKE

READY IN ABOUT: 2 1/2 HOURS
YIELDS: 1 1/2 LB LOAF

INGREDIENTS

- » 1 cup plain yogurt
- » 1/4 cup buttermilk
- » 2 large eggs
- » 1/4 cup vegetable oil
- » 2 teaspoons vanilla extract
- » 2/3 cup light brown sugar
- » 2 1/2 cups unbleached all-purpose flour
- » 1/3 cup unsweetened Dutch-process cocoa powder
- » 1/2 teaspoon baking powder

- » 1 1/2 teaspoons baking soda
- » 1/2 teaspoon instant espresso powder
- » 1/4 teaspoon salt
- » 1 cup white chocolate chips/chunks broken off a bar of white chocolate

INSTRUCTIONS

In the pan, layer the ingredients in the sequence specified in the manufacturer's directions. Set the crust too dark if your machine has that option, and set up the machine for the Quick Bread/Cake cycle; push Start. It will be a thick batter. Check the loaf for doneness when the machine beeps at the end of the cycle. When the cake shrinks from the sides of the pan, the sides are dark brown, and the top is hard when gently pressed with your finger, it is done. When a toothpick or metal skewer is inserted into the center of the bread, it should come out clean.

Take out the pan from the machine as soon as the bread is done. Allow 10 minutes for the bread to cool in the pan before turning it out right side up to cool entirely on a rack before slicing. Wrap securely with plastic wrap and keep refrigerated.

389. SIMPLE KETO BREAD

READY IN ABOUT: 2 1/2 HOURS
YIELDS: 1 1/2 LB LOAF

INGREDIENTS

- » 3 cups almond flour
- » 2 tablespoon inulin
- » 1 tablespoon whole milk
- » 1/2 teaspoon salt
- » 2 teaspoon active yeast
- » 1 1/4 cups warm water
- » 1 tablespoon olive oil

INSTRUCTIONS

Except for the yeast, put all dry ingredients in a small mixing dish. Combine all of the wet ingredients in the bread machine pan. In the bread machine pan, combine all of the dry ingredients from the small mixing bowl. Add the yeast on top. Select the basic bread option on the bread maker. Remove the bread machine pan from the bread machine once the bread is done. Allow cooling before placing to a wire rack to cool completely. The bread can be kept on the counter for up to 5 days and frozen for 3 months.

390. APRICOT JAM

READY IN ABOUT: 2 HOURS

INGREDIENTS

- » 3 cups ripe (firm) apricots, peeled, halved, and pitted
- » 1 Tablespoon low sugar or no sugar pectin
- » 2 cups granulated sugar

INSTRUCTIONS

Using a potato masher or a food processor, mash the fruit. Mix the sugar and flour together in a bowl, then pour the mixture into the bread pan. Start the cycle with the jam or jelly preset. Lift the lid of the machine and set it aside to cool for

30 minutes. Allow 3 hours to rest after carefully pouring or spooning into a jar or jars. Refrigerate until ready to serve. It can be kept in the refrigerator for up to four weeks.

391. EGG PASTA DOUGH

INGREDIENTS

- » 5 large eggs
- » 3 tablespoons water
- » 1/4 cup olive oil
- » 1 1/2 teaspoons salt
- » 4 cups all-purpose flour (unbleached)

INSTRUCTIONS

Combine all ingredients in the order advised by your bread machine manufacturer. Close the cover and start your bread maker with the Pasta Dough program. Take the pan from the baking chamber using potholders and place dough on a gently floured counter. Allow dough to rest for 1/2 hours. Knead the dough a few times by hand once it has rested. If the dough is too wet, add 1 tablespoon of flour at a time until it reaches the appropriate consistency. You can roll pasta by hand or by pasta roller machine.

392. BLUEBERRY LIME JAM

READY IN ABOUT: 1 HOUR
SERVINGS: ABOUT 3 CUPS

INGREDIENTS

- » 1 teaspoon grated fresh lime zest
- » 1 1/3 cup sugar
- » 1/4 cup fresh lime juice
- » 3 1/2 Tablespoon of dry pectin
- » 6 cup blueberries

INSTRUCTIONS

In a medium mixing bowl, combine all of the ingredients and stir well. Place the dough in a bread machine pan fitted with a kneading paddle. Set the machine to the Jam cycle and begin the process according to the instructions.

5 to 10 minutes into the cycle, scrape the sides of the pan. Do this two or three times to ensure that all of the components are well combined. Continue for another 5-6 minutes, and then press the Start/Stop button. Scrape down the mixture and start the baking cycle. Start it and let it run until the cycle is over.

Transfer to clean jars with oven mitts and a wide mouth funnel or a 1/4 cup measuring cup. Allow to cool before covering and storing in the refrigerator for up to 4-6 weeks, or can jars in a water bath and storing once cool (overnight).

393. STRAWBERRY JAM

READY IN ABOUT: 1 1/2 HOUR
SERVINGS: 4 JARS

INGREDIENTS

- » 3 cups of diced strawberries
- » 1 Tablespoon lemon juice
- » 3/4 cup granulated sugar
- » 2 Tablespoon pectin, optional

INSTRUCTIONS

Chop strawberries in half and mash with a fork or a potato masher. Combine strawberries, sugar, lemon juice, and pectin in a bread maker (if using).
Turn on the jam setting. When the cycle is over, dump the contents into a basin with baking mitts and pulse once or twice with an immersion blender.
Pour into jars and set aside to cool before covering with lids and storing in the refrigerator. The jam will thicken in the fridge most of the time, but if you prefer a thicker consistency, add the pectin.

394. SWEET MANGO PICKLE

READY IN ABOUT: 1 1/2 HOUR
SERVINGS: 16 OZ

INGREDIENTS

- » 1 1/2 cup Organic cane sugar
- » 3 cups raw mangoes shredded (2 mangoes)
- » 1 tsp salt
- » 1/4 tsp Turmeric powder
- » 1/4 tsp Red chili powder
- » 1/4 tsp Roasted cumin seed powder

INSTRUCTIONS

Raw mangoes should be washed, peeled, and grated. In the bread machine container, combine the raw mangoes, salt, sugar and turmeric powder. Select the Jam cycle and press start. Remove the mixture from the container and place it in a clean jar once the "Jam" cycle is finished. Mix in the red chili powder and roasted cumin seed powder until thoroughly combined. Allow time for it to cool.

395. APPLE PIE BREAD

READY IN ABOUT: 3 HOURS
YIELDS: 1,5 LB LOAF

INGREDIENTS

- » 1/2 cup water
- » 3 1/4 cups flour
- » 1 1/2 teaspoons salt
- » 1 1/4 cups apple pie filling
- » 1 1/2 tablespoons butter
- » 3 tablespoons dry buttermilk
- » 1 1/2 teaspoons yeast
- » 1 1/2 teaspoons cinnamon

INSTRUCTIONS

In the Bread machine pan, combine all of the ingredients in the sequence stated above.
Select the "White bread" setting or the "Sweet bread" setting if your Bread machine has one. Start by pressing the start button. Allow the bread to cool for 15 minutes on the rack before unmolding. Cool it on the rack for a while longer.

396. GRAPE JELLY

READY IN ABOUT: 1 1/2 HOUR

INGREDIENTS

- » 1 cup sugar
- » 2 cups grape juice
- » 2 Tablespoon reconstituted lemon juice
- » 2 envelopes Knox gelatin

INSTRUCTIONS

Add gelatin to water and dissolve it. Add lemon juice and sugar. Put the mixture in the pan and select Jam or jelly setting. Pour into sterile pint jars as soon as the cycle is complete. Allow to cool for about 3 hours, then refrigerate. Keep in the fridge for up to 4 weeks.

397. RASPBERRY JAM

READY IN ABOUT: 1 1/2 HOUR
YIELDS: 2 HALF-PINT JAR

INGREDIENTS

- » 3/4 cup granulated sugar
- » 3 cups of fresh raspberries
- » 1 teaspoon low sugar
- » 1 Tablespoon lemon juice

INSTRUCTIONS

Using a potato masher or fork, gently mash the raspberries. Combine the mashed raspberries, sugar, lemon juice, and pectin in the bread maker.
On the bread machine, select the jam setting (the typical jam setting on a bread machine runs for about 1 hour and 20 minutes)
When the cycle is finished, carefully remove the pan from the bread machine.
Pour into jars and set aside to cool before covering with lids and storing in the refrigerator.
Carefully take the bread pan from the oven (it will be hot!) using oven mitts. Allow cooling for 45 minutes on a trivet. Store in the refrigerator.

398. DELICIOUS RICE BREAD

READY IN ABOUT: 4 HOURS
YIELDS: 2 LB LOAF

INGREDIENTS

- » 41/2 cups wheat flour
- » 1 cup rice (cooked)
- » 1 whole egg (beaten)
- » 2 tablespoons milk powder
- » 2 teaspoons active dry yeast

- » 2 tablespoons butter
- » 1 tablespoon sugar
- » 2 teaspoon salt
- » 1 1/4 cup water

INSTRUCTIONS

Fill the bread maker bucket with 1 1/4 cups of water. Pour in the beaten egg. Combine the flour, rice, and milk powder in a mixing bowl. Butter, sugar, and salt should all be placed in various corners of the bucket. Make a groove in the center of the flour and sprinkle yeast on top. Set your bread machine's program to Basic/White Bread and the crust type to Medium. Start by pressing the START button. Wait till the cycle is finished. When the loaf is done, take it from the bucket and set it aside to cool for 5 minutes. To remove the bread, gently shake the bucket. Let it cool before slicing and serving.

399. FISH BREAD

READY IN ABOUT: 3 1/2 HOURS
YIELDS: 1 1/2 LB LOAF

INGREDIENTS

- » 2 1/2 cups whole wheat flour
- » 1/2 cup bran
- » 1 1/3 cups warm water
- » 1 1/2 teaspoon salt
- » 1 1/2 teaspoon sugar
- » 1 1/2 tablespoon mustard oil
- » 2 teaspoon powdered milk
- » 1 1/4 teaspoon yeast
- » 1 cup chopped bell pepper
- » 3/4 cup chopped smoked fish
- » 1 chopped and fried onion

INSTRUCTIONS

According to the bread machine's instructions, everything (excluding onion, pepper, and fish) goes into the bread machine. Choose between a basic and a medium crust. After the beep, add the remaining ingredients. When the bread is done, remove it. Allow cooling before slicing and serving.

400. PEACH JAM

READY IN ABOUT: 1/2 HOURS

INGREDIENTS

- » 4 cups fresh peaches (chopped)
- » 1/2 box low sugar pectin
- » Pinch of salt
- » 1 cup sugar

INSTRUCTIONS

Add peaches to the pan of your bread machine. Combine the pectin, sugar, and salt in a mixing bowl. Place the pan back in the bread maker. Using the Jam cycle, cook the ingredients. Remove the pan once the cycle is finished. Pour the mixture into two pint Mason jars with care. Allow time for cooling. Place the Mason jar in the refrigerator with the lid and ring on it. Overnight, the jam will thicken. This jam can be frozen, canned, or used in the refrigerator.

CONCLUSION

A bread maker is a valuable kitchen appliance that allows you to quickly and effortlessly prepare and serve warm, fresh, and tasty homemade bread from the comfort of your own home. A bread machine comprises a built-in bread pan and paddles that are placed in the middle of a compact and manageable multi-purpose oven. This compact oven comes with a built-in microcomputer, which is used to control the bread maker. Depending on the sort of bread you want to bake, the bread maker has multiple settings. White bread, whole wheat bread, French bread, and basic dough like pizza dough are among the options. The bread machine also has a timed setting that automatically turns on and off even if you are not nearby to operate it.

Bread machines are now created by a dozen different companies and come in dozens of versions, each with its own set of settings, functions and sizes. They're not only simple to use, but they also motivate you to create your baking cycles, resulting in bread with thin, crisp crusts and even soft-textured crumbs that rival store loaves and even some bakeries. Baking bread in a bread machine takes so little time that you can experience the luxury of fresh bread every day, as it should be.

The bread machine has won over many people who were previously adept at baking by hand, as well as those who were not motivated to learn how to prepare bread using an earlier approach. They were introduced to the evocative aroma, taste, and texture of baked bread through the bread machine and are now hooked.

Additives, colorants, preservatives, and chemical fixatives are all absent from homemade bread. The bread machine gives you complete control over what goes into your bread, and you can almost always count on it to be of high quality. While handcrafted loaves have a pleasing visual appeal, each machine-baked loaf is the same form as its baking pan.

Loaves of bread are generally defined in baking by the type of flour used, whether they contain yeast or not, their shape, and any additional flavorings, all of which contribute to the bread's unique personality. The recipes in this book vary in these ways, with something for every type of baker— an astonishing diversity of loaves of bread ranging from easy and familiar to innovative and demanding. There is bread for health-conscious individuals, sweet-toothed individuals, and even gluten-free individuals. Bread using familiar and unfamiliar ingredients, imaginative flatbreads, and even artisan bread employing classic techniques adapted for the bread machine is included.

This book has 400 recipes for your bread machine. Even if you are not an expert, a bread machine makes it easy to make and enjoy homemade bread. After just a few loaves in the bread machine, you'll be confident that you're a skilled baker, and you'll be pleased to discover that your loaves are ideal for serving with meals, making sandwiches or toast, or using in other recipes.

APPENDIX 1

MEASUREMENT CONVERSION CHART

Volume Equivalents (Liquid)

US Standard	US Standard (ounces)	Metric (approximate)
2 tablespoons	1 fl. oz.	30 mL
1/4 cup	2 fl. oz.	60 mL
1/2 cup	4 fl. oz.	120 mL
1 cup	8 fl. oz.	240 mL
1 1/2 cups	12 fl. oz.	355 mL
2 cups or 1 pint	16 fl. oz.	475 mL
4 cups or 1 quart	32 fl. oz.	1 L
1 gallon	128 fl. oz.	4 L

Volume Equivalents (Dry)

US Standard	Metric (Approximate)
1/8 teaspoon	0.5 mL
1/4 teaspoon	1 mL
1/2 teaspoon	2 mL
3/4 teaspoon	4 mL
1 teaspoon	5 mL
1 tablespoon	15 mL
1/4 cup	59 mL
1/3 cup	79 mL
1/2 cup	118 mL
2/3 cup	156 mL
3/4 cup	177 mL
1 cup	235 mL
2 cups or 1 pint	475 mL
3 cups	700 mL
4 cups or 1 quart	1 L

Oven temperatures

Fahrenheit	Celsius (Approximate)
250°F	120°C
300°F	150°C
325°F	165°C
350°F	180°C
375°F	190°C
400°F	200°C
425°F	220°C
450°F	230°C

APPENDIX 2

INGREDIENTS CONVERSION CHART

Flours	VOLUME	OUNCES	GRAMS
Unbleached All-Purpose Flour	1 cup	4 1/4	120
9 Grain Flour Blend	1 cup	4 3/8	124
Bread Flour	1 cup	4 1/4	120
French-Style Flour	1 cup	4 1/4	120
Perfect Pizza Blend	1 cup	4 3/8	124
Whole Wheat Flour (traditional)	1 cup	4	113
White Whole Wheat Flour	1 cup	4	113
Whole Wheat Pastry Flour	1 cup	3 3/8	96
All-Purpose Baking Mix	1 cup	4 1/4	120

Gluten-Free Flours	VOLUME	OUNCES	GRAMS
Gluten-Free Flour	1 cup	5 1/2	156
Gluten-Free Brown Rice Flour	1 cup	4 3/4	135
Gluten-Free Whole Grain Flour	1 cup	4 1/4	120
Gluten-Free Baking Mix	1 cup	4 1/4	120

Rye Flours	VOLUME	OUNCES	GRAMS
Medium Rye	1 cup	3 5/8	103
Perfect Rye Blend	1 cup	3 3/4	106
Pumpernickel	1 cup	3 3/4	106
White Rye	1 cup	3 3/4	106

Various Flours	VOLUME	OUNCES	GRAMS
Almond Flour	1 cup	3 3/8	112
Ancient Grains	1 cup	4 5/8	113
Barley flour	1 cup	4	113
Buckwheat Flour	1 cup	4 1/4	120
Chickpea flour	1 cup	3	85
Coconut Flour	1 cup	4 1/2	128

	Volume	Ounces	Grams
Harvest Grains Blend	1/2 cup	2 5/8	74
Hazelnut Flour	1 cup	3 1/8	89
Oat Flour	1 cup	3 1/4	92
Potato Flour	1/4 cup	1 5/8	46
Potato Starch	1 cup	5 3/8	152
Quinoa flour	1 cup	3 7/8	110
Brown Rice Flour	1 cup	5 3/8	152
Rice flour (white)	1 cup	5	142
Semolina Flour	1 cup	5 3/4	163
Sorghum flour	1 cup	4 7/8	138
Soy flour	1/4 cup	1 1/4	35
Spelt Flour	1 cup	3 1/2	99
Sprouted Whole Wheat Flour	1 cup	3 3/4	106
Tapioca Starch or flour	1 cup	4	113
6-Grain Flakes	1 cup	3 3/8	96

Other Ingredients	VOLUME	OUNCES	GRAMS
Almonds (sliced)	1/2 cup	1 1/2	43
Almonds, whole (unblanched)	1 cup	5	142
Apples (dried, diced)	1 cup	3	85
Apples (peeled, sliced)	1 cup	4	223
Baking powder	1 tsp		4
Baking soda	1/2 tsp		3
Bananas (mashed)	1 cup	8	227
Barley (cooked)	1 cup	7 5/8	215
Barley flakes	1/2 cup	1 5/8	46
Basil pesto	2 Tbs.	1	28
Berries (frozen)	1 cup	5	142
Blueberries (dried)	1 cup	5 1/2	156
Blueberries (fresh)	1 cup	6	170
Bread crumbs (dried)	1/4 cup	1	28
Bread crumbs (fresh)	1/2 cup	3/4	21
Baking Sheet brownie mix (dry)	1 cup	5 3/4	163

Buckwheat, whole (kasha)	1 cup	6	170
Bulgur	1 cup	5 3/8	152
Butter	1/2 c, 1 stick	4	113
Buttermilk, yogurt, sour cream	2 Tbs.	1	28
Buttermilk Powder	2 Tbs.	7/8	25
Candied Peel	1/2 cup	3	85
Caraway seeds	2 Tbs.	5/8	18
Cashews (chopped)	1 cup	4	113
Carrots (grated)	1 cup	3 1/2	99
Carrots (cooked and puréed)	1/2 cup	4 1/2	128
Carrots (diced)	1 cup	5	142
Celery (diced)	1 cup	5	142
Cheddar, jack, Swiss(grated)	1 cup	4	113
Cheese powder	1/2 cup	2	57
Cherries (dried)	1/2 cup	2 1/2	71
Cherries (frozen)	1 cup	4	113
Chives (fresh)	1/2 cup	3/4	21
Chocolate (chopped)	1 cup	6	170
Chocolate chips	1 cup	6	170
Cocoa, unsweetened	2 tbls	3/8	11
Coconut, unsweetened (grated)	1 cup	4	113
Coconut milk powder	1/2 cup	2	57
Coconut, sweetened (flakes)	1 cup	3	85
Cookie crumbs	1 cup	3	85
Coffee powder	2 tsp.	1/8	4
Corn (popped)	4 cups	3/4	21
Cornmeal, whole	1 cup	4 7/8	138
Corn syrup	1 cup	11	312
Cornstarch	1/4 cup	1	28
Cranberries (dried)	1/2 cup	2	57
Cranberries (fresh or frozen)	1 cup	3 1/2	99
Cream cheese	1 cup	8	227
Currants	1 cup	5	142

Dates (chopped)	1 cup	5 1/4	149
Egg white (fresh)	1 large	1 1/4	35
Egg whites (dried)	2 Tbs.	3/8	11
Egg yolk (fresh)	1 large	1/2	14
Feta	1 cup	4	113
Flax seed	1/4 cup	1 1/4	35
Figs (dried, chopped)	1 cup	5 1/4	149
Garlic (minced)	2 Tbs.	1	28
Garlic (peeled and sliced)	1 cup	5 1/4	149
Ginger (fresh, sliced)	1/4 cup	2	57
Graham crackers (crushed)	1 cup	5	142
Granola	1 cup	4	113
Grape Nuts	1/2 cup	2	57
Hazelnuts (whole)	1 cup	5	142
Honey	1 Tbs.	3/4	21
Jam or preserves	1/4 cup	3	85
Lard	1/2 cup	4	113
Leeks (diced)	1 cup	3 1/4	92
Lemon powder	2 Tbs.	5/8	18
Lime powder	2 Tbs.	'5/8	18
Macadamia nuts (whole)	1 cup	5 1/4	149
Malted milk powder	1/4 cup	1 1/4	35
Malted Wheat Flakes	1/2 cup	2 1/4	64
Maple sugar	1/2 cup	2 3/4	78
Maple syrup	1/2 cup	5 1/2	156
Mayonnaise	1/2 cup	4	113
Milk, evaporated	1/2 cup	4 1/2	128
Milk, store bought nonfat dry	1/4 cup	3/4	21
Milk, sweetened condensed	1/4 cup	2 3/4	78
Millet (whole)	1/2 cup	3 5/8	103
Molasses	1/4 cup	3	85
Oat bran	1/2 cup	1 7/8	53
Oats, traditional rolled	1 cup	3 1/2	99

Oats, quick cooking	1 cup	3 1/8	89
Oats, steel cut (raw)	1/2 cup	2 7/8	99
Oats, steel cut (cooked)	1 cup	9	255
Oil, vegetable	1 cup	7	198
Olives (sliced)	1 cup	5	142
Onions, baking	1/2 cup	1 3/8	
Onions, fresh (diced)	1 cup	5	142
Orange juice powder	2 Tbs.	5/8	82
Parmesan (grated)	1/2 cup	1 3/4	50
Peaches (peeled and diced)	1 cup	6	170
Peanut butter	1/2 cup	4 3/4	135
Peanuts (whole, shelled)	1 cup	5	142
Pears (peeled and diced)	1 cup	5 3/4	163
Pecans (diced)	1/2 cup	1 7/8	57
Peppers, red or green (fresh)	1 cup	5	142
Pineapple, dried	1/2 cup	2 1/2	71
Pineapple juice powder	2 Tbs.	5/8	18
Pineapple (fresh or canned, diced)	1 cup	8 1/2	43
Pine nuts	1/2 cup	2 1/2	71
Pistachio nuts	1/2 cup	2 1/8	60
Pistachio nut paste	1/4 cup	2 3/4	78
Poppy seeds	2 Tbs.	5/8	18
Potatoes (mashed)	1 cup	7 1/2	213
Pumpkin (canned)	1 cup	9 1/2	269
Quinoa (whole)	1 cup	6 1/4	177
Quinoa (cooked)	1 cup	6 1/2	184
Raisins (loose)	1 cup	5 1/4	149
Raisins (packed)	1/2 cup	3	85
Raspberries (fresh)	1 cup	4 1/4	120
Rhubarb (fresh, medium dice)	1 cup	4 1/4	120
Rice Krispies	1 cup	1	28
Rice, brown (cooked)	1 cup	6	170
Rice, long grain (dry)	1/2 cup	3 1/2	99

Ricotta	1 cup	8	227
Rye flakes	1 cup	4 3/8	124
Scallions (sliced)	1 cup	2 1/4	64
Sesame seeds	1/2 cup	2 1/2	71
Shallots (peeled and sliced)	1 cup	5 1/2	156
Sour cream	1 cup	8	227
Sourdough starter	1 cup	8	227
Strawberries (fresh sliced)	1 cup	5 7/8	167
Sugar (granulated white)	1 cup	7	198
Sugar, dark or light brown	1 cup	7 1/2	213
Sugar, sticky bun	1 cup	3 1/2	99
Sundried tomatoes (dry pack)	1 cup	6	170
Sunflower seeds	1/4 cup	1 1/4	35
Tahini paste	1/2 cup	2 1/2	71
Tapioca (quick-cooking)	2 Tbs.	3/4	21
Toffee chunks	1 cup	5 1/2	156
Vegetable shortening	1/4 cup	1 5/8	46
Vital wheat gluten	2 Tbs.	5/8	18
Walnuts (whole)	1/2 cup	2 1/4	64
Walnuts (chopped)	1 cup	4	113
Water	1/3 cup	2 5/8	74
Wheat berries (red)	1 cup	3 1/2	99
Wheat bran	1/2 cup	1 1/8	32
Wheat (cracked)	1 cup	5 1/4	149
Wheat flakes (malted)	1/4 cup	1	28
Wheat germ	1/4 cup	1	28
Yeast (instant)	2 1/4 tsp.	1/4	7
Yogurt	1 cup	8	227
Zucchini (shredded)	1 cup	5/6	142-170

APPENDIX 3

RECIPE INDEX

Manufactured by Amazon.ca
Acheson, AB